ACE the GMAT®

Brandon Royal

QS Quacquarelli Symonds Limited

QS Quacquarelli Symonds is the world's leading network for education and top careers. QS links graduate, MBA and executive communities around the world with recruiters and education providers through websites, publications, selection services and events. QS helps individuals in their preparation for standardized tests and school selection and applications.

First Edition UK Published November 2003

For more information on MBA admissions, please refer to: www.topmba.com/bookstore

ISBN 978-1-4051-6311-8

BLACKWELL PUBLISHING
350 Main Street, Malden, MA 02148-5020, USA
9600 Garsington Road, Oxford OX4 2DQ, UK
550 Swanston Street, Carlton, Victoria 3053, Australia

All commercial inquiries should be addressed to:
QS Quacquarelli Symonds Ltd
1 Tranley Mews, Fleet Road
London NW3 2DG
UK
www.qsnetwork.com

To contact the author:
G.P.O. Box 440
Central, Hong Kong
brandon@brandonroyal.com
www.brandonroyal.com

Printed and bound in Dubai.

PRAISE FOR 'ACE THE GMAT'

"I can't thank you enough for the clarity and wisdom you impart in Ace the GMAT! In terms of logical organization and exhaustive content, your GMAT guide has no equal."

Kemp Baker
Non-Profit Management Inc.
Washington, DC

"By not wasting a reader's time, 'Ace the GMAT' gives royal treatment to GMAT test takers. He clearly outlines useful strategies to solve real test problems, unlike any other book I have ever seen."

Steve Silbiger
Author: The Ten-Day MBA: The Step-by-Step Guide to Mastering the Skills Taught in America's Top Business Schools

"Rigorous, analytical, thorough. A perfect companion for those wanting to take control of the GMAT."

Rosemaria Martinelli
Associate Dean, Student Recruitment & Admissions
The University of Chicago Graduate School of Business
Former Director of Admissions, The Wharton School

"This author's approach enabled me to increase my score from 650 to 730. I believe that his unique way of categorizing each type of question, giving insightful tips to master these problems, as well as the detailed analysis for each set of problems were key factors in my cracking the test. Moreover, I found in his materials, problems that I did not find anywhere else and which were critical on the D-day when answering a few extra questions right made the difference between a good score and an excellent one."

Cédric Gouliardon
Telecom Specialist
Graduate, INSEAD

"I used Ace the GMAT to achieve a plus 700 GMAT score. One section of the GMAT deals with mathematical concepts and acumen once learned in high school but long forgotten. For me, this book was highly effective in helping to 'recall' such lost math knowledge within a short period of time by selectively concentrating on relevant mathematical problems. Unlike conventional test preparation books which bombard you with irrelevant or overly-simplistic questions, mixed with gimmicks or tricks, Ace the GMAT provides real principles which are ultimately useful over a wide range of problem type and difficulty level."

C. F. Pan
Graduate, Harvard Law School

"For me, the single most important feature of this book was the 'snapshots' that were embedded at the beginning of each problem explanation. Even as a liberal arts major who, upon graduation, worked as an investment banking analyst on Wall Street, I found a good number of these math and verbal tips simple but not immediately obvious and enjoyed having them spelled out for me. I found it a great complement to the GMAT Official Guide, which has gobs of practice problems but doesn't deal with how problems work conceptually. In short, although I was a bit skeptical at first, I thought this book was well deserving of its claim to be 'the #1 skill-building GMAT book.'"

Matt Nelson
MBA Candidate

CONTENTS

ANALITICAL WRITING ASSESSMENT
Analysis of an Argument Essay • Analysis of an Issue Essay

CHAPTER 5: PROBLEM SOLVING

Distance-Rate-Time Problems • Age Problems • Average Problems • Work Problems
• Picture-Frame or Border Problem • Mixture Problems • Group Problems • Matrix Problems
• Price-Cost-Volume-Profit Problems • Least-Common-Multiple Word Problems
• General Algebraic Word Problems • Function Problems • Algebraic Fractions • Fractions and Decimals
• Percentage Problems • Ratios and Proportions • Squares and Cubes • Exponent Problems
• Radical Problems • Inequality Problems • Prime Number Problems • Remainder Problems
• Symbolism Problems • Coordinate Geometry Problems • Plane Geometry Problems
• Solid Geometry Problems • Probability problems • Permutation Problems • Combination Problems

CHAPTER 6: DATA SUFFIENCY

Odds and Evens • Averaging • Positives and Negatives • Integers and Non-Integers • Squares and Cubes

CHAPTER 7: SENTENCE CORRECTION

Subject-Verb Agreement • Pronoun Reference • Modification • Parallelism • Comparisons • Verb Tenses

CHAPTER 8: CRITICAL REASONING

Comparison and Analogy Assumptions • Cause and Effect Assumptions • Representative Sample Assumptions
• Implementation Assumptions • Number-based Assumptions • Logic-based Assumptions

CHAPTER 9: READING COMPREHENSION

CHAPTER 10: ANALYTICAL WRITING

Foreword

A solid GMAT score is sine qua non for acceptance to today's leading business schools. Although the GMAT is said to test "basic skills," it is indeed a tricky exam. What makes the exam especially challenging is that candidates define success in terms of high scores but pursue study within limited timeframes. For aspiring test takers, the operative question is: "What kinds of must-know problems might I face on the exam and what are the best techniques and approaches to use in conquering them?"

Consistent with this book's philosophy, the primary objective is to set the conceptual framework for mastering exam content. Mastery of exam content is the only sure-fire way to conquer the GMAT, and this material is designed to help you understand *how the problems work*. The *Topical Checklist* on the following pages serves to outline topical areas that you ideally need to master prior to sitting for the GMAT exam. Moreover, integral to any successful study program are simulated computer-based tests, which are included here in CD-ROM format.

Best of luck on the journey and at the destination.

Brandon Royal

20-Day Intensive Study Schedule

How long is needed to complete the material in this book? Most candidates will complete their review in 20 days, assuming three to five hours of study time per day, excluding time spent on the CD-ROM tests.

Chapter	Topic	No. of Days
Chapter 1	The GMAT Exam	1 day
Chapter 2	GMAT Test-Taking Strategies	1 day
Chapter 3	The World of Numbers	1 day
Chapter 4	The World of Letters	1 day
Chapter 5	Problem Solving	5 days
Chapter 6	Data Sufficiency	2 days
Chapter 7	Sentence Correction	2 days
Chapter 8	Critical Reasoning	3 days
Chapter 9	Reading Comprehension	2 days
Chapter 10	Analytical Writing Assessment	2 days
		20 days

TOPICAL CHECKLIST

Note: Chapters 1 through 4 are introductory chapters. Chapters 5 through 10 contain designated problems.

MATH   Problem No.

Chapter 5: Problem Solving

▫ Distance-Rate-Time Problems   1-6

▫ Age Problem   7

▫ Average Problems   8-10

▫ Work Problems   11-13

▫ Picture Frame or Border Problem   14

▫ Mixture Problems   15-17

▫ Group Problems   18-20

▫ Matrix Problems   21-23

▫ Price-Cost-Volume-Profit Problems   24-28

▫ Least-Common-Multiple Word Problem   29

▫ General Algebraic Word Problems   30-33

▫ Function Problem   34

▫ Algebraic Fractions   35-36

▫ Fractions and Decimals   37-39

▫ Percentage Problems   40-46

▫ Ratios and Proportions   47-52

▫ Squares and Cubes   53-54

▫ Exponent Problems   55-62

▫ Radical Problems   63-65

▫ Inequality Problem   66

▫ Prime Number Problems   67-68

WRITING

QUIZ

QUIZ – TRUE OR FALSE

Try these ten basic but occasionally tricky math and verbal problems. See page **280** for solutions.

1. If the ratio of gold coins to non-gold coins in a rare coin collection is 1:5, then 20% of the total coin collection represents gold coins.

   ____ T ____ F

2. The probability of tossing a six-sided die twice and getting a six on either the first or second toss is $\frac{1}{3}$, calculated as $\frac{1}{6} + \frac{1}{6}$.

   ____ T ____ F

3. A store item that has been discounted first by 20% and then by 30% is now selling at 50% of its original price.

   ____ T ____ F

4. The ratios of the length of the sides of a right triangle with corresponding angle measures of 30:60:90° is 1:2:√3.

   ____ T ____ F

5. Multiplying a number by 1.2 is the same as dividing that same number by 0.8.

   ____ T ____ F

6. The following is a grammatically correct sentence: "Jonathan not only likes tennis but also golf."

   ____ T ____ F

7. In formal logic, the statement "Every A is a B" may be translated as "Only A's are B's."

   ____ T ____ F

8. Like the Analysis of an Issue essay, the Analysis of an Argument essay is more effective if written using some personal examples and anecdotes.

   ____ T ____ F

9. Whereas the conclusion and evidence of an argument are always explicit, the assumption of an argument may or may not be explicit.

   ____ T ____ F

10. Arguably the best way to read a GMAT Reading Comprehension passage is to read line by line, starting from the top and proceeding to the bottom.

    ____ T ____ F

CHAPTER 1

THE GMAT EXAM

"Chance favors the prepared mind."
(Louis Pasteur)

OVERVIEW

I. What's on the GMAT Exam?
II. How is the GMAT Scored?
III. How Does the CAT Work?
IV. Exam Tactics
V. Attitude and Mental Outlook
VI. Exam Instructions

I. WHAT'S ON THE GMAT EXAM?

The GMAT exam is a 3½-hour, three-section standardized exam consisting of Math, Verbal, and Writing sections. Except for the Writing section (essay format), the Math and Verbal sections follow an entirely multiple-choice format.

Exhibit 1-1: GMAT Exam Snapshot

Section	No. of Questions	Time Allowed
ESSAYS	2	60 minutes
Break		5 minutes
MATH	37	75 minutes
Break		5 minutes
VERBAL	41	75 minutes
	Total Time	4 hours (approx.)

Exam Breakdown:

Analytical Writing Assessment (60 minutes)
- Analysis of an Issue (30 minutes, 1 topic)
- Analysis of an Argument (30 minutes, 1 topic)

Math (Quantitative) Section (75 minutes)
- Problem Solving (23–24 questions)
- Data Sufficiency (13–14 questions)
Total number of questions: 37 (28 scored, 9 unscored*)

Verbal Section (75 minutes)
- Critical Reasoning (14–15 questions)
- Sentence Correction (14–15 questions)
- Reading Comprehension (4 passages, 12–14 questions)
Total number of questions: 41 (30 scored, 11 unscored*)

Note: The two AWA topics (Issue and Argument) may appear in either order on the exam. Within each of the other two sections, the different types of math questions (i.e., Problem Solving and Data Sufficiency) and verbal questions (i.e., Reading Comprehension, Critical Reasoning, and Sentence Correction) are intermixed.

*There are 20 unscored questions shared between the Math and Verbal sections of the GMAT exam; either 9 Quantitative and 11 Verbal Questions or 10 questions from each section are unscored.

II. HOW IS THE GMAT SCORED?

You actually receive four scores from taking the GMAT exam:
1) Total Score, 2) Math (Quantitative) Score, 3) Verbal Score, and 4) AWA (Analytical Writing Assessment) Score. Your Total Score ranges from 200 to 800. Scores on individual Math and Verbal sections range from 0 to 60 and are accompanied by a corresponding percentile rank. Your AWA score, out of 6.0, is totally independent of your Math, Verbal, or Total score.

Scaled scores: Scaled scores of 50 or more out of 60 on the Math section or 45 or more out of 60 on the Verbal section correspond to the 99th percentile. This means that only 1% of all test-takers can achieve either of these respective scores and, as such, these scores are rare. Scaled scores of 750 out of 800 on the combined test correspond to the 99th percentile.

Exhibit 1-2: GMAT Scoring Snapshot

Section	Scaled Scoring	Percentile Rank
Essays	0.0 to 6.0	0% to 99%
Math	0 to 60	0% to 99%
Verbal	0 to 60	0% to 99%
Total (Math + Verbal)	200 to 800	0% to 99%

Naturally, for the purposes of applying to business school, the higher your GMAT Total Score the better. Let's say that a scaled score of 680 (680 out of 800 corresponds to the 90th percentile) is considered a good score and is what most candidates aim for if applying to "top" business schools. There is some credence given to the idea that everyone applying to a leading business school is equal in the admissions process after scoring 680 or above. In other words, if you get rejected with a score of 680 or above, the problem lies not with your GMAT score but with another part of your application. In terms of applying to business school, particularly top business schools, admissions officers typically view GMAT scores (scaled scores) as falling into four arbitrary categories.

Score: *What this likely means:*

Less than 500:   Not acceptable; take the exam over again.
Between 500 and 600:   Marginal; low for a top business school, although you could still get accepted.
Between 600 and 700:   In the "ball park" for a top business school.
Greater than 700:   Excellent!

Remember: The GMAT score is one of several factors that go into the admissions process. In the often quoted words of admissions officers at large: "A high GMAT score does not guarantee acceptance and a low GMAT score does not necessarily preclude it."

Exhibit 1-3: GMAT (Total Math & Verbal) Standardized Test Scores

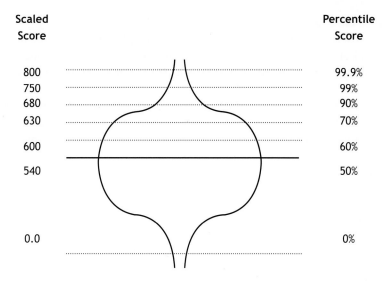

Scaled Score		Percentile Score
800		99.9%
750		99%
680		90%
630		70%
600		60%
540		50%
0.0		0%

The Analytical Writing Assessment (AWA)

The first hour of the GMAT exam consists of two half-hour writing segments. One is called Analysis of an Argument and the other is called Analysis of an Issue. The basic difference between these two exercises is that to analyze the issue, you are required to take a stand and create or "build" an issue essay whereas to analyze an argument, you are required to "break" down an argument by identifying what makes it weak.

Graders (one human and one electronic e-grading machine) score each AWA based on essay content, organization, and grammar. Graders assign scores out of 6.0 based on intervals of 0.5 points. Your overall, final score is an average of both individual scores obtained on the issue and argument essays.

Although it is unclear how business schools use AWA scores in the admissions process, there are three possibilities. Scores could be used in borderline admission decisions. They could be used to identify students who need a remedial writing course. Finally, they could be used to help verify that candidates wrote their admissions essays.

Exhibit 1-4: GMAT (AWA) Standardized Test Scores

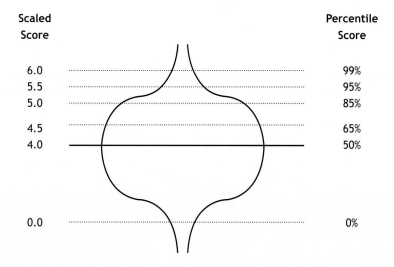

Scaled Score		Percentile Score
6.0		99%
5.5		95%
5.0		85%
4.5		65%
4.0		50%
0.0		0%

III. HOW DOES THE CAT WORK?

CAT stands for Computer Adaptive Test. When starting work on a given Math or Verbal section, each person is assumed to be an average test-taker and the test presents questions of average difficulty (i.e., 500-level test questions). Should the test-taker get these questions correct, he or she is given a series of more difficult problems. As soon as he or she is given an easier question. Eventually, and in theory, there will come a point at which the test-taker can neither get a harder question right nor get an easier question wrong. It is here that the test "draws a line" and assigns a score. If, for example, a test-taker cannot get 720-level questions correct but can get 680-level questions correct, the test assumes that the score to be assigned is 700.

It is not possible to skip a question on the CAT exam without entering an answer; an answer must be entered for every question attempted before attempting additional questions. It is also not possible to go back to a previous question or previous section.

IV. EXAM TACTICS

Mastering the GMAT exam is really a function of mastering two things: content and context. Content refers to the ability to do questions with technical proficiency. Context is about everything else including becoming familiar with the computer, coping with a mix of questions, dealing with time pressure, and maintaining concentration and stamina.

As with many other academic pursuits, content is best mastered "a little at a time"; cumulative practice is preferable. Candidates should try working for at least 15 minutes every day for about a three-month period. If you wait until each weekend in order to try and do, say, two to three hours of GMAT study, you may find your efforts short-changed.

Each section of the GMAT exam is designed to be completed. A common question is, "How can I speed up on my Math or Verbal section?" There are effectively two ways to do this. The first is to do problems quicker; the second is to skip problems. In order to do problems quicker, one has to master content so that individual questions seem easier. And that's what this book is really all about.

In terms of skipping questions, one can skip questions randomly or in blocks. Most of us are good at some types of questions, weaker on others. Learning to identify those types of questions that we are unlikely to get correct gives us the option of skipping them altogether. What if we are fairly certain that we won't be able to finish an entire Verbal section of 41 questions, or a Math section of 37 questions? Because questions toward the end of a GMAT section are deemed less important than earlier questions, in terms of skipping questions, one strategy is to "truncate the exam." This means you simply believe that the Verbal section contains, say, 35 (not 41) questions, and the Math section contains, say, 32 (not 37) questions. Upon doing 35 questions (Verbal section) or 32 questions (Math section), feel free to guess on the remaining questions in light of time running out. Under no circumstances, however, should you allow an exam to finish without having entered answer choices.

V. ATTITUDE AND MENTAL OUTLOOK

Rest assured that few people are truly excited about writing a standardized exam like the GMAT. One way to bring optimism to the process is to talk yourself into believing that you actually like preparing for the exam. Write it on a recipe card, "I like this exam!" and carry it with you. Another approach is to think of it all as a game in which you are greedy for points—you are uncontrollably curious about whether you can keep beating previous practice scores.

The intellectual characteristic of people who score high on standardized exams is the ability to see problems as composed of several smaller, simpler problems. The intellectual characteristic of people who do not score high on standardized exams is the tendency to see a problem as a large, non-dissectible whole. Concentrating on the small steps within each problem will minimize the chances of you losing concentration during the exam. Also, as the GMAT has three sections (i.e., Writing, Math, and Verbal), it is important to refrain from thinking beyond the section you're actually working on. During the exam, think one section at a time, one problem at a time, and only about the specific part of the problem that is before you.

VI. EXAM INSTRUCTIONS

For your reference, here are the actual exam instructions for each question type as seen on the ETS website (mba.com):

Analysis of an Issue
Directions
In this section, you will need to analyze the issue presented and explain your views on it. There is no "correct" answer. Instead, you should consider various perspectives as you develop your own position on the issue.

Writing Your Response: Take a few minutes to think about the issue and plan a response before you begin writing. Be sure to organize your ideas and develop them fully, but leave time to reread your response and make any revisions that you think are necessary.

Valuation of Your Response: College and university faculty members from various subject matter areas, including management education, will evaluate the overall quality of your thinking and writing. They will consider how well you —
  • organize, develop, and express your ideas about the issue presented
  • provide relevant supporting reasons and examples
  • control the elements of standard written English

Analysis of an Argument
Directions
In this section, you will be asked to write a critique of the argument presented. You are NOT being asked to present your own views on the subject.

Writing your response: Take a few minutes to evaluate the argument and plan a response before you begin writing. Be sure to organize your ideas and develop them fully, but leave time to reread your response and make any revisions that you think are necessary.

Valuation of your response: College and university faculty members from various subject matter areas, including management education, will evaluate the overall quality of your thinking and writing. They will consider how well you—
  • organize, develop, and express your ideas about the argument presented
  • provide relevant supporting reasons and examples
  • control the elements of standard written English

Problem Solving
Directions
Solve the problem and indicate the best of the answer choices given.

Numbers
All numbers used are real numbers.

Figures
A figure accompanying a problem solving question is intended to provide information useful in solving the problem. Figures are drawn as accurately as possible EXCEPT when it is stated in a specific problem that the figure is not drawn to scale. Straight lines may sometimes appear jagged. All figures lie in a plane unless otherwise indicated.

Data Sufficiency

Directions

This data sufficiency problem consists of a question and two statements, labeled (1) and (2), in which certain data are given. You have to decide whether the data given in the statements are sufficient for answering the question. Using the data given in the statements, plus your knowledge of mathematics and everyday facts (such as the number of days in July or the meaning of the word counterclockwise), you must indicate whether—

- Statement (1) ALONE is sufficient, but statement (2) alone is not sufficient to answer the question asked.
- Statement (2) ALONE is sufficient, but statement (1) alone is not sufficient to answer the question asked.
- BOTH statements (1) and (2) TOGETHER are sufficient to answer the question asked, but NEITHER statement ALONE is sufficient to answer the question asked.
- EACH statement ALONE is sufficient to answer the question asked.
- Statements (1) and (2) TOGETHER are NOT sufficient to answer the question asked, and additional data specific to the problem are needed.

Numbers

All numbers used are real numbers.

Figures

A figure accompanying a data sufficiency question will conform to the information given in the question but will not necessarily conform to the additional information given in statements (1) and (2).

Lines shown as straight can be assumed to be straight and lines that appear jagged can also be assumed to be straight.

You may assume that the positions of points, angles, regions, etc. exist in the order shown and that angle measures are greater than zero.

All figures lie in a plane unless otherwise indicated.

Note: In data sufficiency problems that ask for the value of a quantity, the data given in the statement are sufficient only when it is possible to determine exactly one numerical value for the quantity.

Reading Comprehension

Directions

The questions in this group are based on the content of a passage. After reading the passage, choose the best answer to each question. Answer all questions following the passage on the basis of what is stated or implied in the passage.

Critical Reasoning

Directions

For each question, select the best of the answer choices given.

Sentence Correction

Directions

This question presents a sentence, part of which or all of which is underlined. Beneath the sentence you will find five ways of phrasing the underlined part. The first of these repeats the original; the other four are different. If you think the original is best, choose the first answer; otherwise choose one of the others.

This question tests correctness and effectiveness of expression. In choosing your answer, follow the requirements of standard written English; that is, pay attention to grammar, choice of words, and sentence construction. Choose the answer that produces the most effective sentence; this answer should be clear and exact, without awkwardness, ambiguity, redundancy, or grammatical error.

CHAPTER 2

GMAT TEST-TAKING STRATEGIES

"Nothing is more difficult, and therefore more precious, than to be able to decide."
(Napoleon)

This chapter summarizes exam strategies and approaches. Examples chosen here are purposely simple.

PROBLEM SOLVING
Strategies and approaches

1. Identify the type of problem and the appropriate *math principle* behind the problem at hand.
2. Decide which *approach* to use to solve the problem—algebra, picking numbers, backsolving, or approximation and eyeballing.
3. After performing calculations, always check again for what is being asked for.
4. Employ guessing or elimination strategies, if necessary, and when possible.

Author's notes

STEP #1: There are many different types of math problems on the GMAT. Each problem in this book comes with a "Classification" to highlight what category a problem belongs to.

STEP #2: There are both direct problem-solving approaches and indirect problem-solving approaches. The direct or algebraic approach involves applying actual math principles or formulas. Because we may not always know the correct algebraic method, we need an indirect or alternative approach. Other times, an indirect approach is plainly easier to apply than the algebraic approach. There are four alternative approaches for Problem Solving and these include: picking numbers, backsolving, and approximation/eyeballing, and guessing/elimination.

STEP #3: Avoid making "Reading Comprehension" errors on the math section. Always re-read the question before choosing an answer, particularly if you have been engrossed in performing a longer computation.

STEP #4: Guess if you must but employ guessing techniques as discussed in point *iv* below.

Here are examples of the four indirect or alternative approaches:

I. Picking Numbers

If a and b are even integers, which of the following is an odd integer?

A) ab + 2
B) a(b - 1)
C) a(a + 5)
D) 3a + 4b
E) (a + 3)(b - 1)

II. Backsolving

If $(x + 2)^2 = -4 + 10x$, then which of the following is the value of x?

A) 2   B) 1   C) 0   D) -1   E) -2

III. Approximation

Approximately what percent of the world's forested area is represented by Finland given that Finland has 53.42 million hectares of forested land of the world's 8.076 billion hectares of forested land.

A) 0.006%   B) 0.06%   C) 0.66%   D) 6.6%   E) 66%

IV. Eyeballing

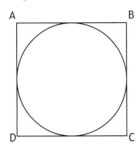

If the figure above is a square with a side of 4 units, what is the *area* of the enclosed circle, expressed to the nearest whole number?

A) π   B) 4   C) 8   D) 13   E) 16

V. Guessing and Elimination

A female broker invested her own money in the stock market. During the first year, she increased her stock market wealth by 50%. In the second year, largely as a result of a slump in the stock market, she suffered a subsequent 30% decrease in the value of her stock investments. What was the net increase or decrease on her overall stock investment wealth by the end of the second year?

A) -5%   B) +5%   C) +15%   D) +20%   E) +80%

ANSWERS:

I. Picking Numbers

Choice E. This key strategy involves first picking numbers and then substituting them into the answer choices. Whenever a problem involves variables, we may consider using this strategy. For this particular problem, pick the numbers a = 2 and b = 4 because both are even integers, yet both are still small and manageable numbers. Now substitute. Answer Choice E is correct. You can be confident that if it works for your chosen set of numbers, it will also work for all other numbers as well. There is no need to try other numbers.

ab + 2	(2 x 4) + 2 = 10 even
a(b - 1)	2(4 - 1) = 6 even
a(a +5)	2(2 + 5) = 14 even
3a + 4b	(3 x 2) + (4 x 4) = 22 even
(a + 3)(b - 1)	(2 + 3)(4 - 1) =15 odd

II. Backsolving

Choice A. The key to *backsolving* is to use the answer choices and see if they work. In this respect, *backsolving* is like picking numbers except that the numbers we pick are one or more of the actual answer choices. Look for the answer which makes both sides equal. In this particular problem, we may choose to start testing on any single answer choice. Choice A is as good a starting point as any.

Choice A. $(2 + 2)^2 = -4 + 10(2)$
$16 = 16$; This is the correct answer since both sides are equal.

Choice B. $(1 + 2)^2 = -4 + 10(1)$
$9 = 6$; This is a wrong answer since both sides are not equal.

Choice C. $(0 + 2)^2 = -4 + 10(0)$
$4 = -4$; This is a wrong answer since both sides are not equal.

Choice D. $(-1 + 2)^2 = -4 + 10(-1)$
$1 = -14$; This is a wrong answer since both sides are not equal.

Choice E. $(-2 + 2)^2 = -4 + 10(-2)$
$0 = -24$; This is a wrong answer since both sides are not equal.

III. Approximation

Choice C. Approximation is a strategy that helps us arrive at less than an exact number and the word "approximately" is an obvious clue. In this case, 8.076B is 8,076M and 1% of 8,000M is 80M. Round 53.42M to 53M. Now stop and compare 53M and 80M. Obviously, the answer is something less than 1%. The answer can only be answer Choices A, B or C. Choice C is correct, $\frac{50M}{80M} \cong 0.66\%$ or two-thirds of 1%.

IV. Eyeballing

Choice D. Eyeballing is a parallel technique to be used on diagrams. Note that whatever the area of this circle may be, it must be less than the area of this square. The area of the square (in square units) is: $A = s^2 = 4 \times 4 = 16$. Therefore, the area of the circle is a little less than 16. Choice D is the only close answer. For the record, the near exact area of the circle is: $A = \pi r^2 = 3.14(2)^2 = 12.56$ or 13. Note that the decimal approximation for π is 3.14 while the fractional approximation is $\frac{22}{7}$.

V. Guessing and Elimination

Choice B. If you must guess, the key strategies of elimination include: (1) eliminate an answer that looks different from the others (2) eliminate answers which look too big or too small, i.e., extreme answers, and (3) eliminate answers which contain the same or similar numbers as given in the question stem or are easy derivatives of the numbers used in the problem. By easy derivatives, think in terms of addition and subtraction, not multiplication and division. For example, eliminate -5% because it is negative, and thus different from the other positive numbers. Eliminate +80% because it is much bigger than any other number (extreme). Eliminate +20% because it is an easy derivative of the numbers mentioned in the stem, (i.e., 50% less 30%). You would then guess Choices B or C. The actual answer is obtained by multiplying 150% by 70% equals 105% ; 105% - 100% = 5%.

DATA SUFFICIENCY

Strategies and approaches

1. Evaluate each stem independently (one at a time); if each stem is insufficient then evaluate both stems together as if they were a single stem.
2. In a "yes/no Data Sufficiency question", each stem is sufficient if the answer is always *yes* or always *no* while a stem is insufficient if the answer is sometimes *yes* and sometimes *no*. In a "value Data Sufficiency question", each stem is sufficient if the answer results in a single value while a stem is insufficient if the answer results in a range of values.
3. When picking numbers, think first in terms of the "big seven" numbers.
4. Employ guessing or elimination strategies, when possible.

Author's notes

STEP #1: It is critical to analyze each statement or stem independently. This entails not letting information from a previous stem be "carried over" to the next stem.

Be sure to memorize the answer pattern of choices for Data Sufficiency.

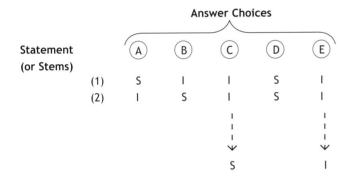

"S" stands for Sufficiency
"I" stands for Insufficiency

If the first statement provides information *sufficient* to answer the question but the second stem provides information that is *insufficient* to answer to question, then the answer is Choice A. If the first stem provides information that is *insufficient* to answer the question but the second stem provides information that is *sufficient* to answer the question, then the answer is Choice B. If both stems individually are *insufficient* but together they are *sufficient*, then the answer is Choice C. If both stems alone are *sufficient* then the answer is Choice D. If both stems individually are *insufficient* and together they are still *insufficient* then the answer is Choice E.

STEP #2: To understand "Sufficiency" and "Insufficiency," let's familiarize ourselves with the two kinds of Data Sufficiency questions: "yes/no" questions and "value" questions. Here are two examples:

"Yes/No" Data Sufficiency question:

Is x an even number ?

(1) x is an integer greater than 1.

(2) x + 1 is an odd integer.

Knowing that $x > 1$, tells us that x could be numbers like 2, 3, 4, 5, etc. Since some of these numbers are even and some are not, we can only answer the question by saying "sometimes *yes* and sometimes *no*". Therefore the first statement is *insufficient*.

Knowing that x + 1 is an odd integer, tells us that x is even. We can answer the question definitively "yes". Therefore the second statement is *sufficient*.

The answer to the above question is Choice B. The first stem is *insufficient* and the second stem is *sufficient*.

"Value" Data Sufficiency question:

What is the value of x?

(1) $x \geq 2$

(2) $x \leq 4$

Knowing that $x \geq 2$, tells us that x could be numbers like 2, 3, 4, 5, etc., not to mention numbers like 2.5, 3.3, etc. We obviously can't tell if x is even. Therefore this stem is *insufficient*.

Knowing that $x \leq 4$, tells us that x could be numbers like 4, 3, 2, 1, etc., not to mention decimals. We obviously can't tell if x is even. Therefore this stem is *insufficient*.

The answer to the above question is Choice E. Since both stems are *insufficient*, we put them together. Knowing that $x \geq 2$ and that $x \leq 4$ tells us that x could be 2, 3 or 4, as well as those decimals in between. We cannot find a single value for x so the answer is *insufficient*.

STEP #3: Picking numbers is a popular and often necessary approach to use on Data Sufficiency problems. The question becomes: "How do I pick numbers for problems?" The secret is to learn how, and when, to use small, manageable numbers to attack problems. The "big seven" numbers are: 2, -2, 1, -1, $\frac{1}{2}$, $-\frac{1}{2}$, and 0.

The beauty of the *Big Seven Numbers* is that they offer a consistent, controlled base of numbers to pick from. Think not only of using these numbers in pairs, but also in terms of hierarchy. Start off with the positive numbers 1 and 2, then the negative numbers -1, and -2. Only if the statements contain squares or cubes should you also consider trying $-\frac{1}{2}$ and $\frac{1}{2}$. Zero is a reserve number. Further discussion of the "big seven" numbers is included in *Chapter 6: Data Sufficiency*. See Author's note, Problem #114, *Reciprocal*, page 181).

STEP #4: In terms of guessing, remember that, "sufficiencies are our friends on Data Sufficiency". Once we discover that a statement is *sufficient*, the odds of us getting the problem right are 50-50. If the first statement is *sufficient*, the answer can only be Choices A or D. If the second stem is *sufficient*, the answer can only be Choices B or D. On the other hand, knowing that a stem is *insufficient* only eliminates two answers, still leaving three choices.

SENTENCE CORRECTION
Strategies and approaches

1. Glance at answer choices looking for *vertical patterns*.
2. Try to determine what the pivotal grammar issue is and if the pivotal issue falls under one of the "big six" grammar categories.
3. Read each answer choice looking for *horizontal patterns*.
4. Choose the best answer—the answer which is *grammatically* correct, *idiomatically* correct, and effective in terms of *style*.

Author's notes

STEPS #1-4: Sentence Correction requires mastering basic *grammar, diction, idioms*, and *style*. Grammar and diction are based on rules of English. Idioms are based on adopted expressions which are deemed right or wrong simply because "that's the way it is said." Style is not considered right or wrong but rather it is viewed as more effective or less effective. Examples of each follow:

Grammar: The choice between "They have arrived" and "They has arrived" is based on a rule of grammar; the plural subject "they" requires the plural verb "have."

Diction: The choice between "fewer pencils" and "less pencils" is based on diction; "fewer" is used with countable items such as pencils.

Idioms: The choice between "I prefer chicken to beef" and "I prefer chicken over beef" is based on idiomatic expression; in this case "to" is the correct preposition.

Style: The choice between "employees of the company" and "company employees" is based on a convention of style—brevity; here the simplest version ("company employees") is deemed more effective.

Sentence Correction questions selected for inclusion in this book focus primarily on the "big six" grammar categories: subject-verb agreement, modification, pronoun reference, parallelism, comparisons, and verb tenses. Consistent with a majority of GMAT questions, grammar and diction are the driving forces while idioms and style are interwoven subcomponents. *Vertical patterns* refer to the first word or words of each answer choice (or the last word or words of each answer choice). It is the first few words of each answer choice that will often offer clues as to where a grammatical distinction lies, that is, those that fall into the "big six" grammar categories. For example, if the first couple of answer choices contain the word "has" and the last three answer choices contain the word "have" then we can deduce that a grammatical distinction centers on *subject-verb agreement*. *Horizontal patterns* may also uncover problems in grammar but more likely they will be used to spot-check idioms and style. We may even use our ear to hone in on the correct answer.

CRITICAL REASONING
Strategies and approaches

1. Read the question.
2. Read the passage.
3. Analyze the argument and try to anticipate what the likely answer is.
4. Eliminate common wrong answer choices including *out-of-scopes, irrelevancies, distortions*, and *opposites*.

Author's notes

STEP #1: There are four common Critical Reasoning questions types. These include: Assumption questions, Weakening questions, Strengthening questions, and Inference questions. Examples of each include: "Which of the following is an <u>assumption</u> in the argument above?...Which of the following would most <u>weaken</u> the   argument?...Which of the following would most

<u>strengthen</u> the above argument?...Which of the following can be <u>logically inferred</u> from the passage above?"

STEPS #2 & #3: There are essentially two ways to analyze an argument. The first is according to classic argument structure. This entails breaking the argument down according to its three parts, namely conclusion, evidence, and assumption. The second and perhaps more effective method is to see if an argument's primary assumption falls under one of the six common categories of assumptions that commonly appear on the GMAT. These include: *Comparisons and Analogy Assumptions*, *Representative Sample* Assumptions, *Cause and Effect* Assumptions, *Implementation* Assumptions, *Number-based* Assumptions, and Logic-based Assumptions.

STEP #4: In terms of common wrong answer choices, *out-of-scope* answer choices may be defined as answer choices which "cannot be answered based on information presented in the passage". *Irrelevancies* are answer choices which are simply not pertinent to the question or issue at hand. *Distortions* are extreme answer choices. *Opposites* are answer choices which reverse meaning.

READING COMPREHENSION
Strategies and approaches

1. Read for content, noting *topic*, *scope*, and *purpose*.
2. Read the first sentence *first*, then scroll down and read the *last* sentence next.
3. Read for structure, noting important *transition words* as well as the number of viewpoints and relationship among viewpoints.
4. Eliminate common wrong answer choices including *out-of-scopes*, *distortions*, and *opposites*.

Author's notes

STEPS #1-4: A GMAT test-taker will encounter four Reading Comprehension passages per Verbal section and each passage will be accompanied by 3 or 4 questions each. Understanding the "purpose" of each passage is fundamental. As you read a passage, keep talking silently to yourself, "What's the purpose...where is the author going?" In other words, ask yourself, "Why did the author sit down to write the passage?" A good tip is to read the first sentence of the passage and then read the last sentence of the passage, then start back reading at the top. Why? Because an author of a passage might conclude on the last line, and if you read this early you will know where the author is going with his or her discussion, and be better able to remember details. Next is structure. Keep close track of transition words such as "however", "but", "moreover", and "hence." These words are important and may influence dramatically the flow of the passage. Second, think in terms of the number of paragraphs and viewpoints presented. Usually one paragraph represents one viewpoint. Frequently, Reading Comprehension passages will contain two viewpoints and it may be helpful to try and simplify everything into simple "black-and-white" terms. For example, take a hypothetical passage written about personality development. Ask yourself what is the relationship between, say, the three paragraphs of the passage. Perhaps, "the first paragraph is the introduction, the second paragraph is how sociologists view personality development, the third paragraph is how biologists view personality development...got it!"

There are three common wrong answer choices on Reading Comprehension. These include: *out-of-scopes*, *opposites*, and *distortions*. Note that although *irrelevancies* are common wrong answer choices in Critical Reasoning, they are not common wrong answer choices in Reading Comprehension.

ANALYTICAL WRITING

AWA - ANALYSIS OF AN ARGUMENT
Strategies and approaches

1. Visualize the *solutions template* for an Analysis of an Argument essay.
2. Identify the conclusion and evidence in the argument.

5. Use transition words to structure your argument essay.

6. Question the use of one vague term used in the argument and ask for clarification.

7. Suggest strengthening the argument by softening its absolute-type wording.

8. Write (or type) a response and proofread your argument essay.

AWA - ANALYSIS OF AN ISSUE
Strategies and approaches

1. Visualize the *solutions template* for an Analysis of an Issue essay.

2. Summarize the pros and cons for your issue.

3. Choose three (or more) pieces of evidence.

4. Begin by restating the issue and by answering the original question.

5. Use transition words to structure your issue essay.

6. Question the use of one vague term used in the issue and ask for clarification and/or draw attention to ambiguity inherent in the issue itself.

7. Use one rhetorical question.

8. Write (or type) a response and proofread your issue essay.

Author's notes

"An in-depth discussion of Analytical Writing is contained in *Chapter 4* while sample essays and solutions appear in *Chapter 10*."

CHAPTER 3

THE WORLD OF NUMBERS

"None of us really understands what's going on with all these numbers."
(David Stockman, former Budget Director, the USA Regan Administration)

FLOWCHARTING THE WORLD OF NUMBERS

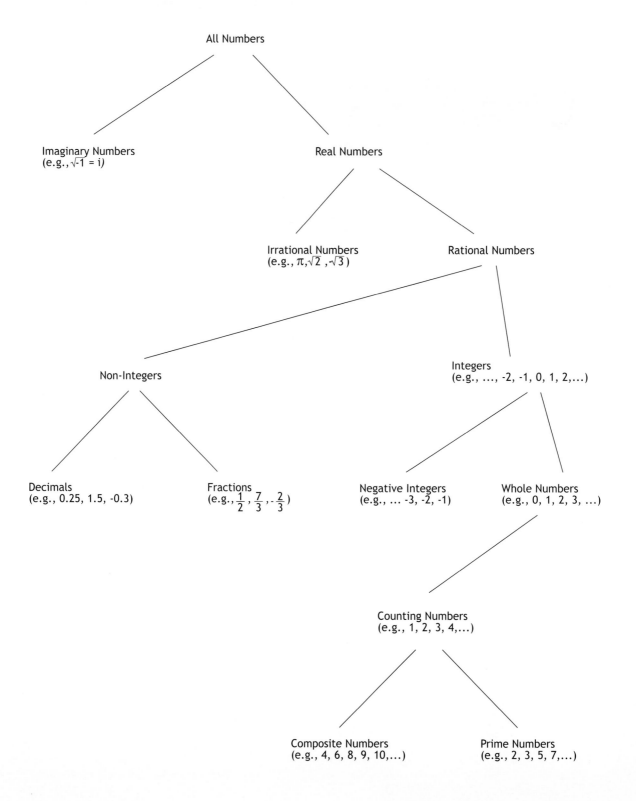

Numbers are first divided into real and imaginary number. Imaginary numbers are not a part of everyday life. *Real* numbers are further divided into rational and irrational numbers. *Irrational* numbers are numbers which cannot be expressed as simple integers, fractions, or decimals; non-repeating decimals are always irrational numbers of which π may be the most famous. *Rational* numbers include integers and non-integers. *Integers* are positive and negative whole numbers while *non-integers* include decimals and fractions.

NUMBER DEFINITIONS

Real numbers: Any number which exists on the number line. Real numbers are the combined group of rational and irrational numbers.

Imaginary numbers: Any number multiplied by i, the imaginary unit. i = $\sqrt{-1}$. Imaginary numbers are the opposite of real numbers and are not part of our everyday life.

Rational: Numbers which can be expressed as a fraction whose top (the numerator) and bottom (the denominator) are both integers.

Irrational: Numbers which can't be expressed as a fraction whose top (the numerator) and bottom (the denominator) are integers. Square roots of non-perfect squares (such as $\sqrt{2}$) are irrational, and π is irrational. Irrational numbers may be described as non-repeating decimals.

Integers: Integers consist of those numbers which are multiples of 1: {...,-2, -1, 0, 1, 2, 3,...}. Integers are "integral": they contain no fractional or decimal parts.

Non-integers: Non-integers are those numbers which contain fractional or decimal parts. E.g., $\frac{1}{2}$ and 0.125 are non-integers.

Whole numbers: Non-negative integers: {0, 1, 2, 3,...}. Note that 0 is a whole number (but a non-negative whole number, since it is neither positive nor negative).

Counting numbers: The subset of whole numbers which excludes 0: {1, 2, 3,...}.

Prime numbers: Prime numbers are a subset of the counting numbers. They include those non-negative integers which have two and only two factors; that is, the factors 1 and themselves. The first 10 primes are 2, 3, 5, 7, 11, 13, 17, 19, 23, and 29. Note that 1 is not a prime number as it only has one factor, i.e., 1. Also, the number 2 is not only the smallest prime but also the only even prime number.

Composite numbers: A positive number that has more than two factors other than 1 and itself. Also, any non-prime number greater than 1. Examples include: 4, 6, 8, 9, 10, etc. Note that 1 is not a composite number and the number 4 is the smallest composite number.

Factors: A factor is an integer that can be divided evenly into another integer ("divides evenly" means that there is no remainder). Example: Factors of 12 are 1, 2, 3, 4, 6 and 12.

Multiples: A multiple is a number that results from a given integer being multiplied by another integer. Example: Multiples of 12 include 12, 24, 36, 48, etc. Proof: 12 x *1* = 12, 12 x *2* = 24, 12 x *3* = 36, and 12 x *4* = 48, etc. Note: Whereas a factor of any number is less than or equal to the number in question, a multiple of any number is equal to or greater than the number itself. That is, any non-zero integer has a finite number of factors but an infinite number of multiples.

THE FOUR BASIC OPERATIONS

The four basic arithmetic operations are addition, subtraction, multiplication, and division. The results of these operations are called sum, difference, product, and quotient, respectively. Two additional operations involve exponents and radicals.

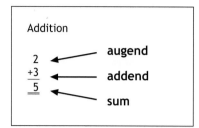

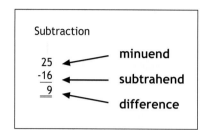

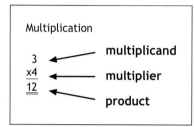

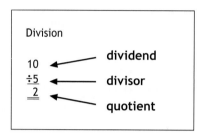

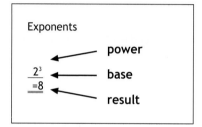

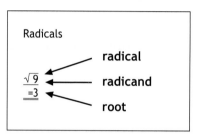

COMMON FRACTIONS AND THEIR PERCENTAGE EQUIVALENTS

Exercise - Fill in the missing percentages to practice changing common fractions in terms of their percent equivalents:

Full
$$\frac{1}{1} = 100\%$$

Halves
$$\frac{1}{2} = 50\% \quad \frac{2}{2} = 100\%$$

Thirds
$$\frac{1}{3} = ?\% \quad \frac{2}{3} = ?\% \quad \frac{3}{3} = 100\%$$

Fourths
$$\frac{1}{4} = ?\% \quad \frac{2}{4} = 50\% \quad \frac{3}{4} = ?\% \quad \frac{4}{4} = 100\%$$

Fifths
$$\frac{1}{5} = ?\% \quad \frac{2}{5} = ?\% \quad \frac{3}{5} = ?\% \quad \frac{4}{5} = ?\% \quad \frac{5}{5} = 100\%$$

Sixths
$$\frac{1}{6} = ?\% \quad \frac{2}{6} = ?\% \quad \frac{3}{6} = 50\% \quad \frac{4}{6} = ?\% \quad \frac{5}{6} = ?\% \quad \frac{6}{6} = 100\%$$

Sevenths
$$\frac{1}{7} = ?\% \quad \frac{2}{7} = ?\% \quad \frac{3}{7} = ?\% \quad \frac{4}{7} = ?\% \quad \frac{5}{7} = ?\% \quad \frac{6}{7} = ?\% \quad \frac{7}{7} = 100\%$$

Eighths
$$\frac{1}{8} = ?\% \quad \frac{2}{8} = ?\% \quad \frac{3}{8} = ?\% \quad \frac{4}{8} = 50\% \quad \frac{5}{8} = ?\% \quad \frac{6}{8} = ?\% \quad \frac{7}{8} = ?\% \quad \frac{8}{8} = 100\%$$

Ninths
$$\frac{1}{9} = 11.1\% \quad \frac{2}{9} = 22.2\% \quad \frac{3}{9} = 33.3\% \quad \frac{4}{9} = 44.4\% \quad \frac{5}{9} = 55.5\% \quad \frac{6}{9} = 66.6\% \quad \frac{7}{9} = 77.7\% \quad \frac{8}{9} = 88.8\% \quad \frac{9}{9} = 100\%$$

Tenths
$$\frac{1}{10} = ?\% \quad \frac{2}{10} = 20\% \quad \frac{3}{10} = ?\% \quad \frac{4}{10} = 40\% \quad \frac{5}{10} = 50\% \quad \frac{6}{10} = 60\% \quad \frac{7}{10} = 70\% \quad \frac{8}{10} = 80\% \quad \frac{9}{10} = 90\% \quad \frac{10}{10} = 100\%$$

Answers

Full
$$\frac{1}{1} = 100\%$$

Halves
$$\frac{1}{2} = 50\% \quad \frac{2}{2} = 100\%$$

Thirds
$$\frac{1}{3} = 33\frac{1}{3}\% \quad \frac{2}{3} = 66\frac{2}{3}\% \quad \frac{3}{3} = 100\%$$

Fourths
$$\frac{1}{4} = 25\% \quad \frac{2}{4} = 50\% \quad \frac{3}{4} = 75\% \quad \frac{4}{4} = 100\%$$

Fifths
$$\frac{1}{5} = 20\% \quad \frac{2}{5} = 40\% \quad \frac{3}{5} = 60\% \quad \frac{4}{5} = 80\% \quad \frac{5}{5} = 100\%$$

Sixths
$$\frac{1}{6} = 16\frac{2}{3}\% \quad \frac{2}{6} = 33\frac{1}{3}\% \quad \frac{3}{6} = 50\% \quad \frac{4}{6} = 66\frac{2}{3}\% \quad \frac{5}{6} = 83\frac{1}{3}\% \quad \frac{6}{6} = 100\%$$

Sevenths
$$\frac{1}{7} = 14.2\% \quad \frac{2}{7} = 28.4\% \quad \frac{3}{7} = 42.8\% \quad \frac{4}{7} = 57\% \quad \frac{5}{7} = 71.4\% \quad \frac{6}{7} = 85.7\% \quad \frac{7}{7} = 100\%$$

Eighths
$$\frac{1}{8} = 12.5\% \quad \frac{2}{8} = 25\% \quad \frac{3}{8} = 37.5\% \quad \frac{4}{8} = 50\% \quad \frac{5}{8} = 62.5\% \quad \frac{6}{8} = 75\% \quad \frac{7}{8} = 87.5\% \quad \frac{8}{8} = 100\%$$

Ninths
$$\frac{1}{9} = 11.1\% \quad \frac{2}{9} = 22.2\% \quad \frac{3}{9} = 33.3\% \quad \frac{4}{9} = 44.4\% \quad \frac{5}{9} = 55.5\% \quad \frac{6}{9} = 66.6\% \quad \frac{7}{9} = 77.7\% \quad \frac{8}{9} = 88.8\% \quad \frac{9}{9} = 100\%$$

Tenths
$$\frac{1}{10} = 10\% \quad \frac{2}{10} = 20\% \quad \frac{3}{10} = 30\% \quad \frac{4}{10} = 40\% \quad \frac{5}{10} = 50\% \quad \frac{6}{10} = 60\% \quad \frac{7}{10} = 70\% \quad \frac{8}{10} = 80\% \quad \frac{9}{10} = 90\% \quad \frac{10}{10} = 100\%$$

RULES FOR ODD AND EVEN NUMBERS

Examples:

Even + Even = Even	2 + 2 = 4	
Odd + Odd = Even	3 + 3 = 6	
Even + Odd = Odd	2 + 3 = 5	
Odd + Even = Odd	3 + 2 = 5	
Even - Even = Even	4 - 2 = 2	[4 + (-2) = 2]
Odd - Odd = Even	5 - 3 = 2	[5 + (-3) = 2]
Even - Odd = Odd	6 - 3 = 3	[6 + (-3) = 3]
Odd - Even = Odd	5 - 2 = 3	[5 + (-2) = 3]
Even x Even = Even	2 x 2 = 4	
Odd x Odd = Odd	3 x 3 = 9	
Even x Odd = Even	2 x 3 = 6	
Odd x Even = Even	3 x 2 = 6	
Even ÷ Even = Even	4 ÷ 2 = 2	
Odd ÷ Odd = Odd	9 ÷ 3 = 3	
Even ÷ Odd = Even	6 ÷ 3 = 2	
Odd ÷ Even = *Not possible	$5 ÷ 2 = 2\frac{1}{2}$	

*An odd number divided by an even number does not result in an even or odd integer, only a non-integer. Also, any of the above numbers could be negative and the rules still hold. For example, (-2) + (-2) = -4; minus four is a negative number but it is even. Remember, for the record, although zero is neither a positive nor negative number, it is considered an even number (integer). For example, 3 + (-3) = 0; since zero is considered an even integer, it still holds that "an odd plus an odd is even."

RULES FOR POSITIVE AND NEGATIVE NUMBERS

Examples:

Positive + Positive = Positive	2 + 2 = 4	
Negative + Negative = Negative	(-2) + (-2) = -4	
Positive + Negative = Depends	4 + -2 = 2	
	2 + -4 = -2	
Negative + Positive = Depends	(-2) + 4 = 2	
	(-4) + 2 = -2	
Positive - Positive = Depends	4 - 2 = 2	[4 + (-2) = 2]
	2 - 4 = -2	[2 + (-4) = -2]
Negative - Negative = Depends	(-2) - (-4) = 2	[-2 + (+4) = 2]
	(-4) - (-2) = -2	[-4 + (+2) = 4]
Positive - Negative = Positive	2 - (-2) = 4	[-2 + (-4) = -6]
Negative - Positive = Negative	(-4) - 2 = -6	[-4 + (-2) = -6]

Positive x Positive = Positive	2 x 2 = 4
Negative x Negative = Positive	(-2) x (-2) = 4
Positive x Negative = Negative	2 x (-2) = -4
Negative x Positive = Negative	(-2) x 2 = -4
Positive ÷ Positive = Positive	4 ÷ 2 = 2
Negative ÷ Negative = Positive	(-4) ÷ (-2) = 2
Positive ÷ Negative = Negative	4 ÷ (-2) = -2
Negative ÷ Positive = Negative	(-4) ÷ 2 = -2

COMMON SQUARES AND CUBES

$1^2 = 1$	$1^3 = 1$	$1^4 = 1$	$1^5 = 1$	$1^6 = 1$
$2^2 = 4$	$2^3 = 8$	$2^4 = 16$	$2^5 = 32$	$2^6 = 64$
$3^2 = 9$	$3^3 = 27$	$3^4 = 81$	$3^5 = 243$	
$4^2 = 16$	$4^3 = 64$	$4^4 = 256$		
$5^2 = 25$	$5^3 = 125$	$5^4 = 625$		
$6^2 = 36$	$6^3 = 216$			
$7^2 = 49$	$7^3 = 343$			
$8^2 = 64$	$8^3 = 512$			
$9^2 = 81$	$9^3 = 729$			
$10^2 = 100$	$10^3 = 1,000$	$10^4 = 10\,k$	$10^5 = 100k$	$10^6 = 1M$

Also:

$10^9 = 1$ billion
$10^{12} = 1$ trillion

Common Squares - From 13 to 30

$13^2 = 169$	$21^2 = 441$	$29^2 = 841$
$14^2 = 196$	$22^2 = 484$	$30^2 = 900$
$15^2 = 225$	$23^2 = 529$	
$16^2 = 256$	$24^2 = 576$	
$17^2 = 289$	$25^2 = 625$	
$18^2 = 324$	$26^2 = 676$	
$19^2 = 361$	$27^2 = 729$	
$20^2 = 400$	$28^2 = 784$	

COMMON SQUARE ROOTS

$\sqrt{2} = 1.4$
$\sqrt{3} = 1.7$
$\sqrt{5} = 2.2$

DIVISIBILITY RULES

No.	Divisibility rule:	Examples:
1.	Every number is divisible by 1.	Not stated.
2.	A number is divisible by 2 if it is even.	Not stated.
3.	A number is divisible by 3 if the sum of its digits is divisible by 3.	651 is divisible by 3 since 6 + 5 + 1 = 12 and "12" is divisible by 3.
4.	A number is divisible by 4 if its last two digits form a number that is divisible by 4.	1,112 is divisible by 4 since the number "12" is divisible by 4.
5.	A number is divisible by 5 if the number ends in 5 or 0.	245 is divisible by 5 since this number ends in "5."
6.	A number is divisible by 6 if it is divisible by 2 and 3.	738 is divisible by 6 since this number is divisible by both 2 and 3, and the rules that govern the divisibility of 2 and 3 apply.
7.	No clear rule.	N.A.
8.	A number is divisible by 8 if its last three digits form a number that is divisible by 8.	2,104 is divisible by 8 since the number "104" is divisible by 8.
9.	A number is divisible by 9 if the sum of its digits is divisible by 9.	4,887 is divisible by 9 since 4 + 8 + 8 + 7 = 27 and "27" is divisible by 9.
10.	A number is divisible by 10 if it ends in 0.	990 is divisible by 10 because 990 ends in 0.

EXPONENTS

Guide: Here are the ten (10) basic rules governing exponents:

Rule #1 $a^b \times a^c = a^{b+c}$

Ex: $2^2 \times 2^2 = 2^{2+2} = 2^4$

Rule #2 $a^b \div a^c = a^{b-c}$

Ex: $2^6 \div 2^2 = 2^{6-2} = 2^4$

Rule #3 $(a^b)^c = a^{b \times c}$

Ex: $(2^2)^3 = 2^{2 \times 3} = 2^6$

Rule #4 $(ab)^c = a^c b^c$

Ex: $6^2 = (2 \times 3)^2 = 2^2 \times 3^2$

Rule #5 $\dfrac{a^c}{b^c} = \left(\dfrac{a}{b}\right)^c$

Ex: $\dfrac{4^5}{2^5} = \left(\dfrac{4}{2}\right)^5 = 2^5$

Rule #6 $a^{-b} = \dfrac{1}{a^b}$

Ex: $2^{-3} = \dfrac{1}{2^3}$

Rule #7 $a^{\frac{1}{2}} = \sqrt{a}$

Ex: $(4)^{\frac{1}{2}} = \sqrt{4} = 2$

$a^{\frac{1}{3}} = \sqrt[3]{a}$

Ex: $(27)^{\frac{1}{3}} = \sqrt[3]{27} = 3$

$a^{\frac{2}{3}} = \left(\sqrt[3]{a}\right)^2$

Ex: $(64)^{\frac{2}{3}} = \left(\sqrt[3]{64}\right)^2 = 4^2 = 16$

Rule #8 $a^b + a^b = a^b(1+1) = a^b(2)$

Ex: $2^{10} + 2^{10} = 2^{10}(1+1) = 2^{10}(2) = 2^{10}(2^1) = 2^{11}$

Rule #9 $a^b + a^c \neq a^{b+c}$

Ex: $2^2 + 2^3 \neq 2^{2+3}$

Rule #10 $a^b - a^c \neq a^{b-c}$

Ex: $2^5 + 2^2 \neq 2^{5-2}$

RADICALS

Guide: Here are the ten (10) basic rules governing radicals:

Rule #1

$(\sqrt{a})^2 = a$

Ex: $(\sqrt{4})^2 = 4$

Proof: $\sqrt{16} = 4$

Rule #2

$\sqrt{a} \times \sqrt{b} = \sqrt{a \times b}$

Ex: $\sqrt{4} \times \sqrt{9} = \sqrt{36}$

Proof: $2 \times 3 = 6$

Rule #3

$\sqrt{a} \div \sqrt{b} = \sqrt{\dfrac{a}{b}}$

Ex: $\sqrt{100} \div \sqrt{25} = \sqrt{4}$

Proof: $10 \div 5 = 2$

Rule #4

$\dfrac{\sqrt[x]{a}}{\sqrt[x]{b}} = \sqrt[x]{\dfrac{a}{b}}$

Ex: $\dfrac{\sqrt[3]{64}}{\sqrt[3]{8}} = \sqrt[3]{\dfrac{64}{8}}$

Proof: $\dfrac{4}{2} = 2$

Rule #5

$b\sqrt{a} + c\sqrt{a} = (b + c)\sqrt{a}$

Ex: $3\sqrt{4} + 2\sqrt{4} = 5\sqrt{4}$

Proof: $3(2) + 2(2) = 5(2)$

Rule #6

$b\sqrt{a} - c\sqrt{a} = (b - c)\sqrt{a}$

Ex: $5\sqrt{9} - 2\sqrt{9} = 3\sqrt{9}$

Proof: $5(3) - 2(3) = 3(3)$

Rule #7

$\dfrac{b}{\sqrt{a}} = \dfrac{b}{\sqrt{a}} \times \dfrac{\sqrt{a}}{\sqrt{a}} = \dfrac{b\sqrt{a}}{a}$

Ex: $\dfrac{6}{\sqrt{3}} = \dfrac{6}{\sqrt{3}} \times \dfrac{\sqrt{3}}{\sqrt{3}} = \dfrac{6\sqrt{3}}{\sqrt{9}} = \dfrac{6\sqrt{3}}{3} = 2\sqrt{3}$

Here (above) we multiply both the numerator and denominator of the original fraction by $\sqrt{3}$ in order to remove the radical from the denominator of this fraction.

Rule #8

$\dfrac{\sqrt{a} + 1}{\sqrt{a} - 1} = \dfrac{\sqrt{a} + 1}{\sqrt{a} - 1} \times \dfrac{\sqrt{a} + 1}{\sqrt{a} + 1}$

Ex: $\dfrac{\sqrt{2} + 1}{\sqrt{2} - 1} = \dfrac{\sqrt{2} + 1}{\sqrt{2} - 1} \times \dfrac{\sqrt{2} + 1}{\sqrt{2} + 1} = 3 + 2\sqrt{2}$

Here (above) we multiply both the numerator and denominator of the fraction by $\sqrt{2} + 1$ in order to remove the radical from the denominator of this fraction.

$\dfrac{\sqrt{a} - 1}{\sqrt{a} + 1} = \dfrac{\sqrt{a} - 1}{\sqrt{a} + 1} \times \dfrac{\sqrt{a} - 1}{\sqrt{a} - 1}$

Ex: $\dfrac{\sqrt{2} - 1}{\sqrt{2} + 1} = \dfrac{\sqrt{2} - 1}{\sqrt{2} + 1} \times \dfrac{\sqrt{2} - 1}{\sqrt{2} - 1} = 3 - 2\sqrt{2}$

By multiplying both the numerator and denominator of the fraction by $\sqrt{2} - 1$, we can remove the radical from the denominator of this fraction.

Rule #9

$\sqrt{a} + \sqrt{b} \neq \sqrt{a + b}$

Ex: $\sqrt{16} + \sqrt{9} \neq \sqrt{25}$

Proof: $4 + 3 \neq 5$

Rule #10

$\sqrt{a} - \sqrt{b} \neq \sqrt{a - b}$

Ex: $\sqrt{25} - \sqrt{16} \neq \sqrt{9}$

Proof: $5 - 4 \neq 3$

BASIC GEOMETRY FORMULAS

Circles

Circumference:
Circumference = π x diameter
C = πd
or C = 2πr   [Where r = radius]

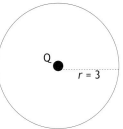

Area:
Area = π x radius^2
A = π r^2

Triangles

Area:

Area = $\dfrac{\text{base x height}}{2}$

A = $\dfrac{bh}{2}$

The Pythagorean Theorem:
c^2 = a^2 + b^2

[where is c the length of the hypotenuse and *a* and *b* are the length of the legs]

3 : 4 : 5 Triangle

In a 3 : 4 : 5 triangle, the ratios of the length of the sides are always 3 : 4 : 5 units.

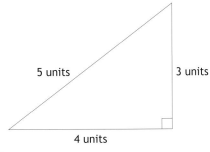

45°- 45°- 90° Triangle

In a 45°- 45°- 90° triangle, the ratios of the length of the sides are 1 : 1 : √2 units; a right-isosceles triangle is another name for a 45°- 45°- 90° triangle.

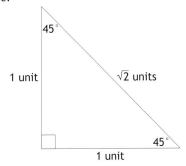

30° - 60° - 90° Triangle

In a 30° - 60° - 90° triangle, the ratios of the lengths of the sides are 1 : $\sqrt{3}$: 2 units.

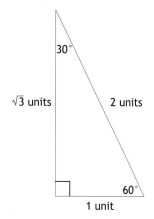

Squares

Perimeter:
Perimeter = 4 x side
P= 4s
Ex: P= 4(2) = 8 units

Area:
Area = side^2
A = s^2
Ex: A = 2^2 = 4 units^2

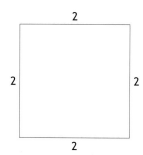

Rectangles

Perimeter:
Perimeter = (2 x length) + (2 x width)
P= 2l + 2w
Ex: P = 2(4) + 2(2) = 12 units

Area:
Area = length x width
A = lw
Ex: A = 4 x 2 = 8 units^2

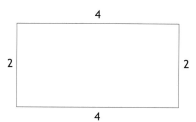

Cubes

Surface Area:
Surface Area = 6 x side^2
SA = 6s^2
Ex: SA = 6(2)^2 = 24 units^2

Volume:
Volume = side^3
V = s^3
Ex: V = 2^3 = 8 units^3

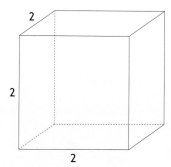

Rectangular Solids

Surface Area:

Surface Area = (2 x length x width) + (2 x length x height) + (2 x width x height)

SA = 2lw + 2lh + 2wh

Ex: Surface Area = 2(4 x 2) + 2(4 x 3) + 2(2 x 3) = 52 units^2

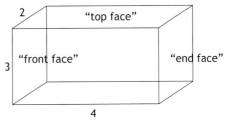

Volume:

v = length x width x height

V= lwh

Ex: A = 4 x 2 x 3 = 24 units^3

Circular Cylinders

Surface Area:

SA = $(2\pi r^2)$ + $(2\pi r^2 h)$

Ex: SA = $[2\pi(2)^2 + 2\pi(2)^2\,5]$

SA = $8\pi + 20\pi = 28\pi$ units^2

Volume:

V = $\pi r^2\,h$

V = $\pi (2)^2\,5 = 20\pi$ units^3

Cone

Volume:

V = $\frac{1}{3}$ Bh = $\frac{1}{3}\pi r^2 h$

Ex: V = $\frac{1}{3}\pi (3)^2\,6 = 18\pi$ units^3

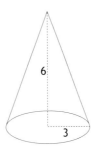

Pyramids

Volume:

V = $\frac{1}{3}$ Bh [where *B* is the area of the base and *h* is the height]

Ex: V = $\frac{1}{3}$ (20)(3) units^3

> Note: The formula for all tapered solids is the same: V = $\frac{1}{3}$ Bh where *B* is the area of the base and *h* is the perpendicular distance from the base to the vertex.

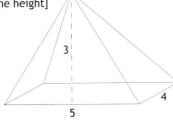

Sphere

Surface Area:

SA = $4\pi r^2$

Ex: SA = $4\pi(3)^2 = 36\pi$ units^2

Volume:

V = $\frac{4}{3}\pi r^3$

Ex: V = $\frac{4}{3}\pi (3)^3 = 36\pi$ units^3

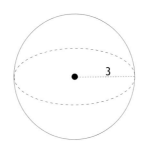

PROBABILITY, PERMUTATIONS & COMBINATIONS

Exhibit 3-1 and *Exhibit 3-2* are strategic flowcharts for use in both previewing and reviewing the material in this segment. What is the difference between probability and permutations & combinations? Probabilities are expressed as fractions, percents, or decimals between 0 and 1 (where 1 is the probability of certainty and 0 is the probability of impossibility). Permutations and combinations, on the other hand, result in outcomes greater than or equal to 1. Frequently they result in quite large outcomes such as 10, 36, 720, etc.

In terms of probability, a quick rule of thumb is to determine first whether we are dealing with an "and" or "or" situation. "And" means multiply and "or" means addition. For example, if a problem states, "what is the probability of x and y," we multiply individual probabilities together. If a problem states, "what is the probability of x or y," we add individual probabilities together.

Moreover, if a probability problem requires us to <u>multiply</u>, we must ask one further question: are the events independent or are the events dependent? Independent means that two events have no influence on one another and we simply multiply individual probabilities together to arrive at a final answer. Dependent events mean that the occurrence of one event has an influence on the occurrence of another event, and this influence must be taken into account.

Likewise, if a problem requires us to <u>add</u> probabilities, we must ask one further question: are the events mutually exclusive or non-mutually exclusive? Mutually exclusive means that two events cannot occur at the same time and there is no "overlap" present. If two events have no overlap, we simply add probabilities. Non-mutually exclusive means that two events can occur at the same time and overlap is present. If two events do contain overlap, this overlap must not be double counted.

With respect to permutations and combinations, permutations are ordered groups while combinations are unordered groups. That is, order matters in permutations; order does not matter in combinations. For example, AB and BA are considered different outcomes in permutations but are considered a single outcome in combinations. In real-life, examples of permutations include telephone numbers, license plates, or electronic codes and passwords. Examples of combinations include selection of members for a team or lottery tickets. In the case of lottery tickets, for instance, the order of numbers does not matter; we just need to get all the numbers, usually six of them.

Note that in problem solving situations, the words "arrangements" or "possibilities" imply permutations; the words "select" or "choose" imply combinations.

Factorials:

Factorial means that we engage multiplication such that:

Ex. 4! = 4 x 3 x 2 x 1

Ex. 7! = 7 x 6 x 5 x 4 x 3 x 2 x 1

Zero factorial equals one and one factorial also equals one:

0! = 1
1! = 1

Coins, Cards, Dice, and Marbles:

Problems in this section include reference to coins, dice, marbles, and cards. For clarification purposes: The two sides of a coin are heads and tails. A die has six sides numbered from 1 to 6, with each having an equal likelihood of appearing subsequent to being tossed. The word "die" is singular; "dice" is plural. Marbles are assumed to be of a single, solid color. A deck of cards contains 52 cards divided equally into four suits—Clubs, Diamonds, Hearts, and Spades—where each suit contains 13 cards including Ace, King, Queen, Jack, 10, 9, 8, 7, 6, 5, 4, 3 and 2. Card problems have not appeared on the GMAT in recent years.

Exhibit 3-1: Probability Flowchart

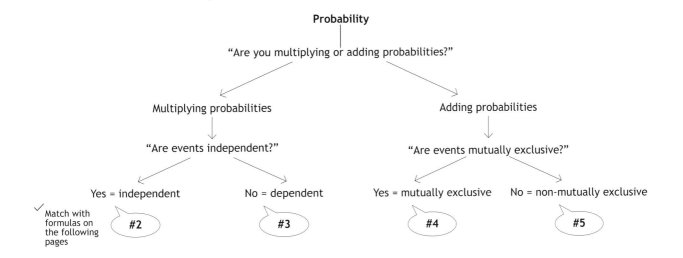

Exhibit 3-2: Permutations and Combinations Flowchart

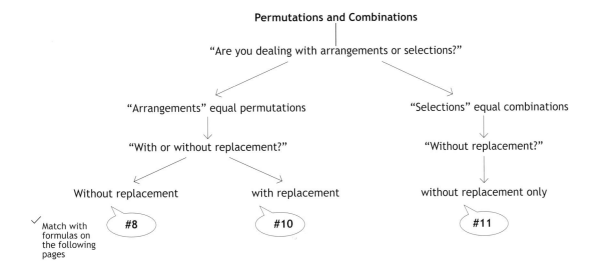

Basic Probability Formulas

Here at a glance are all the basic probability, permutation and combination formulas used in this book.

Universal Formula

$$\text{Probability} = \frac{\text{Selected Events(s)}}{\text{Total Number of Possibilities}}$$

Ex: You buy 3 lotto tickets and there are 1,000,000 tickets sold. What is the probability of winning the lottery?

$$\text{Probability} = \frac{3}{1,000,000}$$

Special Multiplication Rule

$$P(A \text{ and } B) = P(A) \times P(B)$$

If events are independent ("no influence on one another"), we simply multiply them together.

Ex. What is the probability of tossing a coin twice and obtaining heads on both the first and second toss?

$$= \frac{1}{2} \times \frac{1}{2} = \frac{1}{4}$$

General Multiplication Rule

#3

$$P(A \text{ and } B) = P(A) \times P(B/A)$$

[Where P(B/A) equals the probability of B given that A has already occurred]

If events are not independent ("they influence one another"), we must adjust the second event based on its influence from the first event.

Ex: A bag contains six marbles, three blue and three green. What is the probability of blindly reaching into the bag and pulling out two green marbles?

$$= \frac{3}{6} \times \frac{2}{5} = \frac{6}{30} = \frac{1}{5}$$

Special Addition Rule

$$P(A \text{ or } B) = P(A) + P(B)$$

If events are mutually exclusive ("there is no overlap"), then we just add the probability of the events together.

Ex: The probability that Sam will go to prep school in Switzerland is 50%, while the probability that he will go to prep school in the Britain is 25%. What is the probability that he will choose to go to prep school in either Switzerland or Britain?

$$= 50\% + 25\% = 75\%$$

General Addition Rule

P(A or B) = P(A) + P(B) - P(A and B)
[Where P(A and B) equals the probability of both A and B occurring together]

If events are not mutually exclusive ("there is overlap"), then we must subtract out the overlap subsequent to adding the events.

Ex. The probability that tomorrow will be *rainy* is 30%. The probability that tomorrow will be *windy* is 20%. What is the probability that tomorrow's weather will be either rainy or windy?

= 30% + 20% - (30% x 20%)
= 50% - 6% = 44%

Complement Rule

P(A) = 1 - P (not A)

The Complement Rule describes the "subtracting of probabilities" rather than the "adding or multiplying of probabilities."

Ex: What is the probability rolling a pair of dice and not rolling double sixes?

$$= 1 - \frac{1}{36} = \frac{35}{36}$$
[This probability equals one minus the probability of rolling double sixes]

Rule of Enumeration

If there are *X* ways of doing one thing, *Y* ways of doing a second thing, and *Z* ways of doing a third thing, then the number of ways of doing all these things is *X* x *Y* x *Z* This is known as the *Rule of Enumeration*.

Note: Technically, the *Rule of Enumeration* falls under neither the umbrella of probability nor permutation and combination.

Ex: All-Fest Restaurant offers customers a set menu with a choice of one of each of the following: 2 different salads, 3 different soups, 5 different entrees, 3 different desserts, and coffee or tea. How many possibilities are there with respect to how a customer can take his or her dinner?

= 2 x 3 x 5 x 3 x 2 = 180

Permutations

(i) without replacement $$_nP_r = \frac{n!}{(n - r)!}$$
[Where n = total number of items and r = number of items we are taking or arranging]

#9
$_nP_n = n!$
[Shortcut formula when all items are taken together]

Ex: How many ways can a person display (or arrange) four different books on a shelf?

$$_nP_r = \frac{n!}{(n-r)!} \qquad\qquad _4P_4 = \frac{4!}{(4-4)!} = \frac{4!}{0!} = \frac{4!}{1} = 4! = 24$$

Also, shortcut formula: $n! = 4! = 24$

#10

(ii) with replacement $\qquad\qquad n^r$

Ex: How many four-digit codes can be made from the numbers 1, 2, 3, 4 if the same numbers can be displayed more than once?

$n^r \qquad\qquad\qquad\qquad 4^4 = 256$

Note: Permutation with replacement (n^r) technically falls under the *Counting Rule* or *Rule of Enumeration*. It is included here for ease of presentation. To be considered a *permutation*, the permutation formula must be applicable.

Combinations

 #11
$$_nC_r = \frac{n!}{r!(n-r)!}$$
[Where n = total number of items taken and r = the number of items we are choosing]

Ex: How many ways can a person choose three of four colors for the purpose of painting the inside of a house?

$$_nC_r = \frac{n!}{r!(n-r)!}$$

$$_4C_3 = \frac{4!}{3!(4-3)!} = \frac{4!}{3! \times 1!} = 4$$

Other formulas:

Joint Permutations

#12
$$_nP_r \times {}_nP_r = \frac{n!}{(n-r)!} \times \frac{n!}{(n-r)!}$$

Ex: A curator at a local museum has seven panels in which she must display four of five wood carvings and three of four bronze sculptures. How many possibilities are there with respect to how she can arrange these art pieces?

$$= {}_5P_4 \times {}_4P_3$$

$$= \frac{5!}{4!(5-4)!} \times \frac{4!}{3!(4-3)!}$$

$$= \frac{5!}{4!(1)} \times \frac{4!}{3!(1)!}$$

$$= \frac{5 \times 4 \times 3 \times 2 \times 1!}{4 \times 3 \times 2 \times 1! \times 1!} \times \frac{4 \times 3 \times 2 \times 1!}{3 \times 2 \times 1! \times 1!} = 5 \times 4 = 20$$

[Multiplying outcomes, rather than adding them, is consistent with the treatment afforded by the *Counting Rule* or *Rule of Enumeration*].

Joint Combinations

 #13 $_nC_r \times {}_nC_r = \dfrac{n!}{r!(n-r)!} \times \dfrac{n!}{r!(n-r)!}$

Ex. A special marketing task force is to be chosen from five professional golfers and five professional tennis players. If the final task force chosen is to consist of three golfers and three tennis players, then how many different task forces are possible?

$= {}_5C_3 \times {}_5C_3$

$= \dfrac{5!}{3!(5-3)!} \times \dfrac{5!}{3!(5-3)!}$

$= \dfrac{5!}{3!(2)!} \times \dfrac{5!}{3!(2)!}$

$= \dfrac{5 \times 4 \times \cancel{3 \times 2 \times 1}}{\cancel{3 \times 2 \times 1!} \times \cancel{2 \times 1}} \times \dfrac{5 \times 4 \times \cancel{3 \times 2 \times 1}}{\cancel{3 \times 2 \times 1!} \times \cancel{2 \times 1}} = 10 \times 10 = 100$

Repeated Letters or Numbers (Permutations)

#14 $\dfrac{n!}{x!\,y!\,z!}$ where x, y, z and are different but identical letters or numbers.

Ex: How many four-numeral codes can be created using the four numbers 0, 0, 1, 2?

$= \dfrac{4!}{2!} = \dfrac{4 \times 3 \times \cancel{2 \times 1}}{\cancel{2 \times 1}} = 12$

[The two zeros are repeated numbers]

CHAPTER 4

THE WORLD OF LETTERS:

Sentence Correction, Critical Reasoning, Reading Comprehension, and Analytical Writing

"I never let my schooling interfere with my education."
(Mark Twain)

SENTENCE CORRECTION

The ensuing discussion covers the major topical areas of grammar, grouped according to the eight parts of speech. This coverage is not meant to be exhaustive, but rather to focus on common problem areas. Readers who want a more technical, in-depth analysis should consult a handbook of English grammar and usage.

Grammar and the Eight Parts of Speech

There are eight parts of speech in the English language and any given part of speech may have one or more of the following characteristics: gender, number, person, case, voice, mood, and tense. In summary, gender is either masculine or feminine; number is either singular or plural; person may be first person, second person, or third person; case may be subjective, objective, or possessive; voice is either active or passive; mood may be indicative, imperative, or subjunctive; and tense is either simple or progressive. These characteristics are introduced here to familiarize the reviewer with them and to set the foundation when or if doing more in-depth research at a later point.

Note that adjectives, adverbs, conjunctions, and interjections do not have gender, number, person, case, voice, mood, or tense. The matching of a given part of speech with each of the above characteristics is the primary "cause" of grammar.

I. Nouns

II. Pronouns

III. Adjectives

IV. Verbs

V. Adverbs

VI. Prepositions

VII. Conjunctions

VIII. Interjections

I. Nouns

Definition   A noun is a word that names a person, place, or thing.

Example   <u>Sally</u> is a nice person and you can speak freely with her.

Major classification of nouns:

> Proper nouns (specific names)
> Ex: Mrs. Jones, Boston, Budweiser Beer
>
> Common nouns (general classes)
> Ex: man, trout, umbrella
>
> Concrete nouns (tangibles)
> Ex: tree, car, pencil

Abstract nouns (ideas, qualities)
Ex: honor, jealousy

Singular nouns (individuals)
Ex: person, dog, flower

Collective nouns (group)
Ex: crowd, flock, jury

Grammar   Nouns have gender, number, and case but not person, voice, tense, or mood.

Gender   Masculine   Feminine
Ex: John   Ex: Mary

Number   Singular   Plural
Ex: river   Ex: rivers

Case   Subjective
Ex: Sally is going home.

Objective
Ex: The car struck Sally.

Possessive
Ex: Sally's book contains a bibliography.

II. Pronouns

Definition   A pronoun is a word used in place of a noun or another pronoun.

Example   Sally is a nice person and <u>you</u> can speak freely with <u>her</u>.

Major classification of pronouns:

Personal pronouns:
Ex: I, you, he/she, it, we, they

Relative pronouns:
Examples: who, which, what, that

Interrogative pronouns:
Ex: who, which, what

Demonstrative pronouns:
Ex: this, that, these, those

Indefinite pronouns:
Ex: all, anybody, each, either

Reflexive pronouns:
Ex: himself, herself, ourselves, themselves

Grammar   Pronouns have gender, number, person, and case, but not voice, mood, or tense.

Gender   Masculine
              Ex: he, his, him

              Feminine
              Ex: she, hers, her

Exhibit 4-1: Personal Pronouns

The table below presents personal pronouns in terms of all gender, number, person, and case.

Personal Pronouns	Subjective	Possessive	Objective
1st-person singular	I	my, mine	me
2nd-person singular	you	your, yours	you
3rd-person singular	he, she, it	his, hers, its	him, her, it
1st-person plural	we	our, ours	us
2nd-person plural	you	your, yours	you
3rd-person plural	they	their, theirs	them
who	who	whose	whom

Number   Singular   Plural
           Ex: I, you, he   Ex: we, you, they

Person   1st person   2nd person   3rd person
           Ex: I, we   Ex: you   Ex: he, she, they

Case   Subjective   Objective   Possessive
           Ex: <u>He</u> plays tennis.   Ex: I knew <u>her</u>.   Ex: This is <u>our</u> book.

III. Adjectives

Definition   An adjective is a word used to modify or describe a noun or pronoun.

Example   Sally is a <u>nice</u> person and you can speak freely with her.

Grammar   Adjectives do not have gender, number, person, case, voice, mood, or tense.

IV. Verbs

Definition   A verb is a word that expresses an action or a state of being.

Example   Sally <u>is</u> a nice person and you <u>can speak</u> freely with her.

Major classification of verbs:

Principal verbs
Ex: spoken

Auxiliary verbs
Ex: have spoken

Transitive verbs (requires an object)
Ex: She posted a letter.

Intransitive verbs (doesn't require an object)
Ex: He waits.

Regular verbs (form their participle with "ed")
Ex: travel, traveled, have traveled

Irregular verbs (do not form their participle with "ed")
Ex: go, went, have gone

Grammar   Verbs have voice, mood, tense, number, and person but not gender or case.

Number   Singular
Ex: he plays

Plural
Ex: they play

Note: singular verbs often use an "s"; plural verbs usually drop the "s".

Person   1st-person
Ex: I see

2nd-person
Ex: you see

3rd-person
Ex. they see

Voice   Active
Ex: The player hit the ball.

Passive
Ex: The ball was hit by the player.

Mood   Indicative (indicates a statement)
Ex: Athens is the capital of Greece.

Imperative (indicates a suggestion or command)
Ex: Take charge, Harold.

Subjunctive (indicates a wish or hypothetical, contrary-to-fact situation)
Ex: He wishes he were a rich man.

Tense   Simple tense
Ex: present, past, future, present perfect, past perfect, and future perfect

Progressive tense
Ex: present, past, future, present perfect, past perfect, and future perfect

Exhibit 4-2: The Simple and Progressive Verb Forms

	Simple Form	Progressive Form
Present Tense	I travel	I am traveling
Past Tense	I traveled	I was traveling
Future Tense	I will travel	I will be traveling
Present Perfect Tense	I have traveled	I have been traveling
Past Perfect Tense	I had traveled	I had been traveling
Future Perfect Tense	I will have traveled	I will have been traveling

Exhibit 4-3: Visualizing the Six Verb Tenses

Tense	Examples	Summary
Simple Present	I study physics.	Expresses events or situations that currently exist including the near past and near present.
Simple Past	I studied physics.	Expresses events or situations that existed in the past.
Simple Future	I will study physics.	Expresses events or situations that will exist in the future.
Present Perfect	I have studied physics.	Expresses events or situations that existed in the past but that touch the present.
Past Perfect	I had studied physics in high school before I went to college.	Expresses events or situations in the past, one of which occurred before the other.
Future Perfect	By the time I graduate from college, I will have studied for four years.	Expresses events or situations in the future, one of which will occur after the other.

V. Adverbs

Definition   An adverb is a word that modifies a verb, an adjective, or another adverb.

Example   Sally is a nice person and you can speak <u>freely</u> with her.

Grammar   Adverbs do not have gender, number, person, case, voice, mood, or tense.

VI. Prepositions

Definition   A preposition is a word that shows a relationship between two or more words.

Example   Sally is a nice person and you can speak freely <u>with</u> her.

Grammar   Prepositions do not have gender, number, person, case, voice, mood, or tense.

VII. Conjunctions

Definition   A conjunction is a word that joins or connects words, phrases, clauses, or sentences.

Example   Sally is a nice person <u>and</u> you can speak freely with her.

Major classification of conjunctions:

Coordinating Conjunctions:
Ex: and, but, or, nor, for, yet

Subordinating Conjunctions:
Ex: although, because, before, if, since, unless, when, where

Correlative Conjunctions:
Ex: both...and, either...or, neither...nor, not only...but (also), whether...or

Grammar   Conjunctions do not have gender, number, person, case, voice, mood, or tense.

VIII. Interjections

Definition   An interjection is a word or a term that denotes a strong or sudden feeling.

Example   Sally is a nice person and you can speak freely with her. <u>Wow!</u>

Grammar   Interjections do not have gender, number, person, case, voice, mood, or tense.

Grammatical Idioms

Idioms, like grammar, are correct or incorrect, right or wrong. Idioms are phrases or expressions (in any given language) that have gained acceptance through the passage of time and usually have non-literal meaning. Examples of English language idioms include: "You're pulling my leg," or "Keep your eyes peeled." The following *grammatical idioms*, as included here, do not have non-literal meanings, and they usually involve the correct use of a preposition. Here are fifteen recurring grammatical idioms.

1.   **Between X and Y**

Correct: A choice must be made <u>between</u> blue <u>and</u> green.

Incorrect: A choice must be made <u>between</u> blue <u>or</u> green.

2.   **Consider (or Considered)**

Correct: Many doctors <u>consider</u> stress a more destructive influence on one's longevity than is smoking, drinking, or over-eating.

Incorrect: Many doctors <u>consider</u> stress <u>to be</u> a more destructive influence on one's longevity than is smoking, drinking, or over-eating.

Incorrect: Many doctors <u>consider</u> stress <u>as</u> a more destructive influence on one's longevity than is smoking, drinking, or over-eating.

Correct: Until this recent incident, I had <u>considered</u> him a good friend.

Incorrect: Until this recent incident, I had <u>considered</u> him <u>to be</u> a good friend.

Incorrect: Until this recent incident, I had <u>considered</u> him <u>as a</u> good friend.

(Note: "consider" or "considered" is not followed by "to be" or "as").

3. **Credit X with having**

Correct: Many <u>credit</u> Gutenberg <u>with having</u> invented the printing press.

Incorrect Many <u>credit</u> Gutenberg <u>as having</u> invented the printing press.

4. **Depicted as**

Correct: In the movie *Born on the 4th of July*, Tom Cruise is <u>depicted as</u> a war-torn Vietnam veteran, who struggles tempestuously to reconcile his post-war life to the life he once knew.

Incorrect: In the movie *Born on the 4th of July*, Tom Cruise is <u>depicted to</u> be a war-torn Vietnam veteran, who struggles tempestuously to reconcile his post war-life to the life he once knew.

5. **Distinguishing X from Y**

Correct: Only experts can <u>distinguish</u> a masterpiece <u>from</u> a fake.

Incorrect: Only experts can <u>distinguish</u> a masterpiece <u>and</u> a fake.

6. **Do so**

Correct: Although doctors have the technology to perform brain transplants, there is no clear evidence that they can <u>do so</u>.

Incorrect: Although doctors have the technology to perform brain transplants, there is no clear evidence that they can <u>do it</u>.

7. **From X rather than from Y**

Correct: The majority of discoveries result <u>from</u> meticulous research <u>rather than from</u> sudden inspiration.

Incorrect: The majority of discoveries result <u>from</u> meticulous research <u>instead of</u> sudden inspiration.

8. **From X to Y**

Correct: The population of Africa has grown <u>from</u> 530 million in 1960 <u>to</u> 700 million in 1990.

Incorrect: The population of Africa has grown <u>from</u> 530 million in 1960 <u>up to</u> 700 million in 1990.

9. **In Comparison to**

Correct: <u>In comparison to</u> France, Luxembourg is an amazingly small country.

Incorrect: <u>In comparison with</u> France, Luxembourg is an amazingly small country.

10.　　　　**In Contrast to**

Correct:　　　Pete Sampras won Wimbledon with a classic tennis style <u>in contrast to</u> Bjorn Borg, who captured his titles using an unorthodox playing style.

Incorrect:　　Pete Sampras won Wimbledon with a classic tennis style <u>in contrast with</u> Bjorn Borg, who captured his titles using an unorthodox playing style.

11.　　　　**More...than/Less...than**

Correct:　　　There are <u>more</u> students today applying to graduate school <u>than</u> there were 10 years ago.

Incorrect:　　There are <u>more</u> students today applying to graduate school <u>compared to</u> 10 years ago.

Incorrect:　　There are <u>more</u> students today applying to graduate school <u>compared with</u> 10 years ago.

Correct:　　　There were <u>less</u> students applying to graduate school 10 years ago <u>than</u> there are today.

Incorrect:　　There were <u>less</u> students applying to graduate school 10 years ago <u>compared to</u> today.

Incorrect:　　There were <u>less</u> students applying to graduate school 10 years ago <u>compared with</u> today.

12.　　　　**Prefer to**

Correct:　　　I <u>prefer</u> fish <u>to</u> chicken.

Incorrect:　　I <u>prefer</u> fish <u>over</u> chicken.

13.　　　　**Recover from**

Correct:　　　Someday, it may be worthwhile to try to <u>recover</u> salt <u>from</u> saltwater.

Incorrect:　　Someday, it may be worthwhile to try to <u>recover</u> salt <u>out of</u> saltwater.

14.　　　　**Regarded as**

Correct:　　　Rembrandt is <u>regarded as</u> the greatest painter of the Renaissance period.

Incorrect:　　Rembrandt is <u>regarded to be</u> the greatest painter of the Renaissance period.

15.　　　　**Tying X to Y**

Correct:　　　The author does a good job of <u>tying</u> motivational theory <u>to</u> obtainable results.

Incorrect:　　The author does a good job of <u>tying</u> motivational theory <u>with</u> obtainable results.

CRITICAL REASONING

Arguments

What is an argument? An argument is not a heated exchange like the ones you might have had with a good friend, family member, or significant other. An argument, as referred to in logic, is "a claim or statement made which is supported by some evidence." A claim is part of a larger word called "argument."

"Oh, it sure is a nice day today." This statement is certainly a claim but it is not an argument because it contains no support for what is said. To turn it into an argument we could say, "Oh, it sure is a nice day today. We have had nearly five hours of sunshine." Now the claim ("it sure is a nice day") is supported by some evidence ("nearly five hours of sunshine").

Let's get some definitions out of the way.

Definitions

Conclusion   The conclusion is the claim or main point that the author, writer, or speaker is making.

Evidence   The evidence includes any facts, examples, statistics, surveys, and other information or data that the author (writer or speaker) uses in support of his or her conclusion.

Assumption   The assumption is the author's unstated belief ("unstated evidence") about why his or her claim is right. An assumption is that part of the argument that the author, writer, or speaker assumes to be correct without stating so; it is "that which the author takes for granted." More poetically, the assumption may be said to be "the *glue* that holds the evidence to the conclusion."

The ABCs of Argument Structure

The following expresses the relationship between the three elements of classic argument structure:

Conclusion = Evidence + Assumption

or:

Conclusion - Evidence = Assumption

The ability to understand simple but formal argument structure is useful, if not essential, to advance critical thinking. After identifying the conclusion and evidence, we then proceed to examine the third element called the assumption.

So how do we go about identifying the first two elements, the conclusion and evidence?

Identifying the Conclusion and Evidence

Certain words always signal the use of evidence or the start of the conclusion. The chart on the next page lists the most common keywords. If, for example, you hear someone say, "Because the stock market is going up, I'm (therefore) going to invest in real estate," you may presume that the phrase "because the stock market is going up" is evidence. The reason for this is that "because" always signals the use of evidence. The remaining phrase, "I'm going to invest in the stock market" contains the conclusion. Note that these phrases may also be reversed without affecting what is evidence and conclusion. For example, "I'm going to invest in real estate *because* the stock market is going up."

If possible, use "transition words" to identify the conclusion and evidence in an argument.

Words that always signal "evidence"	Words that always signal "conclusion"
• As	• As a result
• As indicated by	• Clearly
• As shown by	• Consequently
• Because	• Hence
• For	• In conclusion
• Given that	• So
• Since	• Therefore
• The reason is that	• Thus

It is important to note that transition words will not always be present to guide you, meaning that you cannot always use transition words to locate the conclusion and the evidence in an argument.

Locating the Assumption

Whereas the conclusion and evidence in an argument are always explicit, the assumption is always implicit. The fact that assumptions are by definition implicit means that they will not be stated, that is, written down on paper by the author or spoken out loud by the speaker. They exist foremost in the mind of the author or speaker. Conclusions and evidence on the other hand are explicit. This means that they will be stated—physically written down on paper or spoken out loud.

Parts of an Argument	Stated or Implied	This means
Conclusion	Explicit	It is stated i.e., written down or spoken out loud.
Evidence	Explicit	It is stated i.e., written down or spoken out loud.
Assumption	Implicit	It is neither stated (written down or spoken out loud), but remains in the mind of the person presenting the argument.

Evaluating Arguments

Evaluating arguments typically translates to attacking arguments. There are effectively two ways to attack an argument: attack the evidence or attack the assumption(s). We can either attack the evidence or attack the assumption. Obviously, in order to attack the assumption, we must be able to identify it.

Dorothy and her College Entrance Exam

Exercise: In order to practice identifying an argument's assumption(s), fill in the missing pieces below.

Argument	As Dorothy achieved a high score on her college entrance exam, she will surely succeed in college.
Conclusion	_____
	_____
	_____
Evidence	_____
	_____
	_____
Assumption	_____
	_____
	_____

The following is a possible solution to the argument on the previous page.

Argument   As Dorothy achieved a high score on her college entrance exam, she will surely succeed in college.

Conclusion   Dorothy will surely succeed in college.

Evidence   She achieved a high score on her college entrance exam.

Assumption   Success on a college entrance exam leads to success in college or, stated another way, success in college requires the same set of skills as is required to perform well on a college entrance exam.

Let's attack this argument.

1.   Attack the evidence

Did Dorothy really score high on her college entrance exam? How high is high? In other words, we need to find out what score she actually got and then verify that it was indeed a "high" score.

2.   Attack the assumption

Furthermore, before Dorothy can succeed in college, she must first be accepted to college. Is a high score on her college entrance exam enough to get her accepted to college? College, for example, requires group work. Succeeding on a test requires no interaction with anyone except yourself. What about other factors such as personal motivation, independence, or emotional stability? In short, Dorothy may not have the personal qualities to succeed in college, even though she loves to take entrance tests!

What are the common categories of assumptions that appear on the GMAT? The six categories include: Comparison and Analogy Assumptions, Representative Sample Assumptions, Cause-and-Effect Assumptions, Implementation Assumptions, Number-based Assumptions, and Logic-based Assumptions.

Comparison and Analogy Assumptions

The general strategy for attack is as follows:

Topic	Formulaically	How to Attack the Comparison
Are two things the same or nearly the same?	Does A = B?	Show that A is different from B and you weaken the comparison.
Are two things different?	Does A ≠ B?	Show that A is similar to B and you weaken the comparison.

What is an analogy? An analogy is a comparison made of two items on the basis that because there are one or more similarities between the two items, we can therefore assume they are alike in one or more other respects. An analogy assumption is different from a representative sample assumption (discussed next) in that an analogy assumption makes a side-by-side comparison of two things whereas a representative sample assumption makes a vertical comparison stating that a "smaller something" is just like the larger whole. An analogy assumes big "A" is equal to big "B" but a representative sample assumption assumes little "a" is equal to big "A".

What are some ways in which two things are typically compared? Basically, we make comparisons based on people, places, things, or situations. For example, we are constantly making comparisons across situations. An analogy is created every time a researcher delves into the realm of biological experimentation and compares the results done on animals, usually mice, to human beings. We also compare two situations (or events) over different time periods. Most corporate decisions are still based on the idea that what has worked in the past will work in the future. International law is also, in large part, based on the principle of historical precedent.

Often two things will be compared under the assumption that they are similar; our goal will be to find dissimilarities in order to show that they are not alike, and in this way weaken the argument. Take the following example: "Martha did such a great job selling cutlery that we're going to promote her and put her in charge of condominium sales." What is being assumed is that sales ability is the key ingredient in making sales and the type of product being sold is of secondary concern. How could we attack this argument? One way is to indicate that you see a big difference between selling cutlery, a commodity product, and selling a condominium, a luxury good. A person effective at selling one type of product may be ineffective when selling another type of product. In the entrepreneurial context, a person successful in one industry may not be successful when switching to another industry.

Sometimes it will be necessary to find ways to show that two things are similar because the arguer believes that two things in question are very much dissimilar. For example, two male sports enthusiasts are having a beer, when one says to the other: "There is no comparison between athletes today and those of yesteryear. Forty years ago, Mark Spitz won seven gold medals in swimming in the Mexico City Olympics, but his winning times are today not even good enough to qualify for any of the men's Olympic swim events." In order to damage this argument, the second sports enthusiast might want to choose an analogy to show how athletes today are in some way comparable to the athletes of yesteryear. For example, Jack Nicklaus's final round score of 271 in 1965 to win the Master's Golf Tournament in Augusta, Georgia could be compared to Tiger Wood's final round score of 272 in 2002 to win the Master's Golf tournament on the exact same course. In this respect, by comparing two athletes in this manner, things do not look so dissimilar after all.

When comparing two things, particularly those across different time frames, we must be careful not to assume that information gathering techniques and, therefore, the quality of the data obtained are comparable. For example, any report comparing the findings of worker satisfaction levels in the 1940s to worker satisfaction levels today would be suspect if, for no other reason, than the difficulty of comparing the results of information gained under differing circumstances.

Finally, at the most fundamental level, we must ensure that the meaning and scope of words and terms used in an argument are consistently applied. Otherwise any comparison is torpedoed.

Representative Sample Assumptions

A sample is a group of people or things selected from a larger number of people or things that is presumably representative of the larger group or, as it is often said, "the population as a whole." We have all heard such statements as, "I've never met a person from Country Z that I liked" or "I highly recommend ABC Restaurant because the three times that I have dined there the food has been delicious."

These two examples show representative sample assumptions in action. The first person obviously has not met all the people from Country Z and the second person obviously has not tried every dish in ABC Restaurant. For a sample to be representative, it must be both *quantitatively* and *qualitatively* representative. For a sample to be quantitatively sound, a large enough sample must be chosen. Obviously, the selection of one or two items is not enough. For a sample to be qualitatively sound, a random or diverse enough cross sample of its "members" must be chosen.

What about a travel agency that claims, "Three out of every four tourists recommend Morocco as a tourist destination." For all we know, there were only eight tourists surveyed and six of these tourists recommended Morocco as a tourist destination. In this hypothetical case, the sample of tourists chosen was too small. Now let's assume that the statistic, three out of every four tourists recommend Morocco, was based on a sufficiently large sample of several hundred tourists. But what if all tourists were from Africa? All of sudden we would have doubts as to whether these several hundred tourists were representative of tourists in general, and the statement three of four tourists recommend Morocco as a tourist destination would become suspect.

For Critical Reasoning test-taking purposes, the rule is: show how a particular person, place, or thing is not representative of the larger "whole" and the argument is weakened or falls apart. On the other hand, show how a particular person, place, or thing is representative of the larger "whole" and the argument is strengthened.

Generally the question will not be whether a sample is large enough but whether a sample is diverse enough. If the sample is not drawn from relevant representative subclasses, the size of the sample is of little consequence. A noteworthy real-life example is the Gallop pole, as devised by George Gallop, and used notably for the purpose of predicting U.S. presidential races. In order to generalize about the opinion of the American people with respect to a given candidate or political issue, data must be gathered from subclasses based on race, age, education, professional status, sex, geography, and even religion. Other subclasses, such as body weight and hair color are deemed irrelevant. Although the U.S. population exceeds 300 million people, the Gallop pole requires a sample size of only about 1,800 people to be statistically accurate.

Cause and Effect Assumptions

Does one event really cause another? Cause and effect is concerned with the relationship (or non-relationship) between two events. The first event we call the cause and the second event we call the *effect*. Formulaically, we use A for the cause and B for the effect, which can be written $A \rightarrow B$.

The first question we have to ask in thinking or reasoning critically (in either a real-life situation or for the purpose of taking a standardized test) is whether a cause and effect relationship really exists between two items. There may not be any plausible relationship, let alone a cause and effect relationship. For example, the street light turned red just before the cat fell out of the tree; therefore, the red light caused the cat to fall out of the tree.

Many times, however, a relationship exists between two events. In short, there are six possibilities as indicted in the chart on the below. If the situation or question leads us to believe that a strong correlation exists between two events, then we must ask if there is merely a low correlation or if it is only coincidence. If a cause and effect relationship is considered near certain to exist (see right hand side of the chart), then we ask one of two questions. If it seems to be cause and effect, check to see if it is instead just a strong correlation. If there really is cause and effect, perhaps an alternative cause is really responsible for the effect, or perhaps reverse causation is at the root of the explanation.

There are six categories under which potential cause and effect relationships arise. These include the following:

No Cause and Effect	Cause and Effect
I. Mere Coincidence	IV. Legitimate Causation
II. Low Correlation	V. Alternative Explanation
III. High Correlation	VI. Reverse Causation

The following provides further explanations of the categories highlighted in the chart above.

I.   Mere Coincidence

"Every time I sit in my favorite seat during a playoff game, our team wins." It is unlikely that your "lucky" seat is causing your sports team to win. And it is equally unlikely that a regular or "bad" seat will cause your team to lose.

II.   Low Correlation

An example of low correlation might be the opening of new health clubs in your city and the general level of fitness among citizens in your city. Obviously, the opening of health clubs including weightlifting classes, aerobic classes, and exercise machines will have some effect on the level of fitness. But practically it will not have a great deal of impact. The direct impact of a small number of health club members on the larger population of a city is limited. Even if there is a general trend toward more fitness in your city, it may be because people walk more, ride bikes more, and take hikes more often. Individuals may partake in these events and not be associated with health clubs.

III.   High Correlation (but not causation)

There are certain items that have a strong correlation. For example, being tall and being an NBA player. Not every player in the NBA is tall but the vast majority of players are. We can safely say that there is a strong correlation between being tall and being an NBA player. A classic example in business is sales and advertising costs in a company. The more a company spends on advertising, the greater a company's sales. (Case in point: The correlation between advertising and sales is approximately 0.8) Other examples might include hot weather and ice cream sales, or rainy weather and umbrella sales. Certain strongly correlated events are often talked about as if they are causally related. It is important to be able to draw the line between high correlation and actual causation.

IV.   Legitimate Causation

The law of gravity is a causal event. I throw an apple up into the air and it comes back down. Other events are so highly correlated that for all practical purposes they are assumed to be causally related. For example, the amount of coffee consumed and the amount of coffee beans used or the number of babies born and the number of baby diapers *used*. Note that it would not be close enough to say the number of coffee beans *grown* or the number of baby diapers *manufactured*.

V.   Alternative Explanation

Alternative explanation can be technically called *alternative causal explanation*. Here we agree on a single conclusion (the effect) but differ as to which is the correct cause. We must always be on guard for the existence of another cause whenever it looks like two events are otherwise causally related. A business may have increased its advertising budget and seen an increase in sales. It is easy to view these two events as causally connected. But advertising may be having no effect on sales. The reason that sales have increased may be due to a major competitor of the company going out of business. Another example occurs when John is speaking to Alice: "It's plain to see that the recent spate of high school shootings is the result of viewing violent TV programming." Who's to say that the high school shootings are not instead the result of more lax gun laws, dwindling educational standards, or weakened religious following? (In this case, it is not A that is causing B but rather C that is causing B). Or maybe there is a third factor causing both A and B. For example, perhaps both the increase in high school shootings and the increase in violent TV programming are the result of a third factor, i.e., breakdown of the family unit. (In this latter case, it is not A that is causing B but rather C that is causing both A and B).

VI.   Reverse Causation

Does your favorite commercial author sell a lot of books because he or she is famous or is he or she famous as a result of selling lots of books? Reverse causation is tricky. You think X is causing Y but in reality it is Y that is causing X. The following example helps illustrate this point. Say you notice that a young woman at work named Sally is always working hard. And you say to yourself one day: "Sally is a hard worker. No wonder our boss gives her the toughest assignments." The argument becomes, "Because Sally is such a hard worker, our boss gives her the toughest assignments." But could the reverse be true? What if Sally is lazy and not naturally such a hard worker but rather works hard only because she happens to be given the toughest projects. That is, the argument actually now goes: "Because Sally is given such tough work projects, she is therefore forced to work hard!" Children may reveal funny examples to illuminate the concept of reverse causation. Young children may believe that firemen cause fires, for every time they see a picture or a video of a fire there are firemen at the scene. Eventually, the reverse is confirmed to be true: "fires cause firemen."

As an historical example, when researchers first started testing the hypothesis that "smoking causes cancer" one of the first things they considered was the reverse hypothesis—the idea that people who have cancer might go looking to start smoking (i.e., cancer causes smoking). Not surprisingly, this hypothesis was not only considered implausible but also proved groundless. However in many other situations it is difficult to tell which is the cause and which is the effect. The statement: "You're good at the things you like." The cause and effect argument becomes, "You like things" (cause), and therefore you become good at them (effect)." But could it be that you find yourself good at some things and then learn to like them?

Implementation Assumptions

Some years ago, an article in a Western travel magazine stated: "Because air travel is becoming so convenient and because people have increasingly higher levels of disposable income, soon everyone will have been to Africa to see the lions."

Yet today, few people outside of Africa can claim to have been to Africa to see the lions. What accounts for the discrepancy between the travel magazine article and people actually going to visit Africa and/or the lions? Was the article wrong about plane travel being convenient or people having higher levels of disposable income? The magazine was not likely wrong in these respects. However, the article was incorrect in its prediction that "everyone" (or less literally "many people") would go to Africa to see the lions. The discrepancy between an otherwise sound plan and action is based on the assumption that a sound plan must necessarily achieve its desired result. This is not necessarily so.

Why do plans not work? There are essentially four major reasons why plans do not work: (1) lack of desire, motivation, or perseverance on the part of an individual or organization; (2) lack of prerequisite skill or technological capability on the part of an individual or organization to carry out the plan; (3) lack of required opportunity or wherewithal i.e., economic resources to commence or complete a given task; and (4) unanticipated bottlenecks or unforeseen consequences (physical, financial, technological, or logistical) arising from implementation of the plan. All of these assumptions may occur in the form of implementation assumptions as a result of assuming that a plan will work because of an absence of the kind of deficiencies cited above.

First, there may be a lack of desire, motivation, or perseverance on the part of an individual or organization carrying out a plan. There is a saying that "one who can read but doesn't is no better than one who cannot read." The ability to do something is not the same thing as actually using that skill. We all know of examples of extremely talented individuals who lack the focus or motivation to achieve their true potential.

Second, there may also be a lack of required skill or technological capability to carry out the plan. Consider the statement made by a high school graduate: "Either I'm going to medical school or I am going to join the military and become a member of the Special Forces." This assumes that a person has the skill and perseverance to get accepted to medical school en-route to becoming a doctor. It equally assumes the physical skill, mental toughness, and temperament to make it through training en route to being selected as a member of the Special Forces.

Third, we cannot assume that an individual or organization has the required opportunity or financial wherewithal, i.e., economic resources to complete a given task. In the example above, the high school graduate assumes that, in the case of medical school, he or she has the ability to also obtain loans and financial aid in order to complete medical studies.

Fourth, in terms of unanticipated bottlenecks or unforeseen consequences, think in terms of what would happen if everyone pursued the said plan or course of action. For example, your office may be considering the installation of a new computer e-mail system, which many believe will resolve your company's communication problems. But what if everyone uses the computer system at the same time? The system might just crash being unable to accommodate all users (technological limitations).

Be suspicious of GMAT problems which propose legislation as the key to resolving an issue. Legislation can certainly be used to discourage or limit undesirable actions but it does not prevent them per se. Legislation to prevent discrimination, for example, may not work if people do not want to stop discrimination. Likewise, passing a law to increase fines for people parking their cars illegally in front of prestigious shopping venues will not necessarily stop shoppers from parking their cars, particularly wealthy consumers who may nonetheless decide to illegally park and accept higher fines.

Number-based Assumptions

Certain Critical Reasoning problems are based in math and an understanding of math may be essential in untangling these types of reasoning problems. The number-based assumptions presented here are broken down into four sub-categories. For the purposes of this overview, each sub-category below is supported with very simple examples.

Percentage vs. Actual Number Scenarios

We generally cannot compare percentages to numbers unless we know the exact numbers represented by the percentages. Percentages (like decimals, fractions, and ratios) are relative measures; actual numbers are absolute measures.

Suppose that there are only three females working at your company. Is this not gender discrimination? Not necessarily. What if there are only six persons working at your company? Then the three females represent 50% of total workers. Another example. In a given company, 10% of the employees in Department A are salespersons whereas 20% of the employees in Department B are salespersons. Does Department B have more salespersons than Department A? The answer is that we cannot tell. It could be that both departments have the same number of total employees, say 100, in which case Department B would definitely have more salespersons than Department A (see Scenario #1). But there could be, say, 100 employees working in Department A and 40 employees working in Department B. In this case, the number of salespersons working in Department A would be greater than the number of salespersons working in Department B (see Scenario #2).

Scenario #1:

	Dept A	Dept B
Number of total employees	100	100
% of employees who are salespersons	10%	20%
Number of salespersons	10	20

Scenario #2:

	Dept A	Dept B
Number of total employees	100	40
% of employees who are salespersons	10%	20%
Number of salespersons	10	8

Is train travel becoming more dangerous? Even if, in a given year, there are more train crashes and regrettably more deaths compared with a previous year, this does not necessarily mean that train travel is becoming more dangerous. We have to examine how many people are riding on trains (or, more precisely, "how many deaths per train miles logged"). If many more people are taking trains, it is likely that the percentage or ratio of train related deaths (to total passengers) is decreasing. In such a case, train travel would be deemed safer, not more dangerous. Ratios (or fractions, decimals, or percents) are necessary tools for drawing conclusions about qualitative measures such as "preferability," "danger," or "safety."

Overlap Scenarios

Overlap scenarios occur when items are members of either one group or another but some items are members of both groups. Typically these are "either...or" situations which contain overlap. For example, a high school admissions office determined that of its 120 senior students, 78 were enrolled in math and 63 were enrolled in physics. Here the total of both math and physics students adds up to 141. Some of these students must be taking both math and physics, and we cannot assume that all students must be either a math or physics student but not both.

Consider the following exchange:

Travel Agent: "Of people who booked through our agency and traveled to Australia or New Zealand this past winter, 65% went to Australia and 55% went to New Zealand."

Customer: "That doesn't sound right. You should check your numbers. How can more than 100% of your tourists travel to Australia or New Zealand?"

The customer's response is likely invalid, because it is entirely possible that some tourists traveled to both Australia and New Zealand during their winter vacation.

In logic parlance, "situations involving either A or B, do not necessarily preclude the possibility of both A and B". Consider the sign: "No eating or drinking allowed." One cannot interpret this sign to mean that because we can neither eat nor drink, we can therefore eat <u>and</u> drink simultaneously in order to avoid the mandate. The overlap created between A and B already takes into account the possibility that A and B will occur together. (P.S. Ditto for the sign that reads: "No cats or dogs allowed.")

Distribution or Allocation Scenarios

It cannot be assumed that data is divided into groups or sets of equal number. Distributions are not always proportional or linear. If a test has 100 problems and is divided into four sections, we can't assume that there are 25 problems per section. Likewise, we wouldn't assume that in a house that has three rooms covering an area of 750 square feet, that all rooms are exactly 250 square feet each.

Total Costs vs. Per Unit Costs Scenarios

There are certain situations in which a distinction must be drawn between total costs and per unit costs. For example, a single piece of *Dove Chocolates* and a single piece of *Valentine Chocolates* are of equivalent size and of comparable quality. Since a box of *Dove Chocolates* cost £5 (British pounds) and a box of *Valentine chocolates* costs £4 (British pounds), can we conclude *Valentine Chocolates* are our best buy. Not necessarily-what if a box of *Dove Chocolates* contains significantly more chocolates as compared with a box of Valentine Chocolates? Or what if the there is the same number of chocolate pieces but substantially larger pieces?

Profit-and-Loss Scenarios

Profit-and-loss scenarios highlight the interplay of the three profit components: price, cost, and volume. Just because a computer store is selling more computers than last year, does not mean that its profits are up. Why? Because an increase (decrease) in the sales volume (i.e., number of unit sales) of a good or service item does not necessarily equal an increase (decrease) in revenues or profits. Likewise, an increase (decrease) in the price of a good or service does not necessarily equal an increase (decrease) in profits. Moreover, an increase (or decrease) in the cost of a good or service does not necessarily equal a decrease (or increase) in profits.

Variations of the *profit formula* appear below:

Revenue - Cost = Profit

$(Price_{per\ unit} - Cost_{per\ unit}) \times Volume = Profit$

$(Price_{per\ unit} \times Volume) - (Cost_{per\ unit} \times Volume) = Profit$

Logic-based Assumptions

To introduce formal logic, consider the following statements:

Original: "If you work hard, you'll be successful."

Now ponder these related statements.

Statement #1:   "If you're successful, then you've worked hard."

Statement #2:   "If you don't work hard, you won't be successful."

Statement #3:   "If you're not successful, then you didn't work hard."

The question becomes: Which of the above statements are logical deductions based on the original statement?

Upon closer examination, Statement #1 isn't necessarily correct. The fact that you're successful (whatever this means!) doesn't mean that you have necessarily worked hard. There could be several other ways to become successful. For example, perhaps you're intelligent or perhaps you're down-right lucky.

Likewise, Statement #2 is not necessarily correct. Just because you don't work hard, doesn't mean that you won't be successful. As already mentioned, you might be lucky or intelligent as opposed to hard working. However, Statement #3 is a perfectly logical deduction based on the original. If you're not successful, then you must not have worked hard. This doesn't mean however that there are not other explanations for why you might not have been successful. For example, perhaps you were neither intelligent in your approach nor lucky in your application.

"If...Then" Statements

"If....then" statements are another way to represent causal relationships. Take the following generic statement: "If A, then B." This is sometimes written in a formulaic manner, i.e., "If A→B." What can we logically infer from this type of statement?

Exhibit 4-5 contains four statements that may seem to the casual observer to be all inferable. However, only the fourth version is correctly inferable. In "If...then" statements, it is important that you read in one direction only as the reverse is not necessarily true. According to formal logic, the *contrapositive* is always correct. That is to say, the only thing we can infer from an "If A, then B statement" is the following: "If not B, then not A."

Consider the statement, "If it is U.S. money (dollar bills), then it is green (colored)." This can also be written: If $US→Green. Based on the original statement ("If it is U.S. money, then it is green"), the only thing we can infer logically from this statement is that it is true that "If it is not green, then it is not U.S. money". Another way to illustrate an "If....then" relationship is to draw circles. The "If" item always represents the innermost circle while the "then" item always represents the outermost circle. *See Exhibit 4.*

Exhibit 4-4: Diagramming "If...then" Statements

If it is U.S. money, then it is green. (If US$ → Green)

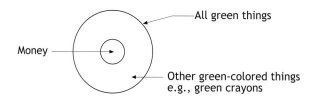

The above diagram illustrates in picture form the relationship between U.S. money and all green things. As previously mentioned, we cannot read in reverse order. That is, we can read from the inside circle to the outside circle but we cannot read from the outside circle to the inside circle. "If U.S. money then green" does not equal "If green then U.S. money."

Another way of understanding "If...then" statements is through an understanding of *necessary vs. sufficient* conditions. A necessary condition must be present for an event to occur but will not, by itself, cause the given event to occur. A sufficient condition is enough, by itself, to ensure that the event will occur. In more technical parlance, a necessary condition is a condition which, if absent, will not allow the event to occur. A sufficient condition is a condition which, if present, will cause the event to occur.

When a person argues "If A then B" and then argues "If B then A," he or she erroneously reverses the conditional statement. The reason that a conditional statement cannot be reversed is that the original "If...then" statement functions as a necessary condition. When it is reversed, an "If...then" statement erroneously turns into a sufficient condition. In the example above, being "green" is a necessary but not a sufficient condition in order for something to be considered U.S. money. Obviously, there are other factors besides "green coloring" that need be present including special watermark paper, special insignia, special size, etc. By reversing the "If...then" statement we erroneously suggest that being green colored is enough of a criterion for something to be considered U.S. money.

Try one more example: "I gave my pet hamster water everyday and he still died." Giving your pet hamster water each day is a necessary condition for keeping him (or her) alive but it is not a sufficient condition. There are many other things that a hamster needs besides water, one of which is food.

Exhibit 4-5: "If...then" Statements

Statement	Reference to formal logic	Are the statements logical inferences based on the original statements?
1) If A, then B	n/a – (original statement)	n/a– (original statement)
2) If B, then A	Known as the *fallacy of affirming the consequence*.	No, incorrect. This is not inferable.
3) If not A, then not B	Known as the *fallacy of denying the antecedent*.	No, incorrect. This is not inferable.
4) If not B, then not A	Known as the *contrapositive*.	Yes, correct. This is always logically inferable based on the original statement.

Exhibit 4-6: American Money

Statement	Are the statements logical inferences based on the original statements?
1) If it is U.S. money, then it is green.	n/a – original statement
2) If it is green, then it is U.S. money.	Incorrect. Why? The reverse is not equivalent because the statement now says that all green things are U.S. money and this is obviously ridiculous. Many things in the universe are green in color and this includes green-colored crayons, Christmas trees, garbage pails, green paint, Kermit the Frog, etc. (Fallacy of Affirming the Consequence)
3) If it is not U.S. money, then it is not green.	Incorrect. Why? For many of the exact reasons mentioned above. (Fallacy of Denying the Antecedent)
4) If it is not green, then it is not U.S. money.	Correct. This is inferable. Why? Because being green is one of the requirements for something being U.S. money.

"No-Some-Most-All" Statements

Many errors are committed in drawing inferences because ordinary speech is inherently ambiguous. For example, take the four statements below:

I.   No As are Bs
II.   All As are Bs
III.   Some As are Bs
IV.   Most As are Bs

To study the meaning of the four Roman Numeral statements (I to IV), refer to *Exhibit 4-7*. You can see that Roman Numeral I unambiguously corresponds to diagram (1), but that Roman Numeral II could mean either diagram (2) or (3), although usually (3). Roman Numeral III could mean any one of the diagrams (4), (5), or (8), although usually (5). Roman Numeral IV could mean either diagrams (6) or (7). This is evidence that ordinary speech can hamper clear thinking, and it is often necessary to use non-verbal symbols to reinforce clear thinking.

There are two major differences between "most" and "some" type statements. First, "most" implies majority ($\geq 50\%$) while "some" implies minority ($< 50\%$). Second, whereas "some statements" automatically imply reciprocality, "most statements" do not necessarily imply reciprocality. For example, the statement, "some doctors are wealthy people" implies that some wealthy people are also doctors. But the statement, "most doctors are wealthy people" does not necessarily mean that most wealthy people are doctors. For example, diagram (6) on the following page does indicate reciprocality; most As are Bs and most Bs are As. However, diagram (7) does not indicate reciprocality; most As are Bs even though most Bs are not As (only some Bs are As).

The diagrams in *Exhibit 4-7* serve to summarize the concepts of mutual inclusivity, mutual exclusivity, and overlap. Either circles are imbedded inside one another, or circles are completely separated, or circles overlap with one another. Basically, there are eight possibilities.

Exhibit 4-8 provides a summary of Logical Equivalency statements. With a better understanding of visuals, the next step is to be able to combine these visuals with verbal-type logic statements expressed in English. This is a translation exercise. For example, within the area of inclusion, we must be able to see that all of the following are equivalent forms: "All cats are mammals"; "Every cat is a mammal"; "If it is a cat then it is a mammal"; "Only mammals are cats"; and "No cat is not a mammal".

Diagramming Mutual Inclusivity and Exclusivity

Exhibit 4-7: Mutual Inclusivity, Exclusivity & Overlap

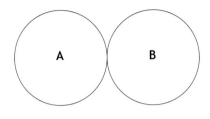

(1)
"A and B are mutually exclusive"
(A and B touch but do not overlap)

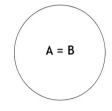

(2)
"A and B coincide"
(A and B overlap perfectly)

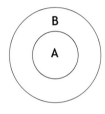

(3)
"A is included in B"
(A is completely inside B)

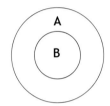

(4)
"B is included in A"
(B is completely inside A)

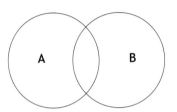

(5)
"A and B overlap"
(A and B overlap partly)

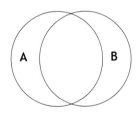

(6)
"A and B overlap"
(most of A is inside B and
most of B is inside A)

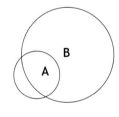

(7)
"A and B overlap"
(most of A is inside B but
most of B is not inside A)

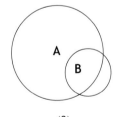

(8)
"A and B overlap"
(most of B is inside A but
most of A is not inside B)

Statements of Logical Equivalency

Exhibit 4-8: Logical Equivalency Statements

	Mutual Inclusivity	Mutual Exclusivity	Reciprocality or Overlap
"All" Type Statements	*All* cats are mammals. Cats are mammals. *Every* cat is a mammal. *Anything* that is a cat is a mammal. *All* non-mammals are non-cats.	*All* cats are not birds. *All* birds are not whales.	n/a
"Only" Type Statements	*Only* mammals are cats. A thing is a cat *only* if it is a mammal.	*Only* things that are not birds are cats. *Only* things that are not cats are birds.	n/a
"No" Type Statements	*No* cat is not a mammal. *Nothing* is a cat unless it is a mammal.	*No* cats are birds. *No* birds are cats. *Nothing* that is a cat is a bird. *Nothing* that is a bird is a cat.	n/a
"If....Then" Type Statements	*If* anything is a cat, *(then)* it is a mammal. *If* anything is not a mammal, *(then)* it is not a cat.	*If* anything is a cat, *(then)* it is not a bird. *If* anything is a bird, *(then)* it is not a cat.	n/a
"Some" Type Statements	n/a	n/a	*Some* mammals live in the sea. *Some* things that live in the sea are mammals.
"Most" Type Statements	n/a	n/a	*Most* mammals do not live in the sea. *Most* things that live in the sea are not mammals.

READING COMPREHENSION

There is an obvious difference between the kind of casual reading that takes place when reading a newspaper and the kind required when one sits for a standardized exam like the GMAT. There are essentially five areas to cover when discussing strategies to tackle Reading Comprehension passages and accompanying multiple-choice questions. Mastering Reading Comprehension involves an understanding of passage type, passage content, passage structure, as well as passage question types and common wrong answer choices.

I.   **Passage Type**

i)   Social Science
ii)   Science

II.   **Passage Content**

i)   Topic
ii)   Scope
iii)   Purpose (= main idea)

III.   **Passage Structure**

i)   Transition words
ii)   Number of paragraphs and their function
iii)   Number of viewpoints and their relationship

IV.   **Passage Question Types**

i)   Overview questions
ii)   Explicit detail questions
iii)   Inference questions
iv)   Tone questions
v)   Passage organization questions

V.   **Common Wrong Answer Choices**

i)   Out of Scope
ii)   Opposite
iii)   Distortion
iv)   Irrelevant
v)   Too General
vi)   Too Detailed

Passage Type

Of the two basic types of Reading Comprehension passages—Social Science and Science—Science passages tend to be objective and generally exist to *describe*. Social Science passages tend to be subjective and typically exist to *argue*. This is because Social Science is typically concerned with putting forth opinions while Science is typically concerned with presenting details.

Ideas, and the flow of ideas, are generally more important in Social Science readings than in Science readings. In terms of understanding a Social Science passage, it is critical to understand "what side the author is on." We must understand the author's stance. A fitting analogy is to say: Social Science passages are "river-rafting rides"; Science passages are "archeological digs." Navigating a Social Science passage is like "a white-water rafting ride"—let's not fall off the raft amid the twists and turns. Science reading, on the other hand, is like "digging for hidden artifacts at an archeological site." Once we determine where to dig, we must keep track of the small pieces—we must be able to memorize and work with details.

Passage Content

Obviously, the better we understand what we have read, the better our chance of answering questions related to the subject at hand. In breaking down passage content, we can subdivide everything into three areas, namely topic, scope, and purpose.

Topic is defined as "the broad subject matter of the passage." Scope is defined as "the specific aspect of the topic that the author is interested in." Purpose is defined as "the author's main reason for writing the passage" or "why did the author sit down to write this passage?" In summary, *topic* and *scope* are "what" a passage is about while *purpose* is about "why" the passage was written.

One tip involves always performing a T-S-P drill. That is, always ask yourself what is the topic, scope, and purpose. Let's test this.

> The whale is the largest mammal in the animal kingdom. When most people think of whales, they think of sluggish, obese animals, frolicking freely in the ocean by day and eating tons of food to sustain themselves. When people think of ants, on the other hand, they tend to think of hardworking underfed creatures transporting objects twice their body size to and from hidden hideaways. However, if we analyze food consumption based on body size, we find that ants eat their full body weight everyday while a whale eats the equivalent of only one-thousandth of its body weight each day. In fact, when we compare the proportionate food consumption of all living creatures, we find that the whale is one of the most food efficient creatures on earth.

What is the topic? The answer is clearly "whales." Don't be fooled into thinking that the topic is the "animal kingdom." This would be an example of an answer that is too general. What is the scope? The answer is "food consumption of whales." What is the purpose of the passage or why did the author sit down to write this? The author's purpose is to say that "whales are food efficient creatures" and to thereby counter the popular misconception that they are "biological gas guzzlers."

One technique worth practicing which may help to gain control over passage content very quickly is to: "read the first sentence first and the last sentence next." That is, after reading the first sentence (to gain some idea of what the passage is about) then read the last sentence before going on to read the whole passage. Occasionally, the author of a passage summarizes on the last line of the passage. Reading the last line early may afford you the opportunity to return to the top of the passage and continue reading knowing exactly where the author is going with his or her discussion. This technique can greatly aid reading comprehension.

Passage Structure

There are essentially two distinct ways to analyze passage structure: the micro and the macro. Micro analysis involves keeping track of transitions, which signal the flow of the passage. Transition words such as "but" and "however" have been called the traffic lights of language. These words serve one of four primary purposes: to show contrast, illustration, continuation, or conclusion See *Exhibit 4-9*.

Macro analysis involves not only noting the number of paragraphs and their function, but more importantly, the number of viewpoints and their relationship. Passages with one or two viewpoints are most common on the GMAT, although three viewpoints within a single Reading Comprehension passage is a possibility.

Paragraphs and their function – The GMAT contains four passages per Verbal section, two of which will likely be two paragraphs in length and two will be either three or four paragraphs in length. In terms of function, the opening paragraph is usually the introduction and each succeeding paragraph takes on a single concept. Concluding paragraphs are rare in Reading Comprehension.

Viewpoints – As already noted, viewpoints are more applicable to Social Science passages than to Science passages because Social Science is typically subjective and argumentative. The relationships between or among viewpoints are finite. *Exhibit 4-10* provides a summary. In the case of two viewpoints, for example, one of three things will occur: (1) each of the two ideas will be presented as separate ideas (non-competing viewpoints); (2) one idea presented will be deemed greater than the other idea (competing viewpoints); (3) one idea will lead to another idea (complementary viewpoints).

Two classic structures arise in Reading Comprehension passages. The first occurs in Science passages. Here two phenomena are described in three paragraphs. The first paragraph will be an introduction, the second paragraph will describe the first phenomenon, and the third paragraph will describe a second phenomenon. Because science passages so often exist to describe, the author is unlikely to criticize or show favor to one side. The second occurs in Social Science passages. Here, two competing viewpoints will be presented over three paragraphs. The first paragraph will be an introduction, the second paragraph will present the first viewpoint, while the third paragraph will present a second contrasting viewpoint. Note that although viewpoints may clash, the author may or may not side with one of these viewpoints.

Exhibit 4-9: Transition Words

RED LIGHT
"Stop and Get Ready to Turn"

I. Contrast
- however
- but
- yet
- on the other hand
- whereas

FLASHING GREEN LIGHT
"Slow Down but Keep Going"

III. Continuation
- moreover
- furthermore
- on the one hand
- undoubtedly
- coincidentally

GREEN LIGHT
"Keep Going"

II. Illustration (or enumeration)
- first, second, third
- for example
- for instance
- in fact
- case in point

YELLOW LIGHT
"You're about to Arrive"

IV. Conclusion
- in conclusion
- finally
- hence
- so
- therefore
- as a result
- thus

Exhibit 4-10: Passage Structure and Viewpoint

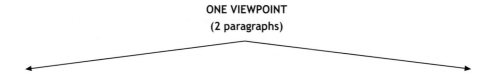

ONE VIEWPOINT
(2 paragraphs)

A single viewpoint is presented with which the author agrees.

Structure: [=Agree]

Ex: "Heredity is the most important factor in personality development. Let me explain."

A single viewpoint is presented with which the author does not agree.

Structure: [=Disagree]

Ex: "Green is <u>not</u> the most versatile color. Let me explain."

TWO VIEWPOINTS
(3 paragraphs)

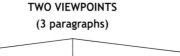

*Non-competing viewpoints
Two viewpoints are presented without comparison or conflict.

Structure: [A,B]

Ex: "Gold is a precious metal and diamonds are precious gems."

Complementary viewpoints
One viewpoint builds on another viewpoint.

Structure: [A→B]

Ex: "The invention of the automobile has paved the way for the invention of the airplane."

**Competing viewpoints
One of two viewpoints is deemed to be the clear winner, the other inferior.

Structure: [A > B or B > A]

Ex: "Our environment is a more important factor in personality development than is heredity."

THREE VIEWPOINTS
(3 or 4 paragraphs)

Non-competing viewpoints
Three viewpoints are presented without comparison or conflict.

Structure: [A, B, C]

Ex: "Fruits, vegetables, and proteins are part of a healthy diet."

Complementary viewpoints
A third superior viewpoint is considered to be the product of two original viewpoints.

Structure: [A + B→C]

Ex: "The invention of the automobile and jet plane have led to the invention of the space craft.

Competing viewpoints
One of the three viewpoints is deemed to be the clear winner, the others inferior.

Structure: [C > A or B]

Ex: "Tablet C is more effective than Tablet A or Tablet B".

Note: *Represents a classic structure in Science passages.
**Represents a classic structure in Social Science passages

Passage Question Types

There are five different types of Reading Comprehension questions. These include: (1) *Overview* questions, (2) *Explicit-Detail* questions, (3) *Inference questions*, (4) *Tone* questions, and (5) *Passage Organization* questions.

Examples of each of these question types are as follows:

Overview questions:	"The primary purpose of this passage is to...?" or "The author's main idea is...?" Not surprisingly, an overview question is sometimes called a *primary purpose* or *main idea* type question.
Explicit-Detail questions:	"According to the passage, the author states...?" An explicit detail question is a question which has a very literal answer. It is something that the reader has read and it can be confirmed based on words actually written in the passage.
Inference questions:	"It can be inferred from the passage that..." or "The author implies...?" The artistry in answering an inference question lies in drawing that magic line between what can be logically inferred based on information in a passage and what is declared outside the scope of the passage.
Tone questions:	"The attitude of the author toward mystics can best be described as...?" A tone question asks the reader to comment on the "temperature" of some aspect of the passage.
Passage Organization questions:	"Which of the following best describes the way in which this passage is organized?"

The four-section grid below, titled *Four-Corner Question Cracker*, can be used to ferret out common wrong answer choices on Reading Comprehension questions. The correct answer always appears in the middle where the bull's-eye is located. The four incorrect answers will almost always appear in one of the four corners.

Exhibit 4-11: Four-Corner Question Cracker

An answer choice is <u>too general</u> to be correct.

An answer choice is <u>outside of scope</u> (we simply don't know the answer) or an answer choice is <u>irrelevant</u>.

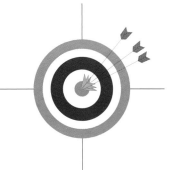

An answer choice is <u>opposite</u> in meaning or an answer choice is a <u>distortion</u>.

An answer choice is <u>too detailed</u> to be correct.

Common Wrong Answer Choices

Out-of-Scope:

An *out-of-scope* answer choice is an answer choice that cannot be answered based on information in the passage. An *out-of-scope* statement may, in fact, be right or wrong but it is not something that can be determined based on information supplied by the passage.

Irrelevant:

An *irrelevant* answer choice is an answer choice that in no way touches the topic; it is completely off target. We might contrast *irrelevant* answer choices with *out-of-scope* answer choices in that an *out-of-scope* answer choice is related tangentially to the passage, whereas the *irrelevant* answer choice is not. Think of an archer with bow and arrow. *Outside of scope* means that the archer is missing the target, but at least he or she is shooting at the right target, and in the right direction. *Irrelevant* means that the archer isn't even shooting at the correct target.

Opposite:

An *opposite* answer choice is an answer choice which is *opposite* in meaning to a statement or viewpoint expressed or implied by the passage. One common way answer choices are used to reverse meaning is through the inclusion or omission of prefixes such as "in", "un," and "dis," or the inclusion or omission of negative words such as "no" or "not." Thus "unfortunately" becomes "fortunately", "advantageous" becomes "disadvantageous," and "not applicable" becomes "applicable."

Distortion:

A *distorted* answer choice is an answer choice that distorts meaning. Saying, for example, that something is "good" is not the same as saying that something is "best." *Distortions* are typically signaled by the use of extreme wording or by the use of categorical words such as "only," "any," "all," "always," "never," and "cannot."

Too General:

This answer choice is relevant only to the Overview-type question; it is not as common therefore as an *out-of-scope*, *opposite*, or *irrelevant* answer choice. Example: A discussion of "South American trade imbalances in the 1950s" is not the same thing as a discussion of "modern global economic practices." The latter is obviously broader in scope: "global" is broader than "South American"; "modern" is broader than "the 1950s"; "economics" encompasses more than just "trade imbalances."

Too Detailed:

This answer choice is also relevant only to Overview-type questions. Example: A discussion of "the propagation of the Venus Fly Trap" is a much more specific topic than is "plant reproductive systems." The correct answer to an Overview-type question is neither too general nor too detailed.

Let's gain further insight into how test-makers may create incorrect answer choices with respect to Reading Comprehension (as well as Critical Reasoning) questions. Take the following easy-to-understand statement:

"Success is a strange phenomenon. You can either be hardworking, intelligent, or lucky."

Here are several concocted statements derived from the original statement which might appear as incorrect answer choices.

Out-of-scope:	"The *most* important ingredient in success is hardwork."
	(No. We don't know whether hardwork is the most important element in achieving success.)
	"Hardwork is a *more* important element in success than is intelligence."
	(Unwarranted comparison—we don't know which element is relatively more important than the other.)
Irrelevant:	"People who are successful sometimes have emotional problems later in life."
	(We are only concerned with how to achieve success, not what might happen beyond that juncture.)
Opposite:	"People who are either hardworking, intelligent, or lucky are *not* likely to achieve success."
	(The word "not" reverses the meaning of the original statement.)
Distortion:	"*Only* through hardwork can one become successful."
	(No, we can also achieve success by being intelligent or lucky.)
	"A person who is hardworking does not run any risk of failure."
	(The word "any" creates a *distortion*; how unlikely is the possibility of engaging in any human endeavor and having no chance of failure. Another way to view this statement is *out-of-scope* because the original statement makes no mention of the word "failure.")
	"A person who is hardworking, intelligent, or lucky can achieve *greatness*."
	(The word "greatness" has an elevated meaning as compared to "success." Another way to view this statement is that it is *out-of-scope* because the original statement does not make mention of what it takes to achieve greatness.)

How might you tackle the different Reading Comprehension Question Types based on an understanding of the Common Wrong Answer Choices?

(1) Overview questions

There are at least three ways to avoid wrong answer choices when tackling Overview questions.

i) Consider eliminating any answer choice which does not contain the words of the *topic*. Test this concept out on Question #1 of the upcoming Passage #1, appearing on **(page 252)**.

ii) Avoid any overly detailed answer choice which may be a factually correct statement but which is too detailed to be the correct answer choice to an overview question.

iii) Use a verb scan, when possible. That is, look at the verb which begins each answer choice and eliminate those verbs which do not fit. Five common verbs found in Reading Comprehension passages include "describe," "discuss," "explain," "argue," and "criticize." "Argue" is found frequently in Social Science-type passages; "describe" is found frequently in Science passages; "discuss" and "explain" are found in both Social Science and Science passages; "criticize" is usually not correct in an overview question involving a Science passage because the author is typically out to describe something and is non-judgmental.

(2) Explicit-Detail questions and (3) Inference questions

Common wrong answer choices on both *Explicit-Detail* questions and *Inference* questions include opposites and out-of-scopes.

Inference questions are especially vulnerable to wrong answer choices that are beyond the scope of the passage. In the context of a standardized test question, the test-taker must be careful not to assume too much. Standardized test questions are notorious for narrowing the scope of what we can infer based on what we read. Contrast this with everyday life in which we generally use a loose framework and assume a lot.

(4) Tone questions

Tone is attitude and there are basically three "temperatures" for tone questions-positive, negative, or neutral. One trick is to avoid answer choices which contain "verbally confused word pairs". For example, the word pairs "supercilious disdain" or "self-mingled pity" are not terribly clear. Testmakers like to include these types of answer choices believing that test-takers will be attracted to confusing, complex sounding wrong answer choices.

(5) Passage Organization questions

Given that the hallmark of Social Science passages is their provocative, subjective, and often argumentative nature, such passages often contain multiple viewpoints. In terms of two viewpoints, a common structure is "A>B." In terms of three viewpoints, a common structure is "C > A or B." Pure science passages, characterized by heavy detail and description, may be structured in the form "A, B" in which two events are simply described but not contrasted.

Note that passage structure may give clues to potential wrong and right answer choices. For example, in a "C >A or B" structure, the author will likely be negative toward item A or B. In an "A + B→C" structure, the author will likely be positive toward A and B because each is an integral building block to get to C.

ANALYTICAL WRITING ASSESSMENT

Here are answers to several frequently asked questions:

How are the two AWA essays different?

There are two analytical writing essays that appear on the GMAT. One type of analytical writing requires a test-taker to analyze a statement or series of statements, called an argument, and discuss what is technically or logically wrong with it. The other type of analytical writing requires one to take one side of an issue and give support to it.

There are distinct differences in the way we should approach the writing of each of these two types of essays. Roughly speaking, an Analysis of an Issue essay (herein called *issue essay*) is a "subjective" essay because we are encouraged to use personal examples, ideas, and opinions to make our case. An Analysis of an Argument essay (herein called *argument essay*) is an "objective" essay because we are not required or encouraged to introduce personal examples, ideas, or opinions to make our case. Note that the GMAT official instructions to the AWA *argument essay* includes the sentence, "You are NOT being asked to present your own views on the subject."

It is also true to say that the *argument essay* is primarily a "breaking down" essay whereas an issue essay is a "building up" essay. Here are two analogies to reinforce the differences between the two essays:

Responding to an *issue essay* is like building a sandcastle. The goal is to pick a spot on the beach and build a sandcastle as big as possible by piling on sand (picking a spot on the beach is analogous to picking one side of an issue and supporting it; sand is analogous to support points). The bigger we build our sandcastle (our essay) in a half-hour (30 minutes of test time), the more points we get.

Responding to *argument essay* requires us to respond to the argument at hand as if we are "overhauling a bicycle." We are required to break the argument down into its three parts, namely conclusion, evidence, and assumptions. This type of essay requires that we also show how to make the argument stronger, a requirement which is analogous to putting a bicycle back together once we have identified the problem areas.

How is the AWA used by Business Schools?

Although it is unclear how business schools use AWA scores in the admissions process, there are three possibilities. Scores could be used in borderline admission decisions. They could be used to identify students who need a remedial writing course. Finally, they could be used to help verify that candidates wrote their admissions essays.

How is the AWA scored?

Graders (one human and one electronic e-grading machine called the "e-rater") score each AWA essay. Graders assign scores out of 6.0 based on intervals of 0.5 points. Your overall, final score is an average of both individual scores obtained on the issue and argument essays. To review a bell-curve showing scaled scores and percentile rank, refer to *Chapter 1: The GMAT Exam*.

What do graders look for in terms of grading AWA essays?

GMAT graders are looking for "good essays", defined in the most general sense as ones which have "good grammar, structure, and content". Content is deemed most important.

For each 30-minute essay, what is the ideal way to allocate my time?

Spend five minutes thinking about and sketching your response; spend twenty minutes writing/typing your essay; and spend the last five minutes proofreading/tweaking your essay. The time allocation for each essay is therefore: 5-20-5.

How long should essays be?

Essays ("good essays") should be five to seven paragraphs, approximately 400 to 500 words in total word length. More is better on the AWA essays. Longer essays, all things being equal, correlate with higher grades.

Where do the AWA essays come from?

A complete list of the approximately 270 essay questions (135 *issue essays* and 135 *argument essays*) may be downloaded from the GMAT website (www.mba.com). During the exam, a random generating device chooses one essay each from the data bank. No one therefore knows which two essays will be chosen. The order in which essays appear may also be random, meaning that either the *issue essay* or *argument essay* may appear first.

Analysis of an Argument Essay

Here is an 8-step approach to use in answering an argument essay:

1.   Visualize the solution template for an argument essay.

2.   Identify the conclusion and evidence in the argument.

3.   Choose three (or more) assumptions contained in your argument.

4.   Begin by restating the argument and by answering the original question.

5.   Use transition words to structure your argument essay.

6.   Question the use of one vague term used in the argument and ask for clarification.

7.   Suggest strengthening the argument by softening its absolute-type wording.

8.   Write (or type) a response using the five-paragraph approach to guide you and proofread your argument essay.

Step #1: Visualize the solution template for an argument essay.

To visualize a solution, think in terms of the following template:

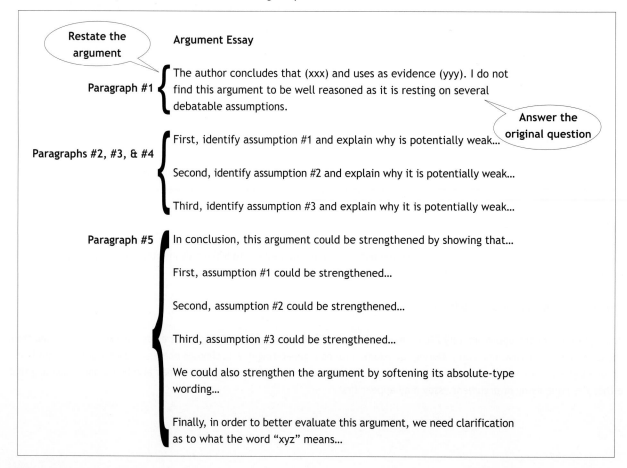

Visualizing the solution template includes visualizing a classic "five-paragraph format"-just as you learned in high school. The introduction is one paragraph, the body is three paragraphs, and the conclusion is one paragraph. Each point in the main discussion represents one paragraph in the body of the essay.

A Variation from the Standard Approach

The recommended structure to use to answer an argument essay is outlined above. This method involves first identifying the assumptions and second showing how these assumptions can be strengthened. An alternative method involves mentioning how to strengthen each assumption directly after identifying a given assumption. These two structures are outlined in *Exhibit 4-12*.

Exhibit 4-12: Outlines for Argument Essay

Standard Outline	Optional Outline
The author concludes that (xxx) and uses as evidence (yyy). I do not find this argument to be well reasoned as it is resting on several debatable assumptions.	The author concludes that (xxx) and uses as evidence (yyy). I do not find this argument to be well reasoned as it is resting on several debatable assumptions.
First, identify assumption #1...	First, identify assumption #1. This argument could be strengthened by showing that...
Second, identify assumption #2...	Second, identify assumption #2. This argument could be strengthened by showing that...
Third, identify assumption #3...	Third, identify assumption #3. This argument could be strengthened by showing that...
This argument could be strengthened by showing that...	We could also strengthen the argument by softening its absolute-type wording...
First, assumption #1 could be strengthened...	In conclusion, in order to better evaluate this argument, we need clarification as to what the word "xyz" means...
Second, assumption #2 could be strengthened...	
Third, assumption #3 could be strengthened...	
We could also strengthen the argument by softening its absolute-type wording...	
In conclusion, in order to better evaluate this argument, we need clarification as to what the word "xyz" means...	

Step #2: Identify the conclusion and evidence in the argument.

Logically, we identify the conclusion first, then the evidence, and finally the assumption. Again, the following formulas express the relationship between these three elements:

Conclusion = Evidence + Assumption
Conclusion - Evidence = Assumption

The conclusion is defined as the claim or main point that the author, writer, or speaker is making. The evidence includes any facts, examples, statistics, surveys, and other data or information that the author uses in support of his or her conclusion. The assumption is defined as "that which the author takes for granted."

Step #3: Choose three (or more) assumptions contained in your argument.

The practical goal of answering an *argument essay* is to identify three (or more) assumptions in the argument presented. Although there is no "right" way to go about finding assumptions, think of assumptions as falling into certain categories, including: *Comparison and Analogy* Assumptions, *Representative Sample* Assumptions, *Cause and Effect* Assumptions, and *Implementation* Assumptions. Use the "assumptions template" per *Exhibit 4-13* to uncover common, recurring assumptions.

Exhibit 4-13: Assumptions Template

1. Comparison Assumptions

Ask: Does the argument make logical comparisons? Are apples being compared to apples (or are apples instead being compared to oranges)? At the most fundamental level, we must ensure that the meaning (or definition) of words and terms used in an argument are applied consistently. Also, watch for "scope shifts" which occur when one term changes as an argument unfolds.

Rule: Show how two things are not logically comparable and the argument is weakened or falls apart.

2. Cause-and-Effect Assumptions

Ask: Does A really lead to B?

Rule: Show that A does not necessarily lead to B and the argument is weakened or falls apart. This may be achieved by finding another cause which explains the presumed cause-and-effect relationship or by showing that the two events in question are only strongly correlated but not causally related.

3. Representative Sample Assumptions

Ask: Does little "a" equal big "A"?

Rule: Show how a "part" does not equal the "whole" or that a sample is not representative of the larger population and the argument is weakened or falls apart.

4. Implementation Assumptions

Ask: Will a plan be implemented or used?

Rule: Show how no one will act on a plan or how the plan cannot be implemented due to financial, physical, logistical, or technological limitations and the argument is weakened or falls apart.

5. Attack the Evidence

Ask: Is the evidence used in the argument really good evidence? Are the numbers or statistics used really good? Are costs really as low as suggested, or are revenues or profits really as high as anticipated?

Rule: Show how the evidence (including any facts, examples, or statistics) is misleading or flawed and the argument is weakened or falls apart.

Author's note: Although it may not always be possible to "check off" all five categories for every given argument essay, the two arguments chosen in Chapter 10 for our review (i.e., *Yuppie Café and Cars vs. Public Transportation*) each contain all five groups of assumptions.

As mentioned, we can evaluate an argument both by attacking its evidence and attacking its assumptions. Of the five categories above, the first four involve attacking assumptions. The fifth category involves attacking the evidence.

There are a few differences between the arguments that appear on the Analysis of an Argument essay (as part of the AWA section) and the Critical Reasoning arguments that appear on the Critical Reasoning section of the GMAT exam. First, whereas the arguments on the Critical Reasoning section center on a single, primary assumption, the arguments on the AWA contain multiple assumptions. Second, we are generally not given the option of attacking evidence when attacking arguments that appear on the Critical Reasoning section of the exam (we can only attack an argument's central assumption). However, when attacking arguments as part of the *argument essay* (AWA), we are free to attack both assumptions and evidence.

It appears that the GMAT AWA does not require the test-taker to make a technical distinction between evidence and assumption(s). Therefore, we can write "this argument assumes" when in fact we are attacking the argument's evidence.

Remember that all arguments have assumptions. It is never possible to say that an argument is weak because it is resting on assumptions. All arguments[1] have assumptions.

[1]Arguments that appear on the AWA Section of the GMAT are inductive as opposed to deductive. Inductive arguments are viewed as stronger or weaker rather than valid or invalid as is the case with deductive arguments.

Step #4: Begin by restating the argument and by answering the original question.

First and foremost, it is recommended that you begin your essay by answering the question at hand. That is, "How well-reasoned do you find this argument." Note that the question of whether or not an argument is actually well-reasoned is essentially unimportant because regardless of whether you think it is or is not well-reasoned, you will still have to proceed to take the argument apart and examine the underlying assumptions. If you believe the argument is not well-reasoned you may state: "I do not believe this argument is well-reasoned as it is resting on several debatable assumptions." This makes real sense since the game of answering an *argument essay* is to attack an argument regardless of its actual reasonableness.

Should you believe the argument is well-reasoned you may state, "I believe this argument is well-reasoned; however, it is resting on several debatable assumptions." It is recommended that you simply replicate one of these two sentences when writing your *argument essay*.

Step #5: Use transition words to structure your argument essay.

As traffic lights of language, *transition words* are extremely important words in the verbal and writing sections of the GMAT exam, and serve one of four primary purposes, namely to show contrast, illustration, continuation, or conclusion.

Perhaps the most relevant transition words that you'll consider using when writing your *argument essay* are the transition words for illustration: *first, second, third*. What you are essentially going to do is to say that: "I don't find this argument to be well reasoned as it contains several debatable assumptions...first (assumption)..., second (assumption)..., and third (assumption)...."

Another way to view overall essay structure, particularly in terms of transition words, is to ponder the "simplest writing approach in the world". *Exhibit 4-14* depicts a sure-fire way to write on just about anything. It might not be the most exciting writing structure but it is clear and it works—take a stance, write your conclusion, say "there are several reasons for this," use transition words, and voila!

Exhibit 4-14: The Simplest Writing Approach

Example: Renaissance

I agree that the Renaissance Period was the most glorious time in human history. There are several reasons for this. First,~~~~~~
~~~~~~
~~~~~~~~~~Second,~~~~~~
~~~~~~
Third,~~~~~~
~~~~~~Fourth,~~~~~~~~~~~~~
~~~~~~
~~~~~~~~~~~~~~~~~~~~~~~~~~~~~~~~~~~~~~Moreover,~~~~~~~~~~~~~~~~~~~~~~~~~~~~~~
~~~~~~
~~~~~~~~~~~~~~~~~~~~~~~~~~~~~~~~~~~~~Finally,~~~~~~~~~~~~~~~~~~~~~~~~~~~~~~~~~
~~~~~~
~~~~~~~~~~~~~~~~~~~~~~~~~~~~~~~~~~~~~~.

Step #6: Question the use of one vague term used in the argument and ask for clarification.

Argument essay questions will contain certain key words which are inherently ambiguous. Examples of such words include "success," "justice," "high-quality," or "increase in business." What do each of these words mean exactly? For example, the phrase "increase in business" could mean more customers coming into a store, higher unit sales, higher revenues, or higher profits. These are not necessarily equivalent terms. Naturally, different people may interpret them differently. A good writing technique includes drawing attention to one vague word (or phrase) per each *argument essay* and suggesting the need for a clearer, more precise interpretation. Perhaps the best place to draw attention to an inherently vague term is in the concluding paragraph of your essay. This is consistent with treatment seen in the sample essays for *Yuppie Café and Cars vs. Public Transportation.*

Step #7: Suggest strengthening the argument by softening its absolute-type wording.

Argument essays appearing on the GMAT are invariably written with absolute-type wordings. The best example of absolute-type wording is the stated or implied "all" meaning. For example, an argument will effectively say that "(all) corporations should do X or Y" or that "(all) people should take A or B course of action." You can make such arguments stronger by suggesting changing such extreme, categorical, or absolute-type wordings. For example, instead of "all corporations" you could suggest that the wording be changed to "*most* corporations should do X or Y." Instead of saying that people "should take ABC course of action," you could say that "people should *probably* take ABC course of action." Arguably the best place to address Step #6 would be at the end of the body of the essay (just before the conclusion) while the best place to address Step #7 would be in the conclusion of the essay.

Step #8: Write (or type) a response using the five-paragraph approach to guide you and proofread your argument essay.

Let the "five-paragraph approach" guide you. In practice, you may use three paragraphs or even seven paragraphs depending on how you choose to structure your writing.

Plan to spend five minutes proofreading your work and looking for typos and spelling errors. Naturally, variations in spelling and punctuation between British English and American English are both recognized and accepted by test graders in New Jersey, USA.

Analysis of an Issue Essay

Here is an 8-step approach to use in answering an *Analysis of an Issue* essay.

1.   Visualize the solution template for an issue essay.

2.   Summarize the pros and cons for your issue.

3.   Choose three (or more) pieces of evidence.

4.   Begin by restating the issue and by answering the original question.

5.   Use transition words to structure your issue essay.

6.   Question the use of one vague term used in the issue and ask for clarification and/or draw attention to ambiguity inherent in the issue itself.

7.   Use one rhetorical question.

8.   Write (or type) a response using the "five-paragraph approach" to guide you and proofread your issue essay.

Step #1: Visualize the solution template for an Issue essay.

First, visualize the solution. Think in terms of the following template:

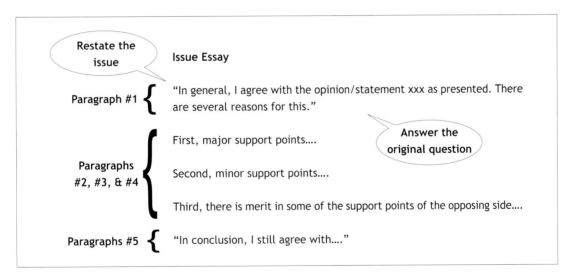

Again, visualizing the solution template involves revisiting the classic "five-paragraph approach." The introduction is one paragraph, the body is three paragraphs, and the conclusion is one paragraph. Each point in the main discussion represents one paragraph in the body of the essay.

A Variation from the Standard Approach

The recommended structure to use to answer an issue essay is seen in the solutions template or standard outline below. This method entails first identifying the major and minor support points on your side of the issue. An alternative method employs a hybrid which involves not only mentioning the support points of your side but also the support points of the opposing side.

Exhibit 4-15 Outlines for Issue Essay

Standard Outline	Optional Outline
In general, I agree with the opinion or statement/opinion xxx as presented. There are seveal reasons for this.	In general, I agree with the opinion or statement/opinion xxx as presented. There are several reasons for this.
First, major support points….	First, major support points….However, the points on the other side include….
Second, more support points….	Second, minor support points….On the other hand, it is important to note that….
Third, there is some merit in the support points of the opposing side….	Third, other support points….Nonetheless, a few points on the other side include….
In conclusion, I still agree with…..	In conclusion, I still agree with…..

Step #2: Summarize the pros and cons for your issue.

Think in terms of the "T-account" below:

Pros	Cons
•	•
•	•
•	•

There are two sides to every issue. The advantages are called "pros" and disadvantages are called "cons." Try to generate three points for each side before beginning to write. Seeing both sides of an issue is the basis for an all-rounded thinking process.

One additional way to summarize the pros and cons is to view each in terms of quantitative and qualitative factors (if possible). Quantitative factors refer to dollar-and-cents issues and, often, to potential increases in revenues or decreases in expenses. Qualitative factors refer to personal factors that are hard to measure in dollar terms: appreciation, beauty, health, intellectual fulfillment, peace of mind, and safety. The distinction between qualitative factors and quantitative factors is somewhat academic, as not all issues can be easily viewed in terms of quantitative and qualitative factors. However, many issues can. The advantages of considering both quantitative and qualitative factors is that it will prevent a test-taker from completely forgetting about addressing the monetary or non-monetary benefits which may be relevant in examining a given topic.

Question: "Do I address both sides of an issue or do I state the strong points of my side and the weak points of the opposing side?" The answer is that we should address both sides of the issue. It is not necessary to discuss the weak points of the opposing side. What then is the objective in answering an Analysis of an Issue essay? It is to "explore" those points that exist on both sides of the issue. Questions are set up to make it ostensibly impossible for an objective, reasonable person to be 100% on one side or the other. Our goal lies not in winning an argument but rather exploring an issue. If we were trying to win an argument, as a politician might do in a political debate, then our strategy would be to state our case, then listen to our opponent's arguments, identifying weak points in his or her argument, and then attack them. By advancing our points while at the same time defeating our opponent's points, we would "win" the debate.

Step #3: Choose three (or more) pieces of evidence.

The practical goal of answering an *issue essay* is to find three (or more) distinct pieces of evidence to support your side of the issue. A common mistake in writing *issue essays* is the inability to personalize writing through the use of personal examples. Personal examples go hand in hand with the use of personal pronouns. Don't shy away from them. The use of first-person pronouns (i.e., I, my, mine, me, we, our, ours, us) forces the writer to relate to the topic at hand in both a personal and usually specific way, not just relating everything in general terms. For example, the statement, "Today, people are too busy to enjoy themselves" is a general statement. "I arrive at work to find some 70 email messages waiting for me, of which 20 are marked urgent. Not only is there work to do by day but I also place calls at night to overseas markets." These sentences show the writer relating to the topic in a more personal way.

Every *issue essay* will likely have need for key personal examples. In the upcoming *issue essay* titled *Is Success Transferable?* examples include, "Italian restaurateurs," "Leilani," "Keith," "friends of my father," and "my brother." In the *issue essay* titled *We Shape Our Buildings*, an example includes the Lippo Centre in Hong Kong, and in the essay titled *An Examined vs. Unexamined Life*, a key personal example is built around the game of golf.

Where is the best place to find personal examples? Think in terms of your work, everyday life, and hobbies. Nearly everyone is an expert on one topic be it tennis, hiking, home decorating, stamp collecting, piano, stock-market picking, shopping, your profession, etc. The better you know a topic, the more information that can be garnered from it. When answering *issue essays*, particularly "open-ended philosophical" *issue essays* (i.e., *An Unexamined Life*), use your "expert knowledge" of hobbies and interests to personalize and deepen your essay. The trick will be to understand how your expert area can be linked to the essay topic at hand.

Your primary concern is to supply a sufficient *amount* of information to support your viewpoint; your secondary concern is to make sure there is a sufficient *variety* of evidence to support your viewpoint. Presenting a variety of information means choosing different kinds of evidence. Think of evidence on three levels—objective, middle, and personal sources. The different levels of support represent different degrees of objectivity. The first (or objective) level of evidence results from citing formal surveys and statistics; the second (or middle-of-the-road) level consists of citing books, newspapers, or magazines; the third (or personal) level consists of drawing from personal experience, observations, opinions, or anecdotes. What you think is important; your personal opinions are totally legitimate and necessary pieces of evidence to support your topic.

Question: "How in the world are you going to be able to employ objective evidence, citing the results of a survey, or employ statistics on the spot?" One thing will likely come as a surprise. For the purpose of writing your *issue essay*, you are allowed to make up evidence. The GMAT Exam allows each test-taker one-half hour to write a response to the *issue essays*. Obviously, you cannot leave the test center to go look for research to support your viewpoint.

This brings us to an interesting question. "If we had a week to write our essay, what would we do?" That is, let's assume that the AWA *issue essay* was a take-home exam. Chances are you would engage an online search engine (or head to the library). What would be the best piece of evidence you could find? Most probably the best evidence would be an authoritative survey or statistic. Say, for example, the sample *issue essay* concerned whether high school students today are more or less prepared for college. A statistic based on a survey conducted by some organization such as the "American Institute of Higher Education" or "British Bureau for Research and Development" that supported the idea of students being more or less prepared for college would go far to support the pro or con side. The two organizations just mentioned were made up; they do not really exist as real as they may seem. However, if you know the names of actual organizations then, by all means, use them. Also, evidence from recognized experts in their fields, in this case those of professional educators, would also fare nicely. Lastly, the opinions of students, friends, parents, and the general public could all be used to produce a forceful, persuasive essay.

It should be noted that the more philosophical an *issue essay* becomes, the less likely will be the need for objective evidence. This is consistent with the writing of the sample essays *We Shape Our Buildings* and *An Unexamined vs. Examined Life*, in which no surveys, statistics, newspaper, or magazine articles are cited.

Step #4: Begin by restating the issue and by answering the original question.

The best way to begin your *issue essay* is to answer the question at hand. The question asked will be, "To what extent do you agree or disagree with the issue at hand?" The best way to begin your essay is to answer this question by saying, "In general I agree with statement/opinion XYZ".

Step #5: Use transition words to structure your issue essay.

Refer to the previous summary contained under Analysis of an Argument essay.

Step #6: Question the use of one vague term used in the issue and/or ask for clarification or draw attention to ambiguity inherent in the issue itself.

Refer to the previous discussion contained within the Analysis of an Argument Essay as well as the proposed solution for each sample essay.

Step #7: Use one rhetorical question.

With respect to your *issue essay*, the *rhetorical question* is a technique worth using. It is a technique that adds a little flair to your writing. Again, note that this technique is not typically used in answering an argument essay.

Rhetorical questions are questions that beg for the adoption of a single answer-the answer that the writer (or speaker) wants the reader (or listener) to adopt. For example, "Who in their right mind would leave for a trip with their door unlocked?" The intended answer is, "No one in his or her right mind". The following are examples of rhetorical questions that could be used if writing an essay on whether high school students today are more or less prepared for college.

In supporting the case that students today are less prepared for college, you could write:

> If basic math skills are difficult for students, how are they going to understand a more advanced area, such as linear programming?

On the other hand, in supporting the side that students today are more prepared for college, you could write:

> Who in their right mind would spend valuable time teaching boring arithmetic calculations instead of spending in-class time learning new multi-media technology?

Step #8: Write (or type) a response using the five-paragraph approach to guide you and proofread your issue essay.

Spend five minutes proofreading your essay. You may find yourself running out of time and compelled to leave the last sentence half finished. Try not to do this. You may think that a grader will feel sympathetic toward you (as if to say that you had so much more to write but only ran out of time), but in fact, any gains in sympathy will be lost due to a lack of professionalism. Make your last sentence short if you cannot finish writing a longer one.

SPECIAL WRITING TECHNIQUES

Consider the use of special writing techniques such as anecdotes, quotes, analogies, similes, and metaphors.

The following are a few literary techniques that can be used to strengthen your *issue essay*. Think of these writing techniques as optional tools.

Anecdotes

Anecdotes are little stories used to embellish a point made by a writer. For example, suppose you are writing on the topic of why we should follow our own path and not be unduly persuaded by the advice of others. You write: "This situation reminds me of the story of a young violinist who is fraught with the dilemma of whether she possesses the talent to continue playing the violin and reach her lofty goal of becoming a virtuoso. Upon a fortuitous meeting with a master violinist, the young girl asks, 'Will you listen to me play and tell me if you think I have the talent to be a virtuoso?' The master then responds, 'If I listen to you play and I feel you do not have the talent, what will you do?' The girl replies, 'Since I value highly your opinion, I will stop playing.' The master remarks, 'If you would quit because of what I would say, then you obviously do not have what it takes to be a virtuoso.'"

Here is an anecdote to convey the idea of greener pastures. Let's call it *Acres of Diamonds*.

> A poor African farmer was tantalized by the stories he had heard of men becoming rich through prospecting for diamonds on the African plains. Determined also to make a fortune, our young man sold his farm and went wandering through the African hinterland in search of diamonds. Years passed and his search finally led him to the side of a wide river where, broke and despondent, he tossed himself into the waters and took his own life. Meanwhile, the man who had bought his farm one day unearthed a big coal-like rock and breaking it open, he discovered a large diamond. Upon closer examination, he found that the whole farm was covered in diamonds-literally acres of them. The original farmer had sold his farm for practically nothing in order to search for diamonds elsewhere, while all the time, they had been beneath his feet.

What might be an interesting way to describe how entrepreneurs succeed despite what others say are realities to the contrary? By not knowing certain information or "truths," entrepreneurs go out and make things happen. Entrepreneurship is very much a "try-first-and-see-what-happens" type of discipline. Not knowing all the facts may actually help a person succeed because he or she doesn't contemplate failure. The way an entrepreneur may succeed is similar to the manner in which a bumblebee flies despite a great danger of crashing.

An entrepreneur can be likened to a bumblebee. NASA has done extensive studies on the bumblebee's flight capabilities based on modern scientific theory. According to studies at NASA, our friend, Mr. Bee, is in imminent danger of crashing. Aeronautically speaking, his wings are too short to support his body weight in flight. Scientists desperately want to communicate to Mr. Bee to tell him that he is in imminent danger of crashing. But scientists do not know "bumblebee language," and in the absence of direct communication, Mr. Bee continues to do what he does best—fly!

Quotes

Citing quotes of famous or well-known people can be persuasive tools. Quotes, when well chosen, make the writer look intelligent. Unfortunately, it is not always easy to recall an applicable quote from mere memory. One possibility involves making up your own quotes. This involves putting quotation marks around your own statements so they appear as actual quotes. An example of such a self-generated quote appears in the essay titled *An Unexamined vs. Examined Life-*"The more we look into life, the more life looks into us."

Analogies

Analogies make comparisons between two otherwise dissimilar things. They can be very effective tools for the writer to use to help the reader see the relationship between two or more otherwise unfamiliar things. For example, suppose you are writing your essay and want to stress the importance of making sales, particularly the relationship between the production department and the sales and marketing department. You might use the following "guns and bullets" analogy. "Production makes the bullets, marketing points the gun, and sales pulls the trigger." This makes clearer the idea that the production department is responsible for making products, while the marketing department is responsible for determining where sales are to be found, and the sales department, for actually going out and making sales.

In the upcoming essay *We Shape Our Buildings*, a climate vs. weather analogy used is: Climate is likened to our fundamental personality traits while weather is likened to our emotions and moods.

Similes

Similes, like metaphors, are figurative comparisons, not actual comparisons. An example of an actual comparison is, "Cindy is taller than Susan." Similes are direct comparisons between two different things usually introduced by "as" or "like." An example of a simile is, "A sharp mind is like a knife that cuts problems open." Similes are relatively easy to use and can be powerful, succinct tools in writing your essay.

Metaphors

A metaphor is an indirect comparison of two dissimilar things in which "as" or "like" is not used. Example: "He has the heart of a lion." Whereas a simile says that one thing is like another, a metaphor says that one thing is another.

CHAPTER 5

PROBLEM SOLVING

"Math Class is Tough."
(Barbie's 1992 voice chip by Mattell)

DISTANCE-RATE-TIME PROBLEMS

1. River Boat ($\int$)

A river boat leaves Silver Town and travels upstream to Gold Town at an average speed of 6 kilometers per hour. It returns by the same route at an average speed of 9 kilometers per hour. What is the average speed for the round-trip in kilometers per hour?

A) 7.0   B) 7.1   C) 7.2   D) 7.5   E) 8.0

2. Forgetful Timothy ($\int$ $\int$)

Timothy leaves home for school, riding his bicycle at a rate of 9 m.p.h. Fifteen minutes after he leaves, his mother sees Timothy's math homework lying on his bed and immediately leaves home to bring it to him. If his mother drives at 36 m.p.h., how far (in terms of miles) must she drive before she reaches Timothy?

A) $\frac{1}{3}$ B) 3   C) 4   D) 9   E) 12

3. P and Q ($\int$ $\int$ $\int$)

P and Q are the only two applicants qualified for a short-term research project that pays 600 dollars in total. Candidate P has more experience and, if hired, would be paid 50% more per hour than Candidate Q would be paid. Candidate Q, if hired, would require 10 hours more than Candidate P to do the job. Candidate's P's hourly wage is how many dollars greater than Q's hourly wage?

A) $10   B) $15   C) $20   D) $25   E) $30

4. Run-Run ($\int$ $\int$)

If Susan takes 9 seconds to run y yards, how many *minutes* will it take her to run x yards at the same rate?

A) $\frac{xy}{9}$ B) $\frac{9x}{60y}$ C) $\frac{60xy}{9}$ D) $\frac{xy}{540}$ E) $\frac{540x}{y}$

5. Submarine ($\int$ $\int$ $\int$)

On a reconnaissance mission, a state-of-the-art nuclear powered submarine traveled 240 miles to reposition itself in the proximity of an aircraft carrier. This journey would have taken 1 hour less if the submarine had traveled 20 miles per hour faster. What was the average speed, in miles per hour, for the actual journey?

A) 20   B) 40   C) 60   D) 80   E) 100

6. Sixteen-Wheeler ($\int$ $\int$ $\int$)

Two heavily loaded sixteen-wheeler transport trucks are 770 kilometers apart, sitting at two rest stops on opposite sides of the same highway. Driver A begins heading down the highway driving at an average speed of 90 kilometers per hour. Exactly one hour later, Driver B starts down the highway toward Driver A, maintaining an average speed of 80 kilometers per hour. How many kilometers *further* than Driver B, will Driver A have driven when they meet and pass each other on the highway?

A) 90   B) 130   C) 150   D) 320   E) 450

AGE PROBLEM

7. Elmer (🐧)

Elmer, the circus Elephant, is currently three times older than Leo, the circus Lion. In five years from now, Leo the circus Lion will be exactly half as old as Elmer, the circus Elephant. How old is Elmer today?

A) 10   B) 15   C) 17   D) 22   E) 25

AVERAGE PROBLEMS

8. Average (🐧 🐧)

The average (arithmetic mean) of four numbers is 4x + 3. If one of the numbers is x, what is the average of the other three numbers?

A) x + 1   B) 3x + 3   C) 5x + 1   D) 5x + 4   E) 15x + 12

9. Fourth Time Lucky (🐧 🐧)

On his first 3 tests, Rajeev received an average score of N points. If on his fourth test, he exceeds his previous average score by 20 points, what is his average score for his first 4 tests?

A) N   B) N + 4   C) N + 5   D) N + 10   E) N + 20

10. Vacation (🐧 🐧)

P persons have decided to rent a van to tour while on holidays. The price of the van is x dollars and each person is to pay an equal share. If d persons cancel their trip thus failing to pay their share, which of the following represents the *additional* number of dollars per person that each remaining person must pay in order to still rent the van?

A) dx   B) $\dfrac{x}{P - d}$ C) $\dfrac{dx}{P - d}$ D) $\dfrac{dx}{P(P - d)}$ E) $\dfrac{x}{P(P - d)}$

WORK PROBLEMS

11. Disappearing Act (🐧 🐧)

Working individually, Deborah can wash all the dishes from her friend's wedding banquet in 5 hours and Tom can wash all the dishes in 6 hours. If Deborah and Tom work together but independently at the task for 2 hours, at which point Tom leaves, how many remaining hours will it take Deborah to complete the task alone?

A) $\dfrac{4}{15}$ B) $\dfrac{3}{11}$ C) $\dfrac{4}{3}$ D) $\dfrac{15}{11}$ E) $\dfrac{11}{2}$

12. Exhibition (🐧 🐧)

If it takes 70 workers 3 hours to disassemble the exhibition rides at a small amusement park, how many hours would it take 30 workers to do this same job?

A) $\dfrac{40}{3}$ B) 11   C) 7   D) $\dfrac{7}{3}$ E) $\dfrac{9}{7}$

13. Legal (🐧 🐧 🐧)

A group of 4 junior lawyers require 5 hours to complete a legal research assignment. How many hours would it take a group of three legal assistants to complete the same research assignment assuming that a legal assistant works at two-thirds the rate of a junior lawyer?

A) 13　　　　　B) 10　　　　　C) 9　　　　　D) 6　　　　　E) 5

PICTURE-FRAME OR BORDER PROBLEM

14. Persian Rug (🐧 🐧)

A Persian Rug set on a dining room floor measures a meters by b meters, which includes the actual rug design and a solid colored border c centimeters wide. Which algebraic expression below represents the *area* of the solid colored border in square centimeters?

A) ab - 4c
B) a + b - [(a - c) + (b - c)]
C) 2a + 2b - [2(a - 2c) + 2(b - 2c)]
D) ab - (a - c)(b - c)
E) ab - (a - 2c)(b - 2c)

MIXTURE PROBLEMS

15. Nuts (🐧)

A wholesaler wishes to sell 100 pounds of mixed nuts at $2.50 a pound. She mixes peanuts worth $1.50 a pound with cashews worth $4.00 a pound. How many pounds of cashews must she use?

A) 40　　　　　B) 45　　　　　C) 50　　　　　D) 55　　　　　E) 60

16. Gold (🐧 🐧)

An alloy weighing 24 ounces is 70% gold. How many ounces of pure gold must be added to create an alloy that is 90% gold?

A) 6　　　　　B) 9　　　　　C) 12　　　　　D) 24　　　　　E) 48

17. Evaporation (🐧 🐧 🐧)

How many liters of water must be evaporated from 50 liters of a 3-percent sugar solution to get a 10-percent solution?

A) 35　　　　B) $33\frac{1}{3}$　　　　C) 27　　　　D) $16\frac{2}{3}$　　　　E) 15

GROUP PROBLEMS

18. Standardized Test (⚲ ⚲)

If 85% of the test-takers taking an old paper and pencil GMAT exam answered the first question on a given math section correctly, and 75% of the test-takers answered the second question correctly, and 5% of the test-takers answered neither question correctly, what percent answered *both* correctly?

A) 60%   B) 65%   C) 70%   D) 75%   E) 80%

19. German Cars (⚲ ⚲ ⚲)

The *New Marketing Journal* conducted a survey of wealthy German car owners. According to the survey, all wealthy car owners owned one or more of the following three brands: BMW, Mercedes, or Porsche. Respondents' answers were grouped as follows: 45 owned BMW cars, 38 owned Mercedes cars, and 27 owned Porsche cars. Of these, 15 owned both BMW and Mercedes cars, 12 owned both Mercedes and Porsche cars, 8 owned both BMW and Porsche cars, and 5 persons owned all three types of cars. How many different individuals were surveyed?

A) 70   B) 75   C) 80   D) 110   E) 130

20. Language Classes (⚲ ⚲ ⚲)

According to the admissions and records office of a major university, the schedules of X first-year college students were inspected and it was found that S number of students were taking a Spanish course, F number of students were taking a French course, and B number of students were taking both a Spanish and a French Course. Which of the following expressions gives the percentage of students whose schedules were inspected who were taking *neither* a Spanish course *nor* a French course?

A) $100 \times \dfrac{X}{(B + F + S)}$

B) $100 \times \dfrac{(B + F + S)}{X}$

C) $100 \times \dfrac{(X - F - S)}{X}$

D) $100 \times \dfrac{(X + B - F - S)}{X}$

E) $100 \times \dfrac{(X - B - F - S)}{X}$

MATRIX PROBLEMS

21. Single (⚲ ⚲)

In a graduate physics course, 70% of the students are male and 30% of the students are married. If two-sevenths of the male students are married, what fraction of the female students is single?

(A) $\dfrac{2}{7}$ B) $\dfrac{1}{3}$ C) $\dfrac{3}{7}$ D) $\dfrac{2}{3}$ E) $\dfrac{5}{7}$

Chapter 5: Problem Solving

22. Batteries (𝄐 𝄐)

One-fifth of the batteries produced by an upstart factory are defective and one-quarter of all batteries produced are rejected by the quality control technician. If one-tenth of the non-defective batteries are rejected by mistake, and if all the batteries not rejected are sold, then what percent of the batteries sold by the factory are defective?

A) 4%   B) 5%   C) 6%   D) 8%   E) 12%

23. Experiment (𝄐 𝄐 𝄐)

Sixty percent of the rats included in an experiment were female rats. If some of the rats died during an experiment and 70 percent of the rats that died were male rats, what was the ratio of the death rate among the male rats to the death rate among the female rats?

A) 7 : 2
B) 7 : 3
C) 2 : 7
D) 3 : 7
E) Cannot be determined from the information given.

PRICE-COST-VOLUME-PROFIT PROBLEMS

24. Garments (𝄐)

If s shirts can be purchased for d dollars, how many shirts can be purchased for t dollars?

A) sdt   B) $\frac{ts}{d}$ C) $\frac{td}{s}$ D) $\frac{d}{st}$ E) $\frac{s}{dt}$

25. Pete's Pet Shop (𝄐 𝄐)

At Pete's Pet Shop, 35 cups of bird seed are used every 7 days to feed 15 parakeets. How many cups of bird seed would be required to feed 9 parakeets for 12 days?

A) 32   B) 36   C) 39   D) 42   E) 45

26. Sabrina to Change Jobs (𝄐 𝄐)

Sabrina is contemplating a job switch. She is thinking of leaving her job paying $85,000 per year to accept a sales job paying $45,000 per year plus 15 percent commission for each sale made. If each of her sales is for $1,500, what is the least number of sales she must make per year if she is not to lose money because of the job change?

A) 57   B) 177   C) 178   D) 377   E) 378

27. Delicatessen (𝄐 𝄐)

A large delicatessen purchased p pounds of cheese for c dollars per pound. If d pounds of the cheese had to be discarded due to spoilage and the delicatessen sold the rest for s dollars per pound, which of the following represents the gross profit on the sale of the purchase? (gross profit equals sales revenue minus product cost)

A) (p - d)(s - c)   B) s(p - d) - pc   C) c(p - d) - ds   D) d(s - c) - pc   E) pc - ds

28. Prototype (🖋 🖋 🖋)

A Prototype Fuel-Efficient Car (P-Car) is estimated to get 80% more miles per gallon of gasoline than does a Traditional Fuel-Efficient Car (T-Car). However, the P-Car requires a special type of gasoline that costs 20% more per gallon than does the gasoline used by a T-Car. If the two cars are driven the same distance, what percent less than the money spent on gasoline for the T-Car is the money spent on gasoline for the P-Car?

A) 16%   B) $33\frac{1}{3}$%   C) 50%   D) 60%   E) $66\frac{2}{3}$ %

LEAST-COMMON-MULTIPLE WORD PROBLEM

29. Lights (🖋 🖋)

The Royal Hawaiian Hotel decorates its Rainbow Christmas Tree with non-flashing white lights and a series of colored flashing lights—red, blue, green, orange, and yellow. The red lights turn red every 20 seconds, the blue lights turn blue every 30 seconds, the green lights turn green every 45 seconds, the orange lights turn orange every 60 seconds, and yellow lights turn yellow every 1 minute and 20 seconds. The manager plugs the tree in for the first time on December 1st precisely at midnight and all lights begin their cycle at exactly the same time. If the five colored lights flash simultaneously at midnight, what is the next time all five colored lights will all flash together at the exact same time?

A) 0:03 AM   B) 0:04 AM   C) 0:06 AM   D) 0:12 AM   E) 0:24 AM

GENERAL ALGEBRAIC WORD PROBLEMS

30. Chili Paste (🖋 🖋)

Each week a restaurant serving Mexican food uses the same volume of chili paste, which comes in either 25-ounce cans or 15-ounce cans of chili paste. If the restaurant must order 40 more of the smaller cans than the larger cans to fulfill its weekly needs, then how many *smaller* cans are required to fulfill its weekly needs?

A) 60   B) 70   C) 80   D) 100   E) 120

31. Snooker (🖋 🖋)

A snooker tournament charges $45.00 for seats in the front rows and $15.00 for seats in the back rows. On a certain night, a total of 320 tickets were sold, for a total cost of $7,500. How many *fewer* tickets were sold that night for seats in the front row than for seats in the back row?

A) 70   B) 90   C) 140   D) 230   E) 250

32. Hardware (🖋)

Hammers and wrenches are manufactured at a uniform weight per hammer and a uniform weight per wrench. If the total weight of two hammers and three wrenches is one-third that of 8 hammers and 5 wrenches, then the total weight of one wrench is how many times that of one hammer?

A) $\frac{1}{2}$ B) $\frac{2}{3}$ C) 1   D) $\frac{3}{2}$ E) 2

33. Premium (⚲ ⚲)

The price of 5 kilograms premium fertilizer is the same as the price of 6 kilograms of regular fertilizer. If the price of premium fertilizer is y cents per kilogram more than the price of regular fertilizer, what is the price per kilogram of premium fertilizer in cents?

A) $\dfrac{y}{30}$ B) $\dfrac{5}{6}y$ C) $\dfrac{6}{5}y$ D) $5y$ E) $6y$

FUNCTION PROBLEM

34. Function (⚲)

If $f(x) = \sqrt{x}$ and $g(x) = \sqrt{x^2 + 7}$, what is the value of $f(g(3))$?

A) 1 B) 2 C) 3 D) 4 E) 5

ALGEBRAIC FRACTIONS

35. Rescue (⚲)

If $a = \dfrac{b - d}{c - d}$, then $d =$

A) $\dfrac{b + a}{c + a}$ B) $\dfrac{b - a}{c - a}$ C) $\dfrac{bc - a}{bc + a}$ D) $\dfrac{b - ac}{1 - a}$ E) $\dfrac{b - ac}{a - 1}$

36. Hodgepodge (⚲)

The expression $\dfrac{\frac{1}{h}}{1 - \frac{1}{h}}$, where h is not equal to 0 and 1, is equivalent to which of the following?

A) $1 - h$ B) $h - 1$ C) $\dfrac{1}{h - 1}$ D) $\dfrac{1}{1 - h}$ E) $\dfrac{h}{h - 1}$

FRACTIONS & DECIMALS

37. Mirage (⚲)

Which of the following has the greatest value?

A) $\dfrac{10}{11}$ B) $\dfrac{4}{5}$ C) $\dfrac{7}{8}$ D) $\dfrac{21}{22}$ E) $\dfrac{5}{6}$

38. Deceptive (⚲)

Dividing 100 by 0.75 will lead to the same mathematical result as multiplying 100 by which number?

A) 0.25 B) 0.75 C) 1.25 D) 1.33 E) 1.75

39. Spiral (⚲)

In a certain sequence, the first term is 2, and each successive term is 1 more than the reciprocal of the term that immediately precedes it. What is the fifth term in this sequence?

A) $\dfrac{13}{8}$ B) $\dfrac{21}{13}$ C) $\dfrac{8}{5}$ D) $\dfrac{5}{8}$ E) $\dfrac{8}{13}$

PERCENTAGE PROBLEMS

40. Micro Brewery (🐦)

Over the course of a year, a certain Micro Brewery increased its output by 70 percent. At the same time, it decreased its total working hours by 20 percent. By what percent did this factory increase its output per hour?

A) 50%   B) 90%   C) 112.5%   D) 210%   E) 212.5%

41. Diners (🐦 🐦)

A couple spends $264 in total while dining out and paid this amount using a credit card. The $264 figure included a 20% tip which was paid on top of the price of the food which already included a sales tax of 10%. What was the actual price of the meal before tax and tip?

A) $184   B) $200   C) $204   D) $216   E) $232

42. Investments (🐦 🐦)

A lady sold two small investment properties, A and B, for $24,000 each. If she sold property A for 20% more than she paid for it, and sold property B for 20% less than she paid for it, then, in terms of the net financial effect of these two investments (excluding taxes and expenses), we can conclude that the lady

A) broke even.
B) had an overall gain of $1,200.
C) had an overall loss of $1,200.
D) had an overall gain of $2,000.
E) had an overall loss of $2,000.

43. Discount (🐦)

A discount of 10 percent on an order of goods followed by a discount of 30 percent amounts to

A) the same as one 13 percent discount.
B) the same as one 27 percent discount.
C) the same as one 33 percent discount.
D) the same as one 37 percent discount.
E) the same as one 40 percent discount.

44. Inflation (🐦)

An inflationary increase of 20 percent on an order of raw materials followed by an inflationary increase of 10 percent amounts to

A) the same as one 22 percent inflationary increase.
B) the same as one 30 percent inflationary increase.
C) the same as an inflationary increase of 10 percent followed by an inflationary increase of 20 percent.
D) less than a inflationary increase of 10 percent followed by an inflationary increase of 20 percent.
E) more than an inflationary increase of 10 percent followed by an inflationary increase of 20 percent.

45. Gardener (⸙)

A gardener increased the length of his rectangle-shaped garden by increasing its length by 40%, and decreasing its width by 20%. The area of the new garden

A) has increased by 20%.
B) has increased by 12%.
C) has increased by 8%.
D) is exactly the same as the old area.
E) cannot be expressed in percentage terms without actual numbers.

46. Squaring Off (⸙ ⸙)

If the sides of a square are doubled in length, the area of the original square is now how many times as large as the area of the resultant square?

A) 25%   B) 50%   C) 100%   D) 200%   E) 400%

RATIOS & PROPORTIONS

47. Earth Speed (⸙ ⸙)

The Earth travels around the Sun at an approximate speed of 20 miles per second. This speed is how many kilometers per hour? [1 km = 0.6 miles]

A) 2,000   B) 12,000   C) 43,200   D) 72,000   E) 120,000

48. Rum & Coke (⸙ ⸙)

A drink holding 6 ounces of an alcoholic drink that is 1 part rum to 2 parts coke is added to a jug holding 32 ounces of an alcoholic drink that is 1 part rum to 3 parts coke. What is the ratio of rum to coke in the resulting mixture?

A) 2 : 5   B) 5 : 14   C) 3 : 5   D) 4 : 7   E) 14 : 5

49. Millionaire (⸙ ⸙)

For every $20 that a billionaire spends, a millionaire spends the equivalent of 20 cents. For every $4 that a millionaire spends, a yuppie spends the equivalent of $1. The ratio of money spent by a yuppie, millionaire, and billionaire can be expressed as

A) 1 : 4 : 400   B) 1 : 4 : 100   C) 20 : 4 : 1   D) 100 : 4 : 1   E) 400 : 4 : 1

50. Fuchsia (⸙ ⸙ ⸙)

At a certain paint store, "Fuchsia" paint is made by mixing 5 parts of red paint with 3 parts of blue paint. "Mauve" paint is made by mixing 3 parts of red paint with 5 parts blue paint. How many litres of blue paint must be added to 24 litres of "Fuchsia" to change it to "Mauve" paint?

A) 9   B) 12   C) 15   D) 16   E) 18

51. Rare Coins ($\int$)

In a rare coin collection, there is one gold coin for every three non-gold coins. If 10 more gold coins are added to the collection, the ratio of gold coins to non-gold coins will be 1 to 2. Based on this information, how many total coins are there now in this collection (after the acquisition)?

A) 40   B) 50   C) 60   D) 80   E) 90

52. Coins Revisited ($\int$ $\int$ $\int$)

In another rare coin collection, one in six coins is gold. If 10 non-gold coins are subsequently traded for 10 gold coins, the ratio of gold coins to non-gold coins will be 1 to 4. Based on this information, how many gold coins are there now in this collection (after the trade)?

A) 50   B) 60   C) 180   D) 200   E) 300

SQUARES AND CUBES

53. Plus-Zero ($\int$ $\int$)

If $x>0$, which of the following <u>could</u> be true?

I. $x^3>x^2$ II. $x^2 = x$ III. $x^2>x^3$

A) I only   B) I & II   C) II & III   D) All of the above   E) None of the above

54. Sub-Zero ($\int$ $\int$)

If $x < 0$, which of the following <u>must</u> be true?

I. $x^2 > 0$ II. $x - 2x > 0$ III. $x^3 + x^2 < 0$

A) I only   B) I & II   C) II & III   D) All of the above   E) None of the above

EXPONENT PROBLEMS

55. Triplets ($\int$ $\int$)

$3^{10} + 3^{10} + 3^{10} =$

A) 3^{11} B) 3^{13} C) 3^{30} D) 9^{10} E) 9^{30}

56. Solar Power ($\smallint$)

The mass of the sun is approximately 2×10^{30} kg and the mass of the moon is approximately 8×10^{12} kg. The mass of the sun is approximately how many times the mass of the moon?

A) 4.0×10^{-18} 　　 B) 2.5×10^{17} 　　 C) 4.0×10^{18} 　　 D) 2.5×10^{19} 　　 E) 4.0×10^{42}

57. K.I.S.S. ($\smallint$ $\smallint$)

If a is a positive integer, then $3^a + 3^{a+1} =$

A) 4^a 　　 B) $3^a - 1$ 　　 C) $3^{2a} + 1$ 　　 D) $3^a(a - 1)$ 　　 E) $4(3^a)$

58. Toughie ($\smallint$ $\smallint$ $\smallint$)

If $m > 1$ and $n = 2^{m-1}$, then $4^m =$

A) $16n^2$ 　　 B) $4n^2$ 　　 C) n^2 　　 D) $\dfrac{n^2}{4}$ 　　 E) $\dfrac{n^2}{16}$

59. The Power of 5 ($\smallint$ $\smallint$ $\smallint$)

If $5^5 \times 5^7 = (125)^x$, then what is the value of x?

A) 2 　　 B) 3 　　 C) 4 　　 D) 5 　　 E) 6

60. Incognito ($\smallint$ $\smallint$ $\smallint$)

Which of the following fractions has the greatest value?

A) $\dfrac{25}{(2^4)(3^3)}$ 　　 B) $\dfrac{5}{(2^2)(3^3)}$ 　　 C) $\dfrac{4}{(2^3)(3^2)}$ 　　 D) $\dfrac{36}{(2^3)(3^4)}$ 　　 E) $\dfrac{76}{(2^4)(3^4)}$

61. Chain Reaction ($\smallint$ $\smallint$ $\smallint$)

If $x - \dfrac{1}{2^6} - \dfrac{1}{2^7} - \dfrac{1}{2^8} = \dfrac{2}{2^9}$, then $x =$

A) $\dfrac{1}{2}$ 　　 B) $\dfrac{1}{2^3}$ 　　 C) $\dfrac{1}{2^4}$ 　　 D) $\dfrac{1}{2^5}$ 　　 E) $\dfrac{1}{2^9}$

62. Bacteria ($\smallint$ $\smallint$)

A certain population of bacteria doubles every 10 minutes. If the number of bacteria in the population initially was 10^5, then what was the number in the population 1 hour later?

A) $2(10^5)$ 　　 B) $6(10^5)$ 　　 C) $(2^6)(10^5)$ 　　 D) $(10^6)(10^5)$ 　　 E) $(10^5)^6$

RADICAL PROBLEMS

63. Simplify (☾)

$$\sqrt{\frac{12 \times 3 + 4 \times 16}{6}} =$$

A) $\frac{5\sqrt{6}}{3}$ B) $\sqrt{22}$ C) $\sqrt{6} + 4$ D) $\frac{8\sqrt{15}}{3}$ E) $16\frac{2}{3}$

64. Strange (☾ ☾)

The expression $\frac{1 - \sqrt{2}}{1 + \sqrt{2}}$ is equivalent to which of the following?

A) $-3 + 2\sqrt{2}$ B) $1 - \frac{2}{3}\sqrt{2}$ C) 0 D) $1 + \frac{2}{3}\sqrt{2}$ E) $3 + 2\sqrt{2}$

65. Radical (☾)

$$\frac{\sqrt{10}}{\sqrt{0.001}} =$$

A) 10,000
B) 1,000
C) 100
D) 1
E) Can be expressed only as a non-integer.

INEQUALITY PROBLEM

66. Two-Way Split (☾)

If $-x^2 + 16 < 0$, which of the following must be true?

A) $-4 > x > 4$ B) $-4 < x > 4$ C) $-4 < x < 4$ D) $-4 \leq x \geq 4$ E) $-4 \geq x \geq 4$

PRIME NUMBER PROBLEMS

67. Odd Man Out (☾ ☾)

If P represents the product of the first 13 positive integers, which of the following must be true?

I. P is an odd number   II. P is a multiple 17   III. P is a multiple 24

A) I only B) II only C) III only D) None of the above E) All of the above

68. Primed (☾)

The "primeness" of a positive integer x is defined as the positive difference between its largest and smallest prime factors. Which of the following has the greatest primeness?

A) 10 B) 12 C) 14 D) 15 E) 18

REMAINDER PROBLEMS

69. Remainder (⸩ ⸩)

When the integer k is divided by 7, the remainder is 5. Which of the following expressions below when divided by 7, will have a remainder of 6?

I. $4k + 7$ II. $6k + 4$ III. $8k + 1$

A) I only   B) II only   C) III only   D) I and II only   E) I, II and III

70. Double Digits (⸩ ⸩)

How many two-digit whole numbers yield a remainder of 3 when divided by 10 and also yield a remainder of 3 when divided by 4?

A) One   B) Two   C) Three   D) Four   E) Five

SYMBOLISM PROBLEM

71. Visualize (⸩ ⸩)

For all real numbers v the operation $v*$ is defined by the equation $v* = v - \dfrac{v}{2}$. If $(v*)* = 3$, then $v =$

A) 12   B) 6   C) 4   D) $\sqrt{12}$ E) -12

COORDINATE GEOMETRY PROBLEMS

72. Intercept (⸩ ⸩)

In the rectangular coordinate system, what is the x-intercept of a line passing through (10,3) and (-6,-5)?

A) 4   B) 2   C) 0   D) -2   E) -4

73. Masquerade ( )

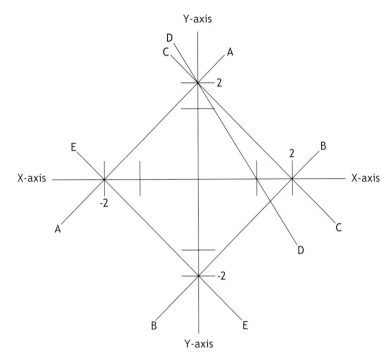

Which of the above lines fit the equation? $y = -2x + 2$

A) Line A   B) Line B   C) Line C   D) Line D   E) Line E

74. Boxed In ( )

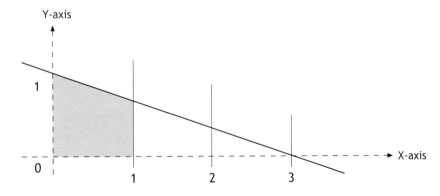

In the rectangular coordinate system above, the shaded region is bounded by a straight line. Which of the following is NOT an equation of one of the boundary lines?

A) $x = 0$ B) $y = 0$ C) $x = 1$ D) $x - 3y = 0$ E) $y + \frac{1}{3}x = 1$

PLANE GEOMETRY PROBLEMS

75. Magic (🐧)

What is the ratio of the circumference of a circle to its diameter?

A) π
B) 2π
C) π^2
D) $2\pi r$
E) varies depending on the size of the circle

76. Circuit (🐧 🐧)

A rectangular circuit board is designed to have a width of w inches, a length of l inches, a perimeter of P inches, and an area of A square inches. Which of the following equations must be true?

A) $2w^2 + pw + 2a = 0$
B) $2w^2 - pw + 2a = 0$
C) $2w^2 - pw - 2a = 0$
D) $w^2 + pw + a = 0$
E) $w^2 - pw + 2a = 0$

77. Victorian (🐧 🐧)

A professional painter is painting the window frames of an old Victorian House. The worker has a ladder that is exactly 25 feet in length which he will use to paint two sets of window frames. To reach the first window frame, he places the ladder so that it rests against the side of the house at a point exactly 15 feet above the ground. When he finishes, he proceeds to reposition the ladder to reach the second window so that now the ladder rests against the side of the house at a point exactly 24 feet above the ground. How much *closer* to the base of the house has the bottom of the ladder now been moved?

A) 7   B) 9   C) 10   D) 13   E) 27

78. Kitty Corner (🐧)

The figure below is a cube with each side equal to 2 units. What is the length (in units) of diagonal BD? (Note: BD is drawn diagonally from bottom left-hand corner in the front to top right-hand corner at the back.)

A) $2\sqrt{2}$
B) $2\sqrt{3}$
C) $3\sqrt{2}$
D) $3\sqrt{3}$
E) $4\sqrt{3}$

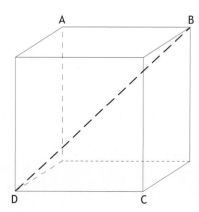

79. QR ($\int \int \int$)

If segment QR in the cube below has length $4\sqrt{3}$, what is the volume of the cube?

A) 16
B) 27
C) 64
D) 81
E) 125

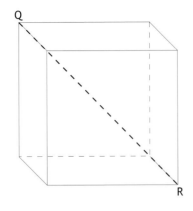

80. Diamond ($\int \int$)

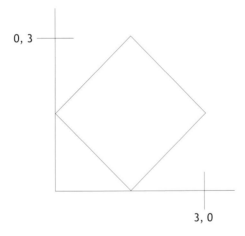

The figure above is a square. What is its perimeter?

A) $6\sqrt{2}$ B) 9   C) 12   D) 12 $\sqrt{2}$ E) 18

81. Cornered (🐦🐦🐦)

Viewed from the outside inward, the figure below depicts a square-circle-square-circle, each enclosed within another. If the area of square ABCD is 2 square units, then which of the following expresses the *area* of the darkened corners?

A) $2 - \frac{1}{4}\pi$

B) $2 - \frac{1}{2}\pi$

C) $1 - \frac{1}{4}\pi$

D) $\frac{1}{2} - \frac{1}{8}\pi$

E) $1 - \frac{1}{2}\pi$

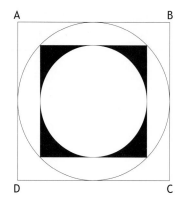

82. AC (🐦🐦)

In the right triangle ABD below, AC is perpendicular to BD. If AB = 5 and AD = 12, then AC is equal to?

A) $\frac{30}{13}$

B) $\sqrt{12}$

C) 4

D) $2\sqrt{5}$

E) $\frac{60}{13}$

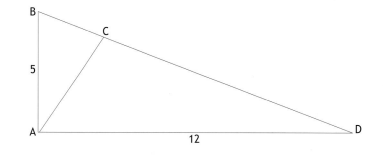

83. Woozy (🐦🐦🐦)

In the equilateral triangle below, each side has a length of 4 units. If PQ has a length of 1 unit and TQ is perpendicular to PR, what is the *area* of region QRST?

A) $\frac{1}{3}\sqrt{3}$

B) $3\sqrt{3}$

C) $\frac{7}{2}\sqrt{3}$

D) $4\sqrt{3}$

E) $15\sqrt{3}$

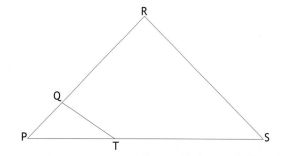

84. Lopsided ($\int$)

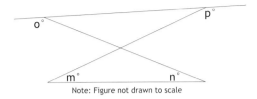

Note: Figure not drawn to scale

In the figure above, $m + n = 110$. What is the value of $o + p$?

A) 70   B) 110   C) 250   D) 270   E) 330

SOLID GEOMETRY PROBLEM

85. Sphere ($\int \int \int$)

A sphere has a radius of x units. If the length of this radius is doubled, then how many times larger, in terms of volume, is the resultant sphere as compared with the original sphere?

A) 1   B) 2   C) 4   D) 8   E) 16

PROBABILITY PROBLEMS

86. Orange and Blue ($\int \int$)

There are 5 marbles in a bag—2 orange and 3 blue. If two marbles are pulled from the bag, what is the probability that at least one will be orange?

A) $\frac{7}{10}$ B) $\frac{3}{5}$ C) $\frac{2}{5}$ D) $\frac{3}{10}$ E) $\frac{1}{10}$

87. Exam Time ($\int$)

A student is to take her final exams in two subjects. The probability that she will pass the first subject is $\frac{3}{4}$ and the probability that she will pass the second subject is $\frac{2}{3}$. What is the probability that she will pass one exam or the other exam?

A) $\frac{5}{12}$ B) $\frac{1}{2}$ C) $\frac{7}{12}$ D) $\frac{5}{7}$ E) $\frac{11}{12}$

88. Sixth Sense ($\int \int$)

What is the probability of getting a six on either the first or second toss of a normal six-sided die?

A) $\frac{1}{36}$ B) $\frac{1}{18}$ C) $\frac{1}{6}$ D) $\frac{11}{36}$ E) $\frac{1}{3}$

89. At Least One (🐧 🐧 🐧)

A student is to take her final exams in three subjects. The probability that she will pass the first subject is $\frac{3}{4}$, the probability that she will pass the second subject is $\frac{2}{3}$, and the probability that she will pass the third subject is $\frac{1}{2}$. What is the probability that she will pass at least one of these three exams?

A) $\frac{1}{4}$ B) $\frac{11}{24}$ C) $\frac{17}{24}$ D) $\frac{3}{4}$ E) $\frac{23}{24}$

90. Coin Toss (🐧 🐧 🐧)

What is the probability of tossing a coin five times and having heads appear *at most* three times?

A) $\frac{1}{16}$ B) $\frac{5}{16}$ C) $\frac{2}{5}$ D) $\frac{13}{16}$ E) $\frac{27}{32}$

91. Antidote (🐧 🐧)

Medical analysts predict that one-third of all people who are infected by a certain biological agent could be expected to be killed for each day that passes during which they have not received an antidote. What fraction of a group of 1,000 people could be expected to be killed if infected and not treated for three full days?

A) $\frac{16}{81}$ B) $\frac{8}{27}$ C) $\frac{2}{3}$ D) $\frac{19}{27}$ E) $\frac{65}{81}$

PERMUTATION PROBLEMS

92. Hiring (🐧)

A company seeks to hire a sales manager, a shipping clerk, and a receptionist. The company has narrowed its candidate search and plans to interview all remaining candidates including 7 persons for the position of sales manager, 4 persons for the position of shipping clerk, and 10 persons for the position of receptionist. How many different hirings of these three people are possible?

A) 7 + 4 + 10 B) 7 x 4 x 10 C) 21 x 20 x 19 D) 7! + 4! + 10! E) 7! x 4! x 10!

93. Fencing (🐧)

Four contestants representing four different countries advance to the finals of a fencing championship. Assuming all competitors have an equal chance of winning, how many possibilities are there with respect to how a first-place and second-place medal can be awarded?

A) 6 B) 7 C) 12 D) 16 E) 24

94. Alternating (🐧 🐧)

Six students—3 boys and 3 girls—are to sit side by side for a makeup exam. How many ways could they arrange themselves given that no two boys and no two girls can sit next to one another?

A) 12 B) 36 C) 72 D) 240 E) 720

95. Banana (𝄞 𝄞)

Which of the following leads to the correct mathematical solution for the number of ways that the letters of the word BANANA could be arranged to create a six-letter code?

A) 6!   B) 6! - (3! + 2!)   C) 6! - (3! x 2!)   D) $\frac{6!}{3! + 2!}$ E) $\frac{6!}{3! \times 2!}$

96. Table (𝄞 𝄞)

How many ways could three people sit at a table with five seats in which two of the five seats will remain empty?

A) 8   B) 12   C) 60   D) 118   E) 120

COMBINATIONS PROBLEMS

97. Singer (𝄞 𝄞 𝄞)

For an upcoming charity event, a famous singer has agreed to sing 4 out of 6 "old songs" and 2 out of 5 "new songs." How many ways can the singer make his selection?

A) 25   B) 50   C) 150   D) 480   E) 600

98. Reunion (𝄞 𝄞 𝄞)

If 11 persons meet at a reunion and each person shakes hands exactly once with each of the others, what is the total number of handshakes?

A) 11 x 10 x 9 x 8 x 7 x 6 x 5 x 4 x 3 x 2 x 1
B) 10 x 9 x 8 x 7 x 6 x 5 x 4 x 3 x 2 x 1
C) 11 x 10
D) 55
E) 45

99. Display (𝄞 𝄞 𝄞)

A computer wholesaler sells eight different computers and each is priced differently. If the wholesaler chooses three computers for display at a trade show, what is the probability (all things being equal) that the two most expensive computers will be among the three chosen for display?

A) $\frac{15}{56}$ B) $\frac{3}{28}$ C) $\frac{1}{28}$ D) $\frac{1}{56}$ E) $\frac{1}{168}$

100. Outcomes (𝄞 𝄞)

Given that $_nP_r = \frac{n!}{(n - r)!}$ and $_nC_r = \frac{n!}{r!(n - r)!}$, where n is the total number of items and r is the number of items taken or chosen, which of the following Roman Numeral statements are *true* in terms of the number of outcomes generated?

I. $_5P_3 > {}_5P_2$ II. $_5C_3 > {}_5C_2$ III. $_5C_2 > {}_5P_2$

A) I only   B) I & II only   C) I & III only   D) II & III only   E) I, II & III

ANSWERS AND EXPLANATIONS

1. River Boat (𝄢)

Choice C
Classification: Distance-Rate-Time Problem
Snapshot: The easiest way to solve this problem is to supply a hypothetical distance over which the riverboat travels. It may therefore be referred to as a "hypothetical distance D-R-T problem."

To find a hypothetical distance over which the riverboat travels, take the Lowest Common Multiple (LCM) of 6 and 9. In other words, assume that the distance is 18 kilometers each way. If the boat travels upstream ("going") at 6 kilometers per hour, it will take 3 hours to complete its 18 kilometer journey. If the boat travels downstream ("returning") at 9 kilometers per hour, it will take 2 hours to complete its 18 mile journey.

$$R = \frac{D}{T} = \frac{18 + 18}{2 + 3} = \frac{36}{5} = 7.2 \text{ km per hour}$$

The trap answer (Choice D) is 7.5 kilometers per hour, which is derived from simply averaging 9 kilometers per hour and 6 kilometers per hour. That is:

$$R = \frac{D}{T} = \frac{9 + 6}{2} = \frac{15}{2} = 7.5 \text{ km per hour}$$

Author's note: For the record, the "algebraic method" for solving this problem is as follows:

$$R = \frac{D_1 + D_2}{T_1 + T_2}$$

$$R = \frac{x + x}{\frac{x}{6} + \frac{x}{9}} = \frac{2x}{\frac{3x + 2x}{18}} = \frac{2x}{\frac{5x}{18}} = \frac{36x}{5x} = \frac{36}{5} = 7.2 \text{ km per hour}$$

2. Forgetful Timothy (𝄢 𝄢)

Choice B
Classification: Distance-Rate-Time Problem
Snapshot: *Forgetful Timothy* may be called a "catch up D-R-T problem." A slower individual (or machine) starts first and a faster second person (or machine) must catch up.

Like so many difficult D-R-T problems, the key is to view distance as a constant. In other words, the formulas become: $D_1 = R_1 \times T_1$ and $D_2 = R_2 \times T_2$ where $D_1 = D_2$. The key, therefore, is to set the two formulas equal to one another such that $R_1 \times T_1 = R_2 \times T_2$.

	Rate		Time	Distance
Timothy:	9	x	T	= 9T
Mother:	36	x	$T - \frac{1}{4}$	= $36(T - \frac{1}{4})$

Note: 15 minutes should be translated as $\frac{1}{4}$ hour.

First, we solve for "T"

$$D_{1 \text{ Timothy}} = D_{2 \text{ Mother}}$$
$$(R_1 \times T_1)_{\text{Timothy}} = (R_2 \times T_2)_{\text{Mother}}$$
$$9T = 36(T - \frac{1}{4})$$

$9T = 36T - 9$

$-27T = -9$

$T = \dfrac{-9}{-27}$

$T = \dfrac{1}{3}$ hour

Second, we solve for "D":

So, if Timothy rode for $\dfrac{1}{3}$ hour at 9 m.p.h., the distance he covered was 3 miles. It is also true that his mother drove for 3 miles:

$D = 36$ m.p.h. $\times (\dfrac{1}{3}$ hrs $- \dfrac{1}{4}$ hrs$)$

$= 36$ m.p.h. $\times \dfrac{1}{12}$ hrs $= 3$ miles

3. P & Q (🦶 🦶 🦶)

Choice A
Classification: Distance-Rate-Time Problem
Snapshot: In this D-R-T problem, output is a constant although the rates and times of two working individuals differ and must be expressed relative to each other.

The formula, $D_1 = R_1 \times T_1$, links Candidate P and Candidate Q in so far as distance or output is a constant (i.e., in this case, "total pay" is $600). Set $P = R_1 \times T_1$ and $Q = R_2 \times T_2$. If the work rate of Candidate Q is 100% or 1.0, then the work rate of Candidate P is 150% or 1.5. If Candidate P takes T hours, then Candidate Q takes T + 10 hours.

D_1 Candidate P $= D_2$ Candidate Q
$(R_1 \times T_1)$Candidate P $= (R_2 \times T_2)$Candidate Q
$1.5(T) = 1.0(T + 10)$
$1.5T = T + 10$
$0.5T = 10$
$T = \dfrac{10}{0.5}$
$T = 20$ hours

Candidate P takes 20 hours (i.e., 10 + 10). Thus Candidate P's hourly rate is, $600 ÷ 20 hours = $30 per hour.

Candidate Q's time in hours to complete the research equals T + 10 or 20 + 10 = 30 hours. Thus Candidate Q's hourly rate is, $600 ÷ 30 hours = $20 per hour. Therefore, since Candidate P earns $30 per hour and Candidate Q earns $20 per hour, Candidate P earns $10 more per hour than Candidate Q does.

4. Run-Run (🏃 🏃)

Choice B
Classification: Distance-Rate-Time Problem
Snapshot: This D-R-T problem expresses its answer in terms of an algebraic expression. Often such problems also require time conversions.

The problem is asking for *time* and $T = \frac{D}{R}$. We have algebraic expressions for both speed and distance. *Speed* is $\frac{y}{9}$ seconds (not 9 seconds over y yards) and *distance* is x yards. Therefore:

$$T = \frac{D}{R} = \frac{x \text{ yards}}{\frac{y \text{ yards}}{9 \text{ sec}}}$$

$$T = \frac{D}{R} = x \text{ \cancel{yards}} \times \frac{9 \text{ seconds}}{y \text{ \cancel{yards}}}$$

$$T = \frac{9x \text{ \cancel{seconds}}}{y} \times \frac{1 \text{ min}}{60 \text{ \cancel{seconds}}} = \frac{9x}{60y} \text{ minutes}$$

Note: When solving for <u>distance</u> or <u>rate</u>, we *multiply* by 60 when converting from minutes to hours (or seconds to minutes) and *divide* by 60 when converting from hours to minutes (or minutes to seconds). When solving for <u>time</u>, we *divide* by 60 when converting from minutes to hours (or seconds to minutes) and *multiply* by 60 when converting from hours to minutes (or minutes to seconds).

Additional Examples:

Solving for distance:

Ex. At the rate of d miles per q minutes, how many <u>miles</u> does a bullet train travel in x hours?

$$D = R \times T$$

$$= \frac{d \text{ miles}}{q \text{ \cancel{minutes}}} \times x \text{ \cancel{hours}} \times \frac{60 \text{ \cancel{minutes}}}{1 \text{ \cancel{hour}}} = \frac{60dx}{q} \text{ miles}$$

Solving for rate (or speed):

Ex. A bullet train completes a journey of d miles. If the journey took q minutes, what was the train's <u>speed</u> in miles per hour?

$$R = \frac{D}{T}$$

$$= \frac{d \text{ miles}}{q \text{ \cancel{minutes}}} \times \frac{60 \text{ \cancel{minutes}}}{1 \text{ hour}} = \frac{60d}{q} \text{ m.p.h}$$

Solving for time:

Ex. Another high-speed bullet train completes a journey of d miles. If this train traveled at a rate of z miles per minute, how many <u>hours</u> did the journey take?

$$T = \frac{D}{R}$$

$$= \frac{d \text{ \cancel{miles}}}{z \text{ \cancel{miles} / \cancel{minute}}} \times \frac{1 \text{ hour}}{60 \text{ \cancel{minutes}}} = \frac{d}{60z} \text{ hours}$$

5. Submarine (〄 〄 〄)

Choice C
Classification: Distance-Rate-Time Problem
Snapshot: *Submarine* is a complicated word problem and one which involves factoring. Again, the key is to view "distance" as a constant where $D_1 = D_2$. The key, therefore, is to set the two formulas equal to one another such that $R_1 \times T_1 = R_2 \times T_2$.

	Rate		Time		Distance
Actual:	R	x	T	=	240
Hypothetical:	R + 20	x	T - 1	=	240

We now have two distinct equations:

i) R x T = 240
ii) (R + 20)(T - 1) = 240

We need to substitute for one of the variables (i.e., "R" or "T") in order the solve for the remaining variable. Practically, we want to find "R," so we solve for "R" in the second equation by first substituting for "T" in the second equation.

To do this, we solve for "T" in the first equation ($T = \frac{240}{R}$) in order to substitute for "T" in the second equation:

$$(R + 20)\left(\frac{240}{R} - 1\right) = 240$$

$$240 - R + \frac{20\,(240)}{R} - 20 = 240$$

Next multiply through by "R."

$$(R)(240) - (R)(R) + (R)\left(\frac{20\,(240)}{R}\right) - (R)(20) = (R)(240)$$

$$240R - R^2 + 4,800 - 20R = 240R$$
$$-R^2 - 20R + 4,800 = 0$$

Next multiply through by -1.

$$(-1)(-R^2) - (-1)(20R) + (-1)(4,800) = (-1)(0)$$
$$R^2 + 20R - 4,800 = 0$$

Factor for "R."

$$(R + 80)(R - 60) = 0$$
$$R = -80 \text{ or } 60$$
$$R = 60$$

We choose 60 and ignore -80 because it is a negative number and time (or distance) can never be negative.

An alternative approach involves backsolving:

Algebraic setup:

Slower time - faster time = 1 hour

$$\frac{240}{R} - \frac{240}{R + 20} = 1 \text{ hour}$$

Now backsolve.

That is, take the various answer choices and substitute them into the formula above and see which equals 1 hour. Our correct answer is 60 m.p.h.

$$\frac{240}{60} - \frac{240}{60 + 20} = 1$$

$$\frac{240}{60} - \frac{240}{80} = 1$$

$$4 - 3 = 1 \text{ hour}$$

6. Sixteen-Wheeler ($\int \int \int$)

Choice B

Classification: Distance-Rate-Time Problem
Snapshot: This problem is a variation of a "two-part D-R-T" problem. Distance is a constant, although individual distances and rates and times are different. The formula is: $D = (R_1 \times T_1) + (R_2 \times T_2)$.

Distance is a constant because the combined distances traveled by the two drivers will always be the same.

$$D = \text{Distance}_{(Driver\ A)} + \text{Distance}_{(Driver\ B)}$$
$$D = (\text{Rate}_1 \times \text{Time}_1) + (\text{Rate}_2 \times \text{Time}_2)$$

The distance covered by Driver A is $90(T + 1)$. The distance covered by Driver B is $80t$.

$$80T + 90(T + 1) = 770 \qquad (\text{ Where } T \text{ equals the time of Driver B})$$
$$80T + 90T + 90 = 770$$
$$170T = 680$$
$$T = \frac{680}{170}$$
$$T = 4 \text{ hours}$$

Given that Driver B took 4 hours, Driver A took 5 hours (i.e., $T + 1$). We now calculate how far each person has traveled and take the difference:

Driver A:

$$D = R \times T$$
$$D = 90(T + 1) = 90(4 + 1) = 90(5) = 450 \text{ Kilometers}$$

Driver B:

$$D = R \times T$$
$$D = R \times T = 80T = 80(4) = 320 \text{ Kilometers}$$

$$\therefore 450 - 320 = 130 \text{ Kilometers}$$

Note: This problem could also have been solved by expressing "time" in terms of Driver A:

$$90T + 80(T - 1) = 770$$
$$90T + 80T - 80 = 770$$
$$170T = 850$$

$$T = \frac{850}{170}$$

$$T = 5 \text{ hours}$$

In this case, whereas Driver A took 5 hours, Driver B still took 4 hours.

7. Elmer (🐘)

Choice B
Classification: Age Problem
Snapshot: In cases where an age problem states, "Alan is twice as old as Betty," the math translation is A = 2B, not 2A = B. In cases where an age problem states, "10 years from now Sam will be twice as old as Tania", the math translation is S + 10 = 2(T + 10). In this latter situation, remember to add 10 years to both sides of the equation because both individuals will have aged 10 years.

First Equation:

"Elmer is currently three times older than Leo."

E = 3L

Second Equation:

"In five years from now, Leo will be exactly half as old as Elmer."

2(L + 5) = E + 5

Next, we substitute for the variable "E" in order to solve for "L." That is, substitute "3L" (First Equation) for the variable "E" (Second Equation).

2(L + 5) = 3L + 5
2L + 10 = 3L + 5
-L = -5
L = 5

Therefore, since Leo, the circus Lion, is 5 years old, this means that Elmer, the circus Elephant, is 15 years old. This calculation is derived from the first equation, E = 3L.

8. Average (🎵 🎵)

Choice D

Classification: Average Problem

Snapshot: If the average of eight numbers is 7, their sum must be 56. This simple revelation provides a key step in solving most average problems.

$$\text{Average} = \frac{\text{Sum of Terms}}{\text{Number of Terms}}$$

$$= \frac{4(4x + 3) - x}{3} = \frac{16x + 12 - x}{3} = \frac{15x + 12}{3} = 5x + 4$$

9. Fourth Time Lucky (🎵 🎵)

Choice C

Classification: Average Problem

Snapshot: This average problem requires a solution in the form of an algebraic expression.

$$\text{Average} = \frac{\text{Sum of Terms}}{\text{Number of Terms}}$$

$$= \frac{3N + (N + 20)}{4}$$

$$= \frac{(4N + 20)}{4} = \frac{4N}{4} + \frac{20}{4} = N + 5$$

Note: Since Rajeev received an average score of N points on his first 3 tests, his total points is 3N.

10. Vacation (🎵 🎵)

Choice D

Classification: Average Problem

Snapshot: The special type of average problem may be referred to as a "Dropout Problem." Specifically, we want to know how much *additional* money each individual must pay as a result of others dropping out. This problem type also requires mastery of algebraic fractions.

First Equation:

$\frac{x}{P}$ represents the amount each person was originally going to pay before the dropouts.

Second Equation:

$\frac{x}{P - d}$ represents the total amount each person has to pay after the dropouts.

Accordingly, $\frac{x}{P - d} - \frac{x}{P}$ will yield the additional amount that each person must pay. Note that the amount that each person has to pay after the dropouts is greater per person than the amount before. Therefore we subtract the First Equation from the Second Equation, not the other way around. The algebra here requires dealing with algebraic fractions which can be a bit confusing. Multiply each term through by the common denominator of P(P - D).

$$\frac{x}{P - d} - \frac{x}{P}$$

$$= \frac{P(P - d) \frac{x}{P - d} - P(P - d) \frac{x}{P}}{P(P - d)}$$

$$= \frac{Px - [(P-d)x]}{P(P-d)}$$

$$= \frac{Px - xP + dx)}{P(P-d)}$$

$$= \frac{dx}{P(P-d)}$$

Author's note: See Problem #36, *Hodgepodge*, which provides another example of working with algebraic fractions.

11. Disappearing Act (𝄞 𝄞)

Choice C
Classification: Work Problem
Snapshot: This problem is a "walk-away work problem." Two people (or two machines) will set to work on something and, after a stated period of time, one of the individuals gets up and leaves (or one of the machines breaks down), forcing the remaining person (or machine) to finish the task.

Since an hour is an easy unit to work with, think in terms of how much of the task each person working alone could complete in just one hour. Deborah could do the job in 5 hours, so she does $\frac{1}{5}$ of it in an hour; Tom could do the job in 6 hours, so he does $\frac{1}{6}$ of it in one hour. Working together for 2 hours, they complete $\frac{11}{15}$ of that job, which leaves $\frac{4}{15}$ of the task for Deborah to complete alone. Deborah can complete $\frac{4}{15}$ of the task in $1\frac{1}{3}$ hours.

The solution unfolds in three steps:

Amount of work they both do in 2 hours:

$$2\left(\frac{1}{5}+\frac{1}{6}\right) = 2\left(\frac{6}{30}+\frac{5}{30}\right) = 2\left(\frac{11}{30}\right) = \frac{22}{30} = \frac{11}{15}$$

Amount of work left to do:

$$1 - \frac{11}{15} = \frac{4}{15}$$

Time it takes Deborah to complete the task:

$$\text{Time} = \frac{\text{Amount of Work}}{\text{Deborah's Work Rate}}$$

$$T = \frac{\frac{4}{15}}{\frac{1}{5}} = \frac{4}{15} \times \frac{5}{1} = \frac{20}{15} = \frac{4}{3} = 1\frac{1}{3} = \text{hours}$$

Author's note: The general formula for work problems is "$\frac{1}{A}+\frac{1}{B}=\frac{1}{T}$", where *A* and *B* represent the time it takes a given person or machine to individually complete a task and *T* represents the total time it takes both persons or machines to complete the task working together but independently.

12. Exhibition (⟨ ⟨)

Choice C

Classification: Work Problem

Snapshot: For problems which involve the work rates for a group of individuals (or machines), calculate first the work rate for a single person (or machine) and then multiply this rate by the number of persons (or machines) in the new group. The time necessary to complete the new task will be 1 divided by this number.

Solution in four steps:

Find how much of the job 70 workers could do in 1 hour.

Result: If 70 workers can do the job in 3 hours then the 70 workers can do $\frac{1}{3}$ of the job in one hour.

Find out how much of the job a single worker can do in 1 hour.

Result: $\frac{1}{70} \times \frac{1}{3} = \frac{1}{210}$. This is the hourly work rate for an individual worker.

Multiply this rate by the number of new workers.

Result: $30 \times \frac{1}{210} = \frac{30}{210} = \frac{1}{7}$. This is the work rate for the group of new workers.

Take the reciprocal of this number and voila—the answer!

Result: $\frac{1}{7}$ becomes $\frac{7}{1}$ = 7 hours

Alternative Solution:

If 70 men could do the work in 3 hours, then how long would it take 30 men to the do the same job?

$$30h = 70 \times 3$$
$$30h = 210$$
$$h = \frac{210}{30} = 7 \text{ hours}$$

13. Legal (⟨ ⟨ ⟨)

Choice B

Classification: Work Problem

Snapshot: Again the key is to think in terms of a "work rate" for a single individual. Next, multiply this figure by the total number of new group members to find a "group rate", and finally, divide this number by 1 to find total hours.

Five steps:

Find how much of the job 4 junior lawyers could do in 1 hour.

If 4 junior lawyers can do the job in 5 hours then the 4 junior lawyers can do $\frac{1}{5}$ of the job in one hour.

Find out how much of the job a single worker can do in 1 hour.

Result: $\frac{1}{4} \times \frac{1}{5} = \frac{1}{20}$. This is the work rate for a single junior lawyer.

Adjust this work rate for the rate of legal assistants vs. junior lawyers.

Result: $\frac{1}{20} \times \frac{2}{3} = \frac{2}{60}$. This is the adjusted work rate for single legal assistant.

Multiply this rate by the number of legal assistants.

Result: $3 \times \frac{2}{60} = \frac{6}{60}$. This is the work rate for the group of three legal assistants.

Take the reciprocal of this number and voila—the answer!

Result: $\frac{6}{60}$ becomes $\frac{60}{6}$ = 10 hours

Alternative Solution:

$3 \times \frac{2}{3} \times h = 4 \times 5$

$\frac{6}{3} h = 20$

$h = \frac{20}{\frac{6}{3}}$

$h = 20 \times \frac{3}{6} = \frac{60}{6} = 10$ hours

14. Persian Rug (🌶 🌶)

Choice E

Classification: Picture-Frame or Border Problem

Snapshot: Don't forget that a frame or border surrounding a picture or carpet contains a border on all sides. The expression $(w - 2b)(l - 2b)$ represents the measure of a framed painting where w and l are the combined width and length of both picture and frame and b is the measure of the width of the frame itself.

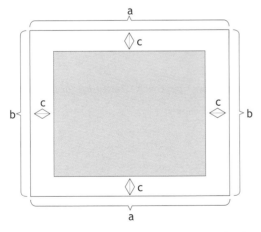

The key is to subtract the area of the entire rug (rug plus border) from the area of the rug itself (rug minus border).

What is the area of the entire rug (rug plus border)?

Answer: a x b.

What is the area of the rug itself (rug minus border)?

Answer: (a - 2c)(b - 2c).

Therefore what is the area, in square centimeters, of the strip alone?

Answer: ab - (a - 2c)(b - 2c).

The answer is not Choice D which assumes that the frame is only on one side of the picture. A border on a rectangle or square object occurs on all sides of the object. Answer Choice C represents the difference in perimeters. It would have been the correct answer had the question been: "Which algebraic expressions below represents the positive difference in the measure of the perimeter of the rug and the rug design?"

15. Nuts ($\int$)

Choice A
Classification: Mixture Problem
Snapshot: This is a dry mixture. We need to calculate the <u>amounts</u> of <u>two</u> different <u>nut</u> mixtures to arrive at a final mixture.

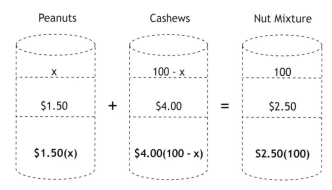

$1.50(x) + $4.00(100 - x) = $2.50(100)
$1.50x + $400 - $4.00x = $250
-$2.5x = -$150
$x = \dfrac{$150}{$2.5}$
x = 60 pounds of peanuts
∴100 - 60 = 40 pounds (of cashews)

The following is an alternative solution using a "two-variables-two-equations" approach. Substitute for one of the variables, *x* or *y*, and solve:

i) $1.50x + $4.00y = $2.50(100)
ii) x + y = 100
    y = 40 pounds (of cashews)

Author's note: Mixture problems are best solved using the *barrel method* which summarizes information similar to a 3-row by 3-column table.

This problem garners one-chili rating partly because it is easy to backsolve, especially given the fact that the answer is Choice A and we would likely begin choosing answer choices beginning with Choice A. From the information given in the problem, we know we are looking for a final mixture that costs $2.50 per pound. We also know the individual prices per pound. Choice A tells us that we have 40 pounds of cashews and, by implication, 60 pounds of peanuts. Will this give us an answer of $2.50? Yes it does, and the answer is Choice A.

40 pounds x $4.00 = $160.00 (cashews)
60 pounds x $1.50 = $90.00 (peanuts)
                     $250.00
Total pounds   100
Price per pound $2.50

16. Gold (𝄞 𝄞)

Choice E

Classification: Mixture Problem

Snapshot: This is a dry mixture, which involves percentages. We need to calculate the <u>amount</u> of <u>pure gold</u> that needs to be added to arrive at a final alloy. When adding pure gold, we use 100%. If we were to add a pure non-gold alloy, the percentage would be 0%.

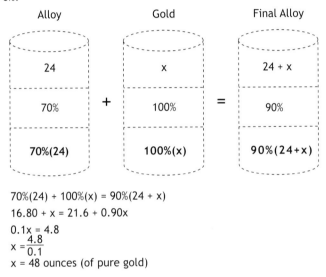

70%(24) + 100%(x) = 90%(24 + x)

16.80 + x = 21.6 + 0.90x

0.1x = 4.8

$x = \dfrac{4.8}{0.1}$

x = 48 ounces (of pure gold)

17. Evaporation (𝄞 𝄞 𝄞)

Choice A

Classification: Mixture Problem

Snapshot: This is a wet mixture. We need to calculate the amount of pure water that needs to be subtracted to arrive at a final solution. The percentage for pure water is 0% because pure water (whether added or subtracted) lacks any "mixture." This causes the middle term in the equation to drop out.

This is a wet mixture. We need to calculate the amount of <u>pure water</u> that needs to be <u>subtracted</u> to arrive at a final solution.

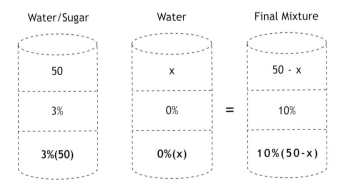

$$3\%(50) + 0\%(x) = 10\%(50-x)$$
$$1.5 + 0 = 5 - 0.10x$$
$$0.10x = 3.5$$
$$x = \frac{3.5}{0.1}$$
$$\therefore x = 35 \text{ liters (of pure water)}$$

18. Standardized Test (⸮ ⸮)

Choice B

Classification: Group Problem

Snapshot: This category of problem deals most often with situations which are not mutually exclusive and will therefore contain overlap; this overlap must not be double counted, otherwise the number of members or items in a group will exceed 100% due to mutual inclusivity. In short, group problems will either give you "neither" and ask for "both" or give you "both" and ask for "neither."

The Venn-Diagram below lends a pictorial. Note that 100% is what is in the "box"; it includes Q1 & Q2 and "neither" but it must not include "both" because "both" represents overlap that must be subtracted out; otherwise the overlap will be double counted.

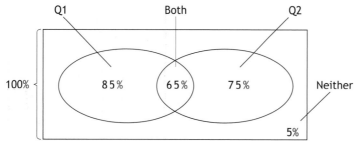

The following is the mathematical solution to this problem.

Two Groups Formula:	Solve:
+ Group A	+85%
+ Group B	+75%
- Both	-x%
+ Neither	+5%
Total	100%

Calculation:

$$\text{Group A} + \text{Group B} - \text{Both} + \text{Neither} = \text{Total}$$
$$85\% + 75\% - x + 5\% = 100\%$$
$$165\% - x = 100\%$$
$$x = 65\%$$

Author's note: Some group problems involve two overlapping circles and some involve three overlapping circles. The formulas below are the key to solving these types of problems with a minimum of effort.

Summary of Templates:

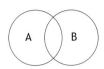

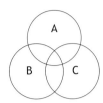

Two Groups Formula:

Add:	Group A	x
Add:	Group B	x
Less:	Both	<x>
Add:	Neither	x
	Total	xx

Three Groups Formula:

Add:	Group A	x
Add:	Group B	x
Add:	Group C	x
Less:	A & B	<x>
Less:	A & C	<x>
Less:	B & C	<x>
Add:	All of A & B & C	x
Add:	None of A or B or C	x
	Total	xx

19. German Cars (𝄞 𝄞 𝄞)

Choice C

Classification: Group Problem

Snapshot: This problem involves three overlapping circles. For the purpose of answering this question in two minutes, it is highly suggested that candidates use the "indirect shortcut" method outlined below.

There are at least two ways to solve this problem: the direct method and indirect method. The direct method is highly analytical and requires breaking the problem down into non-overlapping areas while finding individual values for all seven areas. That's right!—there are seven distinct areas created when three groups overlap in this manner.

Direct Method:

$$27 + 16 + 12 + 10 + 7 + 3 + 5 = 80$$

BMW only + Mercedes only + Porsche only + [(BMW & Mercedes) + (Mercedes & Porsche) + (BMW & Porsche)] + (BMW & Mercedes & Porsche).

Indirect "Short-Cut" Method:

$$B + M + P - BM - BP - MP + BMP + None = Total$$
$$45 + 38 + 27 - 15 - 12 - 8 + 5 = 80$$

Total number of BMW, Mercedes, and Porsche owners less each double overlapping area but adding back one triple overlapping area. This method is the fastest, relying directly on the numbers found in the problem. That is, "add the singles, subtract the doubles, and add back one triple."

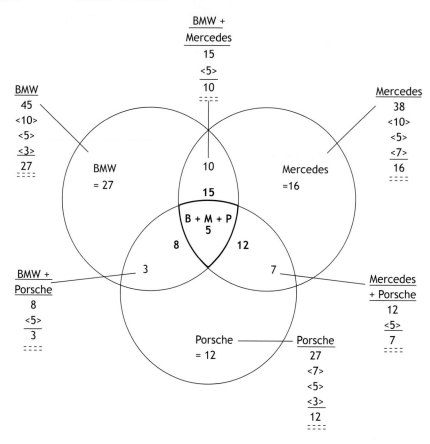

20. Language Classes (🌶️ 🌶️ 🌶️)

Choice D
Classification: Group Problem
Snapshot: This type of Group Problem requires that we express our answer in algebraic form.

This problem is more difficult and garners a three-chili rating in so far as it requires an answer that is expressed in terms of an algebraic expression.

Use the classic "group" formula:

Group A + Group B - Both + Neither = Total

Applied to the problem at hand:

Spanish + French - Both + Neither = Total Students

S + F - B + N = X

N = X + B - F - S

Therefore, expressed as a percent:

$$\text{Neither} = 100\% \times \frac{X + B - F - S}{X}$$

21. Single (𝄞)

Choice D

Classification: Matrix Problem

Snapshot: A matrix can be used to summarize data, particularly data that is being contrasted across two variables and which can be sorted into four distinct outcomes. Use a table with nine boxes and fill-in the data.

For this problem, assume for simplicity's sake that there are 100 students in the course and fill in given information, turning percentages into numbers.

Two-thirds of the women are single (i.e., $\frac{20}{30} = \frac{2}{3}$). For this problem, assume for simplicity's sake that there are 100 students in the course and fill in the given information, turning percentages into numbers.

First, fill in the given information:

	Male	Female	
Married	20		30
Single		?	
	70	?	100

Second, complete the matrix by filling in the remaining boxes:

	Male	Female	
Married	20	10	30
Single	50	20	70
	70	30	100

22. Batteries (𝔖 𝔖 𝔖)

Choice A
Classification: Matrix Problems
Snapshot: To solve difficult matrix problems try "picking numbers", particularly the number 100, if possible.

To obtain the percent of batteries sold by the factory that are defective, we fill in the information per the matrix below to obtain $\frac{3}{75}$ or $\frac{1}{25}$ or 4%. As in the previous problem, the technique of picking of the number "100" greatly simplifies the task at hand.

First, fill in the information directly from the problem:

	Defective	Not Defective	
Rejected		$\frac{1}{10}$ (80) = 8	$\frac{1}{4}$ (100) = 25
Not Rejected	?		100 - 25 = 75
	$\frac{1}{5}$ (100) = 20	100 - 20 = 80	100

Second, complete the matrix:

	Defective	Not Defective	
Rejected	17	8	25
Not Rejected	3	72	75
	20	80	100

23. Experiment (🐧 🐧 🐧)

Choice A
Classification: Matrix Problems
Snapshot: This is a difficult, odd-ball problem in which it is not possible to employ a traditional matrix!

There are two ways to solve this problem: the "picking numbers" approach and the "algebraic" approach.

"Picking Numbers" Approach:

Let's pick numbers. Say the total number of rats is 100, of which 60 are female and 40 are male. Let's say that 50 rats die, which means 15 were female and 35 were male. Calculation for dead rats: 30% x 50 = 15 female rats versus 70% x 50 = 35 male rats.

	Male	Female	
Rats that died	35	15	50
Rats that lived			
	40	60	100

Thus, the ratio of death rate among male rats to the death rate among female rats is calculated as follows:

$$= \frac{\dfrac{\text{male rat deaths}}{\text{male rats (total)}}}{\dfrac{\text{female rat deaths}}{\text{female rats (total)}}} = \frac{\dfrac{35}{40}}{\dfrac{15}{60}} = \frac{35}{40} \times \frac{60}{15} = 7:2$$

Algebraic Approach:

$$= \frac{\dfrac{0.7 \text{ died}}{0.4 \text{ total}}}{\dfrac{0.3 \text{ died}}{0.6 \text{ total}}} = \frac{0.7 \text{ died}}{0.4 \text{ total}} \times \frac{0.6 \text{ total}}{0.3 \text{ died}} = \frac{0.42^7}{0.12^2} = \frac{7}{2} = 7:2$$

The trap answer, Choice B, occurs by multiplying the respective death rates for male and female rats by the percentage of male and female rats. However, this is erroneous since we do not know how many rats died. In other words, we are dealing with two different groups of rats. The first group represents the total number of rats and the second group represents the rats that died. No direct link can be drawn between these two groups so we cannot directly multiply these percentages.

The trap answer is as follows:

$$= \frac{\dfrac{70\% \times 40\%}{40\%}}{\dfrac{30\% \times 60\%}{60\%}} = \frac{\dfrac{28\%}{40\%}}{\dfrac{18\%}{60\%}} = \frac{28\%}{40\%} \times \frac{60\%}{18\%} = 7:3$$

24. Garments ($\int$)

Choice B
Classification: "Price-Cost-Volume-Profit" Problems
Snapshot: When Profit, Cost, or Usage problems are presented in the form of algebraic expressions, it is best to first find a per unit figure: "dollar per unit" or "dollar per individual", "usage per unit" or "usage per individual."

This problem requires us to calculate *number of units* or *volume*. Start with the basic "cost" formula and solve for "number of units" as follows:

$$\text{Cost}_{\text{per unit}} \times \text{Number of units} = \text{Total Cost}$$

$$\therefore \frac{\text{Total Cost}}{\text{Cost}_{\text{per unit}}} = \text{Number of units}$$

$$\frac{t \text{ dollars}}{\frac{d \text{ dollars}}{s \text{ shirts}}} = t \text{ dollars} \times \frac{s \text{ shirts}}{d \text{ dollars}} = \frac{ts}{d} \text{shirts}$$

In summary, since the "price per unit" equals $\frac{d}{s}$, we divide t by $\frac{d}{s}$ to arrive at $\frac{ts}{d}$.

25. Pet's Pet Shop ($\int$ $\int$)

Choice B
Classification: "Price-Cost-Volume-Profit" Problems
Snapshot: The key is to find a "usage per unit" figure, then work outward.

This problem requires that we calculate a "usage per unit" figure.

$$\frac{\frac{35 \text{ cups}}{15 \text{ birds}}}{7 \text{ days}} = \frac{35 \text{ cups}}{15 \text{ birds}} \times \frac{1}{7 \text{ days}} = \frac{1}{3} \text{ cups per bird per day}$$

After 6 birds are sold, there are 9 birds left. Therefore the number of cups of bird seed to feed 9 birds for 12 days is:

$$\frac{1}{3} \text{ cups per bird per day} \times 9 \text{ birds} \times 12 \text{ days} = 36 \text{ cups}$$

26. Sabrina to Change Jobs ($\int$ $\int$)

Choice C
Classification: "Price-Cost-Volume-Profit" Problems
Snapshot: This problem tests break-even point in terms of total revenue.

The difference between Sabrina's current base salary $85,000, and $45,000 is $40,000. Divide $40,000 by (15%)($1500) to get 177.77 sales. In the equation below, *x* stands for the number of sales.

$$\text{Revenue}_{\text{Option 1}} = \text{Revenue}_{\text{Option 2}}$$
$$\$85,000 = \$45.000 + (0.15)(\$1,500)(x)$$
$$\$40,000 = (0.15)(\$1,500)(x)$$

$$x = \frac{\$40,000}{0.15 \times \$1,500}$$

$$x = 177.77$$
$$\therefore = 178 \text{ sales}$$

Don't be tricked by tempting wrong answer Choice B. A total of 177 sales isn't enough to break even. This number must be rounded up to 178 in order to avoid losing money. The actual number of sales is discrete, and can only be represented by whole numbers, not decimals.

27. Delicatessen ($\int$ $\int$)

Choice B
Classification: "Price-Cost-Volume-Profit" Problems
Snapshot: This type of problem shows how to calculate gross profit (or gross margin) when expressed in algebraic terms.

A variation of the "profit" formula is:

$$\text{Profit} = (\text{Price}_{\text{per unit}} \times \text{No. of units}) - (\text{Cost}_{\text{per unit}} \times \text{No. of units})$$

$$= s\frac{\text{dollars}}{\text{pound}}\left(P \text{ pounds} - {}^{d} \text{ pounds}\right) - \left(c\frac{\text{dollars}}{\text{pound}} \times P \text{ pounds}\right)$$

$$= s(p - d) - cp$$

Note: "Gross profit" is *sales revenue* minus *product cost*. Sales revenue is price per unit multiplied by the number of units: s(p - d). Product cost is *cp*. Therefore, gross profit is s(p - d) - cp. The algebraic expressions *cp* and *pc* are identical.

28. Prototype ($\int$ $\int$ $\int$)

Choice B
Classification: "Price-Cost-Volume-Profit" Problems
Snapshot: This type of problem highlights the concepts of *efficiency* and *cost efficiency*.

First, we set up the problem conceptually:

$$\left(1.0\frac{\text{dollar}}{\text{liter}}\right) \times (1.0 \text{ liter}) - {}^{x} \text{ dollar savings} = \left(1.2\frac{\text{dollar}}{\text{liter}}\right) \times \left(\frac{5}{9} \text{ liters}\right)$$

Second, we solve for "x" which represents the cost savings when using the P-Car.

Let's convert $1.2 to $\frac{6}{5}$ for simplicity.

$$\$(1.0)(1.0) - \$x = \$\left(\frac{6}{5}\right)\left(\frac{5}{9}\right)$$

$$\$1.0 - \$x = \$\left(\frac{6}{5}\right)\left(\frac{5}{9}\right)$$

$$\$1.0 - \$x = \$\frac{2}{3}$$

$$x = \$\frac{1}{3} \text{ or } 33\frac{1}{3}\%$$

Since we save one-third of a dollar for every dollar spent, our percentage savings is $33\frac{1}{3}$. Note that the figure $\frac{5}{9}$ is perhaps the most perplexing part of this problem. An 80% increase in efficiency could be expressed as $\frac{180\%}{100\%}$ or $\frac{9}{5}$. The reciprocal of $\frac{9}{5}$ is $\frac{5}{9}$. This means that the P-Car needs only five-ninths as much fuel to drive the same distance as does the T-Car. Therefore, although the cost of gas for the P-Car is more expensive, it results in an overall cost efficiency.

For the record, whereas 80% represents how much more *efficient* the P-Car is compared to the T-Car, the correct answer, $33\frac{1}{3}\%$ represents how much more *cost efficient* the P-Car is compared to the T-Car.

29. Lights (〕 〕)

Choice D
Classification: Least-Common-Multiple Word Problems
Snapshot: This problem highlights the use of prime factorization in solving L.C.M. Word Problems. To find the point at which a series of objects "line up," find the Least Common Multiple of the numbers involved.

There are two ways to solve L.C.M. problems including prime factorization and trail and error. First the *Prime Factor Approach*. Find least common multiple of 1 minute, 1 minute, 3 minutes, 1 minute, and 4 minutes. You should get 12 minutes. Therefore, every twelve minutes all lights will flash together. The columns below are useful in organizing data; the final column contains key information.

"Prime Factor" Method:

Color:	Prime Factors:
Red	2 x 2 x **5** = 20 seconds
Blue	2 x 3 x 5 = 30 seconds
Green	**3** x **3** x 5 = 45 seconds
Orange	2 x 2 x 3 x 5 = 60 seconds
Yellow	**2** x **2** x **2** x **2** x 5 = 80 seconds

Therefore:

$$2 \times 2 \times 2 \times 2 \times 3 \times 3 \times 5 = 720 \text{ seconds}$$

$$720 \text{ seconds} \times \frac{1 \text{ minute}}{60 \text{ seconds}} = 12 \text{ minutes}$$

"Trial-and-Error" Method:

Color:	Flash Time:	Cycles:	Time:
Red	20 seconds	3 cycles	1 minute
Blue	30 seconds	2 cycles	1 minute
Green	45 seconds	4 cycles	3 minutes
Orange	60 seconds	1 cycle	1 minute
Yellow	80 seconds	3 cycles	4 minutes

The trial-and-error method pivots on cycles. "How can the number of seconds for "Flash Time" be turned into cycles?" Observing the numbers in the "Time" column, you ask, "What is the least common multiple of 1 minute, 1 minute, 3 minutes 1 minute, and minutes?" "Voila!" The answer is 12 minutes.

30. Chili Paste (🌶 🌶)

Choice D

Classification: General Algebraic Word Problem

Snapshot: This problem contrasts one-variable vs. two-variable problem-solving approaches. Four scenarios are possible in terms of this particular problem:

x = small cans *and* y = large cans

Scenario #1: $\frac{x}{15} - \frac{x}{25} = 40$ (where x = weekly needs)

x = 1,500 ounces;
∴ 1,500 ÷ 15 = 100 cans

This is the subtlest of all of the four scenarios, using only a single variable and relating "x" as weekly needs.

Scenario #2: $15x = 25(x - 40)$ (where x = small cans)
x = 100 small cans

Scenario #3: $25y = 15(y + 40)$ (y = large cans)
y = 60 large cans
∴ x = 100 small cans

Scenario #4: i) $x = y + 40$ (where x = small cans)

ii) $y = \frac{15}{25}x$ (or x $= \frac{25}{15}y$)

Substituting equation ii) into equation i) above:

∴ $x = \frac{3}{5}x + 40$
x = 100 small cans

The above is a classic two-variable, two equations approach. This last scenario is tricky because the second equation utilizes a relationship involving volume, i.e., $\frac{15}{25}$ ounces.

Author's note: *Chili Paste* is an interesting problem, highlighting multiple solutions. That's what's really interesting about math—"you can get downtown by taking many different roads." In other words, there are often many different approaches that lead to one single correct answer.

31. Snooker (⌇ ⌇)

Choice C

Classification: General Algebraic Word Problem

Snapshot: The classic way to solve GMAT algebraic word problems is to identify two distinct equations and then substitute for one of the variables.

Set-up: x = back seats and y = front seats.

First equation:

$$x + y = 320$$
$$\therefore y = 320 - x$$

Second equation:

$$\$15x + \$45y = \$7,500$$
$$\therefore \$x + \$3y = \$500$$

In the equation above, we divide each term by the number 15 in order to simplify the equation.

Substituting for the variable "y" in the second equation, we solve for "x":

$$\$x + \$3(320 - x) = \$500$$
$$\$x + \$960 - \$3x = \$500$$
$$\$-2x = -\$460$$
$$x = 230 \text{ tickets}$$

Therefore, using the first equation (or, equally, the second equation), we substitute, x = 230, and solve for front seats:

$$230 + y = 320$$
$$y = 90$$

Finally, the difference between 230 and 90 is 140. This represents how many more back seat tickets were sold than front seat tickets.

32. Hardware (⌇)

Choice A

Classification: General Algebraic Word Problem

Snapshot: This problem further highlights the need to translate words into math. If we have twice as many pencils as crayons, the algebraic expression is, P = 2C not 2P = C.

The total weight of 2 hammers and 3 wrenches is one-third that of 8 hammers and 5 wrenches:

$$3(2h + 3w) = 8h + 5w$$
$$6h + 9w = 8h + 5w$$
$$4w = 2h$$
$$w = \frac{2}{4}h$$

$$w = \frac{1}{2}h$$

Choosing the correct answer is perhaps the trickiest step because the mathematical result may seem counterintuitive and may be interpreted in reverse. Since w = $\frac{1}{2}$ h or 2w = h, this means that 2 wrenches are as heavy as 1 hammer. Stated another way, a single wrench is half the weight of one hammer.

33. Premium (∫ ∫)

Choice E
Classification: General Algebraic Word Problem
Snapshot: This problem involves three variables and requires an answer expressed in terms of a third variable, in this case "y".

Likely the easiest way to solve this problem is to identify two equations and substitute for one of the variables.

First Equation:

$$5p = 6r$$

The price of 5 kilograms of premium fertilizer is the same as the price of 6 kilograms of regular fertilizer.

Second Equation:

$$p - y = r \qquad or \qquad r = p - y$$

The price of premium fertilizer is y cents per kilogram more than the price of regular fertilizer.

Now we substitute for "r" in the first equation and solve for "p":

$$5p = 6(p - y)$$
$$5p = 6p - 6y$$
$$-p = -6y$$
$$(-1)(-p) = (-1)(-6y)$$
$$p = 6y$$

Author's note: In the penultimate step above, we multiply both sides by -1 in order to express the final answer in terms of positive outcome.

34. Function (∫)

Choice B
Classification: Function Problem
Snapshot: This problem focuses on how to work with compound functions. A function is a process that turns one number into another number. Usually this involves just plugging one number into a formula. Although it is not the only variable that can be used, the letter f is commonly used to designate a function.

Let's refer to the two equations as follows:

First equation:

$$f(x) = \sqrt{x}$$

Second equation:

$$g(x) = \sqrt{x^2 + 7}$$

Start by substituting "3" into the second equation:

$f(g(x))$ means apply g first, and then apply f to the result.

$$g(x) = \sqrt{x^2 + 7}$$
$$g(3) = \sqrt{(3^2) + 7} = \sqrt{9 + 7} = \sqrt{16} = 4$$

Second, substitute "4" into the first equation:

$$f(x) = \sqrt{x}$$
$$f(4) = \sqrt{4} = 2$$

Here are two more function problems:

Ex. Assuming identical information in the original problem, what would be the solution to $g(f(9))$?

$g(f(x))$ means apply f first, and then apply g to the result.

First, simply substitute "9" into the first equation:

$$f(x) = \sqrt{x}$$
$$f(9) = \sqrt{9} = 3$$

Second, substitute "3" into the second equation:

$$g(x) = \sqrt{x^2 + 7}$$
$$g(3) = \sqrt{x^2 + 7} = \sqrt{(3^2) + 7} = \sqrt{9 + 7} = \sqrt{16} = 4$$

Ex: What is $f(x)g(x)$ if $f(9) = \sqrt{x}$ and $g(3) = \sqrt{x^2 + 7}$?

$f(x)g(x)$ means apply f and g separately, and then multiply the results.

$$f(9) = \sqrt{x} = \sqrt{9} = 3$$
$$g(3) = \sqrt{x^2 + 7} = \sqrt{(3)^2 + 7} = \sqrt{16} = 4$$
$$\text{Result} : f(x)g(x) = 3 \times 4 = 12$$

35. Rescue (♫)

Choice D
Classification: Algebraic Fractions
Snapshot: This problem highlights the "factoring out of a common term" as a key to solving algebraic fraction problems.

$$a(c - d) = b - d$$
$$ac - ad = b - d$$
$$d - ad = b - ac$$
$$d(1 - a) = b - ac$$
$$d = \frac{b - ac}{1 - a}$$

36. Hodgepodge (∫)

Choice C
Classification: Algebraic Fractions
Snapshot: This problem tests the ability to deal with common denominators in solving algebraic fraction problems.

First, we need to simplify the expression $1 - \dfrac{1}{h}$. The key is to pick the common denominator ("1x") for "x" and "1":

$$1 - \frac{1}{h} = \frac{1}{1} - \frac{1}{h} = \frac{(1h)\frac{1}{1} - \frac{1}{h}(1h)}{(1)(h)} = \frac{h - 1}{h}$$

Now the simplified calculation becomes:

$$\frac{\frac{1}{h}}{\frac{h-1}{h}} = \frac{1}{h} \times \frac{h}{h-1} = \frac{1}{h-1}$$

Likely, the trickiest step with this problem is simplifying the fraction in the denominator of the fraction. Take this very simple example:

$$= \frac{1}{2} - \frac{1}{3}$$

$$= \frac{{}^{3}6\left(\frac{1}{2}\right) - {}^{2}6\left(\frac{1}{3}\right)}{(2)(3)}$$

$$= \frac{3-2}{6} = \frac{1}{6}$$

In this simple example, we instinctively place the difference (i.e., 1) over the common denominator. It is easy to forget this step when dealing with the more difficult algebraic expression presented in this problem.

37. Mirage (∫)

Choice D
Classification: Fractions and Decimals
Snapshot: This problem tests the ability to determine fraction size in a conceptual way, without the need to perform calculations.

Whenever we add the same number to both the numerator and denominator of a fraction less than 1, we will always create a bigger fraction. In this problem we are effectively adding 1 to both the numerator and denominator. Take the fraction $\frac{1}{2}$ for example. If we add 1 to both the numerator and denominator of this fraction, the fraction becomes conspicuously larger.

$$\frac{1}{2} = 50\% \qquad \frac{1+1}{2+1} = \frac{2}{3} = 66\frac{2}{3}\%$$

$$\therefore 50\% \text{ becomes } 66\frac{2}{3}\%$$

This memorable example adds 1 million to both the numerator and denominator of a fraction less than 1:

$$\frac{1}{2} = 50\% \qquad \frac{1+1,000,000}{2+1,000,000} = \frac{1,000,001}{1,000,002} \cong 100\%$$

$$\therefore 50\% \text{ becomes almost } 100\%$$

Alternatively, adding the same number to both the numerator and denominator of a fraction <u>greater</u> than 1 will always result in a smaller fraction.

Ex: Which of the following has the greatest value?

A) $\frac{11}{10}$ B) $\frac{5}{4}$ C) $\frac{8}{7}$ D) $\frac{22}{21}$ E) $\frac{6}{5}$

Choice B has the greatest value while Choice D has the smallest value.

38. Deceptive ( )

Choice D
Classification: Fractions and Decimals
Snapshot: Dividing by any number is exactly the same as multiplying by that number's reciprocal (and vice-versa).

Dividing 100 by 0.75 is the same as multiplying 100 by the reciprocal of 0.75. The reciprocal of 0.75 is 1.33, not 1.25!

39. Spiral ( )

Choice A
Classification: Fractions and Decimals
Snapshot: This problem highlights reciprocals in the context of a numerical sequence.

The first five terms in this sequence unfold as follows:

$$2 \rightarrow \frac{3}{2} \rightarrow \frac{5}{3} \rightarrow \frac{8}{5} \rightarrow \frac{13}{8}$$

First term: 2

Second term: $1 + \frac{1}{2} = \frac{3}{2}$

Third term: $1 + \frac{2}{3} = \frac{5}{3}$

Fourth term: $1 + \frac{3}{5} = \frac{8}{5}$

Fifth term: $1 + \frac{5}{8} = \frac{13}{8}$

40. Micro-Brewery ( )

Choice C
Classification: Percentage Problem
Snapshot: This problem highlights the difference between "percent increase" and "percent of an original number."

Note that this problem is in essence asking about productivity: productivity = output ÷ work hours. Use 100% as a base, and add 70% to get 170% and then divide 170% by 80% to get 212.5%. An even simpler calculation involves the use of decimals:

$$\frac{1.7}{0.8} = 2.125 \times 100\% = 212.5\%.$$

Now calculate the percent increase:

$$\frac{New - Old}{Old} \qquad \frac{212.5\% - 100\%}{100\%} = \frac{112.5\%}{100\%} = 112.5\%$$

Encore! What if the wording to this problem had been identical except that the last sentence read:

"The year-end factory output per hour is what percent of the beginning of the year factory output per hour?"

A) 50%   B) 90%   C) 112.5%   D) 210%   E) 212.5%

The answer would be Choice E. This problem is not asking for a percent increase, but rather "percent of an original number."

Percent of an original number:

$$\frac{New}{Old} \qquad \frac{212.5\%}{100\%} = 2.125 \times 100\% = 212.5\%$$

Author's note: The fact that two of the answer choices (Choices C and E) are 100% apart alerts us to the likelihood that a distinction must be made between "percent increase" and "percent of an original number."

41. Diners (🍴 🍴)

Choice B
Classification: Percentage Problem
Snapshot: This problem highlights a subtle mathematical distinction. In terms of percentages, an increase from 80% to 100% is not the same as an increase from 100% to 120%.

Ho, ho, ho—this nice, round number represents the cost before tax (and tip).

Let "x" be the cost of food <u>before</u> tip:

$$\frac{x}{\$264} = \frac{100\%}{200\%}$$

$$120\%(x) = 100\%(\$264)$$

$$\frac{120\%}{120\%}(x) = \frac{\$264\,(100\%)}{120\%}$$

$$x = \frac{\$264\,(100\%)}{120\%}$$

$$x = \frac{\$264\,(1.0)}{1.2}$$

$$x = \$220$$

Now let "x" be the cost of food <u>before</u> tip <u>and</u> tax:

$$\frac{x}{\$220} = \frac{100\%}{110\%}$$

$$110\%(x) = 100\%(\$220)$$

$$\frac{110\%}{110\%}(x) = \frac{\$220(100\%)}{110\%}$$

$$x = \frac{\$220(100\%)}{110\%}$$

$$x = \frac{\$220(1.0)}{1.1}$$

$$x = \$200$$

Note: The quick method is to divide $264 by 1.2 and then by 1.1. That is, [($264 ÷ 1.2) ÷ 1.1)] = $200. Likewise, we can divide $264 by 1.32. That is, $264 ÷ (1.2 x 1.1) $264 ÷ 1.32 = $200

42. Investments ($\int$ $\int$)

Choice E

Classification: Percentage Problem

Snapshot: You cannot add or subtract the percents of different wholes. "Twenty percent of a big number results in a larger value than 20% of a small number."

Below are the calculations for gain and loss expressed as proportions:

Gain on Sale of Property A:

$$\frac{120\%}{100\%} = \frac{\$24,000}{x}$$

$$120\%(x) = 100\%(\$24,000)$$

$$x = \frac{\$24,000(100\%)}{120\%}$$

$$x = \frac{\$24,000(1.0)}{1.2}$$

$$x = \$20,000$$
$$\therefore \$24,000 - \$20,000 = \$4000 \text{ gain}$$

Loss on the Sale of Property B:

$$\frac{100\%}{80\%} = \frac{x}{\$24,000}$$

$$100\%(\$24,000) = 80\%(x)$$

$$80\%(x) = 100\%(\$24,000)$$

$$x = \frac{\$24,000(100\%)}{80\%}$$

$$x = \frac{\$24,000(1.0)}{0.8}$$

$$x = \$30,000$$
$$\therefore \$30,000 - \$24,000 = \$6,000 \text{ loss}$$

Therefore, we have an overall loss of $2,000 (net $6,000 loss and $4,000 gain). Note that the following provide shortcut calculations:

Gain: $24,000 ÷ 1.2 = $20,000
       $24,000 ÷ $20,000 = $4,000

Loss: $24,000 ÷ 0.8 = $30,000
       $30,000 - $24,000 = $6,000

43. Discount (𝄋)

Choice D
Classification: Percentage Problem
Snapshot: Percentage problems are easily solved by expressing the original price in terms of 100%.

A 10% discount followed by a 30% discount amounts to an overall 37% discount based on original price.

> 90% x 70% = 63%
> 100% x 63% = 37%

Note that we cannot simply add 10% to 30% to get 40% because we cannot add (or subtract) the percents of different wholes.

44. Inflation (𝄋)

Choice C
Classification: Percentage Problem
Snapshot: This problem highlights the commutative property of multiplication in which *order* doesn't matter.

> 120% x 110% = 132%
> 110% x 120% = 132%

It does not matter the *order* in which we multiply numbers, the answer remains the same. In this case, a 20% inflationary increase followed by a 10% inflationary increase is the same as an inflationary increase of 10% followed by an inflationary increase of 20%. Either way we have an overall inflationary increase of 32%.

In contrast with the previous problem entitled *Discount*, this problem does not require the actual amount of overall increase but rather the relationship between the two inflationary increases. For the record, a 10 percent discount followed by a 30 percent discount is the same as a 30 percent discount followed by a 10 percent discount. Test: 0.9 x 0.7 = 0.63 = 63% and 0.7 x 0.9 = 0.63 = 0.63%. Either way we have an overall discount of 37%.

Author's note: The *commutative law* of mathematics states that order doesn't matter. This law holds for addition and multiplication but it does <u>not</u> hold for subtraction or division.

Addition:	Multiplication:
Ex. a + b = b + a	Ex. a x b = b x a
2 + 3 = 3 + 2	2 x 3 = 3 x 2

BUT NOT:

Subtraction:	Division:
Ex. a - b ≠ b - a	Ex. a ÷ b ≠ b ÷ a
4 - 2 ≠ 2 - 4	4 ÷ 2 ≠ 2 ÷ 4

45. Gardener (𝄞)

Choice B
Classification: Percentage Problem
Snapshot: This problem introduces percentage increase and decrease problems as they relate to geometry.

View the area of the original rectangular garden as having a width and length of 100%. The new rectangular garden has a length of 140% and a width of 80%. A 20% decrease in width translates to a width of 80% of the original width.

Area of original garden:

Area = length x width = (100% x 100%) = 100%

Area of resultant garden:

Area = length x width = (140% x 80%) = 112%

Percent change is as follows:

$$\frac{\text{New - Old}}{\text{Old}} = \frac{(112\% - 100\%)}{100\%} = 12\%$$

Note: A short-cut calculation involves decimals:

1.4 x 0.8 = 2.12
2.12 - 1.0 = 1.12 or 112%

46. Squaring Off (𝄞 𝄞)

Choice A
Classification: Percentage Problem
Snapshot: A number of tricky geometry problems can be solved by picking numbers such as 1, 100, or 100%.

Original Square:

Area = side²
A = (1)² = 1 square unit

Resultant Square:

Area = side²

A = (2)² = 4 square units

$$\frac{\text{original square}}{\text{resultant square}} = \frac{1}{4} = 25\%$$

Author's note: As a matter of form, we generally express a larger number in terms of a smaller number. For example, we tend to say that A is three times the size of B rather than saying that B is one-third the size of A. But it's not technically wrong to express the smaller value in terms of the larger value. Here the resultant square is four times the size of the original square. It is equally correct to say that the smaller, original square is one quarter (or 25 percent) the size of the resultant square.

47. Earth Speed ( )

Choice E
Classification: Ratios and Proportions
Snapshot: Observe how quantities expressed in certain units can be changed to quantities in other units by "smartly" multiplying by 1.

This problem proves a bit more cumbersome. Here is a three-step approach:

Visualize the end result:

$$\frac{20 \text{ miles}}{1 \text{ second}} \times \frac{?}{?} \times \frac{?}{?} \times \frac{?? \text{ km}}{\text{hour}}$$

Anticipate the canceling of units:

$$\frac{20 \text{ miles}}{1 \text{ second}} \times \frac{? \text{ seconds}}{1 \text{ hour}} \times \frac{1 \text{ km}}{? \text{ mile}} \times \frac{?? \text{ km}}{\text{hour}}$$

Enter conversions and cancel units:

$$\frac{20 \ \cancel{\text{miles}}}{1 \ \cancel{\text{second}}} \times \frac{3,600 \ \cancel{\text{seconds}}}{1 \text{ hour}} \times \frac{1 \text{ km}}{0.6 \ \cancel{\text{mile}}} \times \frac{??\text{km}}{\text{hour}}$$

$$\frac{20 \times 3,600}{0.6} \times \frac{72,000}{0.6} = 120,000 \text{ km/hr}$$

48. Rum & Coke ( )

Choice B
Classification: Ratios and Proportions
Snapshot: Part-to-part ratios are not the same as part-to-whole ratios. 'If the ratio of married to non-married people at a party is 1:2', the percentage of married persons at the party is one out of three persons or $33\frac{1}{3}$ (not 50%). This would give 1 married to every 2 non-married and hence the $33\frac{1}{3}\%$

The trap answer is Choice A because it erroneously adds component parts of the two different ratios. That is, 1 : 2 + 1 : 3 does not equal 1 + 1 : 2 + 3 = 2 : 5. This could only be correct if ratios represent identical volumes. We cannot simply add two ratios together unless we know the numbers behind the ratios.

	Total	Rum	Coke
Solution #1	6	2	4
Solution #2	32	8	24
Totals		10	28
Ratios		5	14

The ratio of 10 : 28 simplifies to 5 : 14.

Supporting Calculations:

$$6 \times \frac{1}{3} = 2 \text{ Two ounces of Rum in Solution \#1.}$$

$$6 \times \frac{2}{3} = 4 \text{ Four ounces of Coke in Solution \#1.}$$

$$32 \times \frac{1}{4} = 8 \text{ Eight ounces of Rum in Solution \#2.}$$

$$32 \times \frac{3}{4} = 24 \text{ Twenty-four ounces of Coke in Solution \#2.}$$

49. Millionaire (∫ ∫)

Choice A
Classification: Ratios and Proportions
Snapshot: Triple ratios (3 parts) are formed by making the middle term of equivalent size.

Correct answers would include any and all multiples of 1 : 4 : 400, including 2 : 8 : 800, 4 : 16 : 1600, etc. However, the latter choices are not presented as options here.

Visualize the Solution:

Billionaire	Millionaire	Yuppie
$20 ⬅⋯⋯⋯⋯⋯➤	$0.20	
	$4 ⬅⋯⋯⋯⋯⋯➤	$1

Do the Math:

Billionaire	Millionaire	Millionaire	Yuppie	
$20	$0.20	$4	$1	Original Ratio
x 20	x 20	x 1	x 1	Adjusting Multipliers
$400	$4	$4	=$1	Resultant Ratio

Choose the Answer:

B to M to Y ⟶ $400 to $4 to $1
∴ Y to M to B ⟶ $1 to $4 to $400

Author's note: Triple ratios (e.g., $A : B : C$) are formed from two pairs of ratios by making a middle term of equivalent size.

50. Fuchsia (🐧 🐧 🐧)

Choice D
Classification: Ratios and Proportions
Snapshot: Fuchsia is considered a difficult ratio problem. The first step is to break the 24 litres of Fuchsia into "red" and "blue." This requires using a part-to-whole ratio (i.e., $\frac{3}{8}$ th's blue and $\frac{5}{8}$ th's red). Our final ratio is a part-to-part, comparing red and blue paint in Fuchsia to the red and blue paint in Mauve.

First we know that there are 24 liters of "Fuchsia" in a ratio of 5 parts red to 3 parts blue. We breakdown this amount into the actual amount of red and blue in 24 liters of "Fuchsia."

Blue: 5 parts red to 3 parts blue:

$$\frac{3}{5+3} = \frac{3}{8} \times 24 = 9 \text{ litres (of blue paint)}.$$

Red: 5 parts red to 3 parts blue:

$$\frac{5}{5+3} = \frac{5}{8} \times 24 = 15 \text{ litres (of red paint)}.$$

So the final formula, expressed as a proportion, becomes:

$$\frac{15\text{red}}{9\text{blue} + {}^{x}\text{ blue}} = \frac{3\text{red}}{5\text{blue}}$$

$$(15)(5) = 3(9 + x)$$
$$75 = 3(9 + x)$$
$$3x + 27 = 75$$
$$3x = 48$$
$$x = 16 \text{ litres (of blue paint)}$$

51. Rare Coins (🐧)

Choice E
Classification: Ratios and Proportions
Snapshot: This problem highlights two different problem solving approaches for ratio type problems: *the two-variable, two-equations approach* and the *multiples approach.*

There are two ways to solve this problem algebraically. The first approach is to use the "two-variable, two-equations" approach. The second approach is to use the "multiples approach."

"Two-variable, two-equations" Approach:

Using this approach, we identify two equations and substitute one variable for another.

First equation:

$$\frac{1}{3} = \frac{G}{N} \qquad or \qquad N = 3G$$

Second equation:

$$\frac{G + 10}{N} = \frac{1}{2} \qquad or \qquad N = 2(G + 10)$$

Since N = 3G and N = 2(G + 10), we can substitute for one of these variables and solve for the other

> 2(G + 10) = 3G
> 2G + 20 = 3G
> G = 20 and, therefore, N = 60

Per above, we substitute G = 20 into either of the two original equations and obtain N = 60.

Finally, 20 (gold coins) *plus* 60 (non-gold coins) *plus* 10 (gold coins added) *totals* 90 total coins.

"Multiples" Approach:

The secret behind this approach is to view "x" as representing multiples of the actual number of coins. Given a ratio of 1 to 3, we can represent the actual number of gold coins vs. non-gold coins as "1x" and "3x" respectively. The solution is as follows:

$$\frac{1x + 10}{3x} = \frac{1}{2}$$

> 2(1x + 10) = 3x
> x = 20

Substituting "20" for "x" in the original equals:

$$\frac{\text{coins (gold)}}{\text{coins (non-gold)}} = \frac{1x}{3x} = \frac{1(20)}{3(20)} = \frac{20}{60}$$

∴ 20 (gold coins) *plus* 60 (non-gold coins) *plus* 10 (gold coins added) *equals* 90 total coins

Author's note: In the event of guessing, since the final ratio is 2 to 1, this means that the total number of coins must be a multiple of 3. Only answer choices C (60) or E (90) could therefore be correct.

52. Coins Revisited (ſ ſ ſ)

Choice B
Classification: Ratios and Proportions
Snapshot: *Coins Revisited* differs from the problem Rare Coins in that the total number of coins in the collection (per *Coins Revisited*) does not change. Mathematically, 10 coins are subtracted from the denominator and added to the numerator. In the problem, *Rare Coins*, the 10 coins added serve to increase the total number in the collection. Also in *Coins Revisited*, the second statement, "If 10 more gold coins…," is merely hypothetical. If asked about the actual number of gold coins or non-gold coins in the collection, then the answer is simply 50 gold coins and 250 non-gold coins for a total of 300 coins.

The secret to this particular problem lies in first translating the part-to-whole ratio of 1 to 6 to a part-to-part ratio of 1 to 5.

"Two-variable-two-equations" Approach:

First equation:

$$\frac{1}{5} = \frac{G}{N} \qquad\qquad N = 5G$$

Second equation:

$$\frac{G + 10}{N - 10} = \frac{1}{4} \qquad\qquad 4(G + 10) = 1(N - 10)$$

Since N = 5G and 4(G + 10) = 1(N - 10) we can substitute and solve for G (or N).

> 4(G + 10) = 1(5G - 10)
> 4G + 40 = 5G - 10
> -G = -50
> G = 50
> G = 50 and, therefore, N = 250

Therefore, there are 60 gold coins after the trade (i.e., 50 gold coins plus 10 gold coins added).

For the record, there are 300 gold coins in the collection (both before and after the trade). Before the trade, there are 50 gold coins and 250 non-gold coins. After the trade, there are 60 gold coins and 240 non-gold coins.

"Multiples" Approach:

Here "1x" and "5x" can be viewed as representing multiples of the actual number of gold coins and non-gold coins, respectively. The solution is as follows:

$$\frac{1x + 10}{5x - 10} = \frac{1}{4}$$

> 4(1x + 10) = 1(5x - 10)
> x = 50

Substituting "50" for "x" in the original equals:

$$\frac{\text{coins (gold)}}{\text{coins (non-gold)}} = \frac{1x}{5x} = \frac{1(50)}{5(50)} = \frac{50}{250}$$

∴ 50 (gold coins) *plus* 250 (non-gold coins) equals 300 coins

53. Plus-Zero (🍷 🍷)

Choice D
Classification: Squares and Cubes
Snapshot: First, consider which of the seven numbers—2, -2, 1, -1, $\frac{1}{2}$, -$\frac{1}{2}$ and 0—satisfy each of the conditions presented in Roman Numerals I through III. When a problem states x > 0, three numbers should immediately come to mind: 2, 1 and $\frac{1}{2}$.

Roman Numeral I:

> Could x^3 be greater than x^2?
> Answer—yes.
>
> Ex. $2^3 > 2^2$
> ∴ 8 > 4

Roman Numeral II:

Could x^2 be equal to x?
Answer—yes.

Ex. $1^2 = 1$
$\therefore 1 = 1$

Roman Numeral III:

Could x^2 be greater than x^3?
Answer—yes.

Ex. $\left(\frac{1}{2}\right)^2 > \left(\frac{1}{2}\right)^3$
$\therefore \frac{1}{4} > \frac{1}{8}$

54. Sub-Zero (∫ ∫)

Choice B
Classification: Squares and Cubes
Snapshot: When a problem states $x < 0$, three numbers should immediately come to mind: 2, -1 and $-\frac{1}{2}$.

Roman Numeral I:

Is x^2 greater than 0?
Answer—absolutely. As long as x is negative, it will, when squared, become positive.

Roman Numeral II:

Is $x - 2x$ greater than 0 ?
Answer—absolutely. As long as x is negative the expression "$x - 2x$" will be greater than zero.

Roman Numeral III:

Is $x^3 + x^2$ less than 0?
Answer—not necessarily.

Ex. $\left(-\frac{1}{2}\right)^3 + \left(-\frac{1}{2}\right)^2$

$= \left(-\frac{1}{8}\right) + \frac{1}{4} = \frac{1}{8}$

$\frac{1}{8} > 0$

55. Triplets (🦢 🦢)

Choice A
Classification: Exponent Problems
Snapshot: Consistent with *Exponent Rule* #8, (see Chapter 3), we can simplify this expression by factoring out a common term (i.e., 3^{10}).

$$3^{10} + 3^{10} + 3^{10}$$
$$= 3^{10} (1 + 1 + 1)$$
$$= 3^{10} (3)$$
$$= 3^{10} \times 3^1 = 3^{11}$$

Here's a bonus question:

$$\frac{2^{15} - 2^{14}}{2} = ?$$

A) 1   B) 2   C) 2^7 D) 2^{13} E) 2^{14}

Calculation:

$$\frac{2^{15} - 2^{14}}{2} = \frac{2^{14}(2^1 - 1)}{2} = \frac{2^{14}(2 - 1)}{2} = \frac{2^{14}(1)}{2} = \frac{2^{14}}{2^1} = 2^{13}$$

Choice D is therefore correct.

56. Solar Power (🦢)

Choice B
Classification: Exponent Problems
Snapshot: This problem tests the ability to manipulate exponents.

$$= \frac{2 \times 10^{30}}{8 \times 10^{12}} = 0.25 \times 10^{18} = 2.5 \times 10^{17}$$

Note that by moving the decimal one place to the right, (i.e., 0.25 to 2.5), we reduce the power by one (10^{18} becomes 10^{17}).

57. K.I.S.S. (🦢 🦢)

Choice E
Classification: Exponent Problems
Snapshot: "Picking numbers" may be used as an alternative approach in solving exponent problems.

Algebraic Method:

$$3^a + 3^{a+1}$$
$$= 3^a + 3^a \times 3^1 = 3^a (1 + 3^1)$$
$$= 3^a(4) \text{ or } 4(3^a)$$

"Picking Numbers" Method:

Another method which can be used to solve this problem is substitution (picking numbers).

Take the original expression: $3^a + 3^{a+1}$.
Substitute the "easiest integer." That is, let's substitute a = 1.
Therefore, $3^1 + 3^{1+1} = 3^1 + 3^2 = 3 + 9 = 12$. We ask ourselves: "Which answer choice gives us 12 when we substitute a =1 into that equation?" Answer: Choice E.
Proof: $4(3^a) = 4(3^1) = 12$.

58. Toughie (🌶🌶🌶)

Choice B
Classification: Exponent Problems
Snapshot: This problem highlights a more difficult exponent problem containing two variables. It also highlights *Exponent Rule #4* (see Chapter 3).

There are two ways to solve this problem. The first is the *algebraic method* and the second is the *picking numbers* method.

Algebraic Method:

$n = 2^{m-1}$
$n = 2^m \times 2^{-1} = \frac{2^m}{2^1}$
$2n = 2^m$

$4^m = (2 \times 2)^m = 2^m \times 2^m$ (Per Exponent Rule #4)
$4^m = 2n \times 2n = 4n^2$ (Note: $2n = 2^m$)

Note that in the penultimate step above, $4^m = 2^m \times 2^m$, and since $2^m \times 2n$, the final calculation becomes $2n \times 2n$.

"Picking Numbers" Method:

Since $m > 1$, pick m = 2,
so $n = 2^{m-1} = 2^{2-1} = 2^1 = 2$

When m = 2 it is also true that $4^m = 4^2 = 16$
So the question becomes: When m = 2 which answer, when substituting n = 2, will result in an answer of 16.
Choice B is correct: $4n^2 = 4(2)^2 = 16$

59. The Power of 5 (🐧 🐧 🐧)

Choice C
Classification: Exponent Problems
Snapshot: This problem highlights the multiplying of exponents consistent with *Exponent Rule #3*—"power of a power" (see Chapter 3).

Notes:

$5^5 \times 5^7 = (125)^x$

$5^{12} = (125)^x$ Per Exponent Rule #1

$5^{12} = (5^3)^x$ Per Exponent Rule #3

$5^{12} = (5^3)^4$ Therefore x = 4

$5^{12} = 5^{12}$

Note that in the penultimate step above, since the bases are equal in value, the exponents must also be equal in value.

Here's a somewhat easier scenario:

Notes:

$10^3 \times 10^5 = (100)^x$

$10^8 = (100)^x$ Per Exponent Rule #1

$10^8 = (10^2)^x$ Per Exponent Rule #3

$10^8 = (10^2)^4$ Therefore x = 4

$10^8 = 10^8$

60. Incognito (🐧 🐧 🐧)

Choice E
Classification: Exponent Problems
Snapshot: This problem shows how fractions can be simplified through factoring. The spotlight is on *Exponent Rule #8*.

The key is to first factor out "$(2^2)(3^2)$" from each of the denominators: This treatment is consistent with *Exponent Rule #8*.

A) $\dfrac{25}{(2^4)(3^3)} \longrightarrow \dfrac{25}{(2^2)(3^1)} = \dfrac{25}{12} = 2\dfrac{1}{12}$

B) $\dfrac{5}{(2^2)(3^3)} \longrightarrow \dfrac{5}{(1)(3^1)} = \dfrac{5}{3} = 1\dfrac{2}{3}$

C) $\dfrac{4}{(2^3)(3^2)} \longrightarrow \dfrac{4}{(2^1)(1)} = \dfrac{4}{2} = 2$

D) $\dfrac{36}{(2^3)(3^4)} \longrightarrow \dfrac{36}{(2^1)(3^2)} = \dfrac{36}{18} = 2$

E) $\dfrac{76}{(2^4)(3^4)} \longrightarrow \dfrac{76}{(2^2)(3^2)} = \dfrac{76}{36} = 2\dfrac{4}{36} = 2\dfrac{1}{9}$

Author's note: One theory in terms of guessing on GMAT math problems relates to "Which of the following" questions (also known as "WOTF" math questions). In this question type, test makers tend to manifest answers deep in the answer choices meaning that Choices D and E have a disproportional chance of ending up as correct answers. Why is this? "Which of the following" questions require the test-taker to work with the answer choices and most candidates logically work from A to E. This presents two opportunities. If we need to guess on these questions, it is best to guess Choices D or E. Also, it is judicious to start checking answers in reverse order, starting with Choice E.

61. Chain Reaction (𝄢 𝄢 𝄢)

Choice D
Classification: Exponent Problems
Snapshot: This follow-up problem is a more difficult problem than the preceding one but the suggested approach is identical.

$$\text{If, } x - \frac{1}{2^6} - \frac{1}{2^7} - \frac{1}{2^8} = \frac{2}{2^9}$$

$$\text{then } x = \frac{2}{2^9} + \frac{1}{2^8} + \frac{1}{2^7} + \frac{1}{2^6}$$

Now factor out $\frac{1}{2^6}$ from each of the terms in the denominator:

$$\text{So } x = \frac{1}{2^6}\left(\frac{2}{2^3} + \frac{1}{2^2} + \frac{1}{2^1} + 1\right)$$

$$= \frac{1}{2^6}\left(\frac{2}{8} + \frac{1}{4} + \frac{1}{2} + 1\right)$$

$$= \frac{1}{2^6}(1 + 1) = \frac{1}{2^6}(2) = \frac{1}{2^5}$$

62. Bacteria (𝄢 𝄢)

Choice C
Classification: Exponent Problems
Snapshot: This problem shows the multiplicative power of numbers.

Visualize the solution. We start with 10^3 then multiply by 2 for each 10-minute segment. Since there are six 10-minute segments in one hour, we arrive at $[2 \times 2 \times 2 \times 2 \times 2 \times 2 \times (10^5)]$. Thus, $(2^6)(10^5)$ represents the number of bacteria after one hour.

63. Simplify (𝄢)

Choice A
Classification: Radical Problems
Snapshot: This problem illustrates how to simplify radicals and brings into play *Radical Rule #7* (see Chapter 3).

$$\sqrt{\frac{(12 \times 3) + (4 \times 16)}{6}} = \sqrt{\frac{36 + 64}{6}} = \sqrt{\frac{100}{6}} = \sqrt{\frac{50}{3}}$$

$$= \sqrt{\frac{50}{3}} = \frac{\sqrt{25 \times 2}}{\sqrt{3}} = \frac{\sqrt{25} \times \sqrt{2}}{\sqrt{3}} = \frac{5\sqrt{2}}{\sqrt{3}}$$

$$= \frac{5\sqrt{2}}{\sqrt{3}} \times \frac{\sqrt{3}}{\sqrt{3}} = \frac{5\sqrt{2 \times 3}}{\sqrt{9}} = \frac{5\sqrt{6}}{3}$$

Note that you cannot break up the radical at the addition sign into two parts:

$$\neq \frac{\sqrt{12 \times 3} + \sqrt{4 \times 16}}{6} = \frac{\sqrt{36} + \sqrt{64}}{6} = \frac{6 + 8}{6} = \frac{14}{6} = 2\frac{1}{3}$$ This result is incorrect!

64. Strange (𝄞 𝄞)

Choice A

Classification: Radical Problems

Snapshot: This problem illustrates how the "multiplicative inverse" can be used to simplify radical equations; it tests *Radical Rule #8* (see Chapter 3).

The solutions approach is to multiply the denominator of the fraction by its multiplicative inverse.

$$\left(\frac{1-\sqrt{2}}{1+\sqrt{2}}\right) \times \left(\frac{1-\sqrt{2}}{1-\sqrt{2}}\right) = \frac{1-\sqrt{2}-\sqrt{2}+\sqrt{4}}{1-\sqrt{2}+\sqrt{2}-\sqrt{4}} = \frac{1-2\sqrt{2}+\sqrt{4}}{1-\sqrt{4}}$$

$$= \frac{1-2\sqrt{2}+2}{1-2} = \frac{3-2\sqrt{2}}{-1} = \frac{3-2\sqrt{2}}{-1} \times \frac{-1}{-1} = \frac{-3+2\sqrt{2}}{1}$$

$$= -3+2\sqrt{2}$$

65. Radical (𝄞)

Choice C

Classification: Radical Problems

Snapshot: This problem highlights *Radical Rule #3* (see Chapter 3).

$$\frac{\sqrt{10}}{\sqrt{.001}} = \sqrt{\frac{10}{.001}} = \sqrt{10,000} = 100$$

66. Two-Way Split (𝄞)

Choice A

Classification: Inequality Problems

Snapshot: This problem tests our ability to express an inequality solution in a single solution, with a single variable *x*. Also, when multiplying through by a negative number, we reverse the direction of the inequality sign.

Note that another correct answer could have been expressed as following: $x < -4$ or $x > 4$, which is an alternative way of writing the former expression.

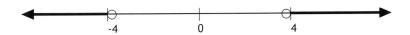

Perhaps the best way to process is to multiply the original expression, $-x^2 + 16 < 0$, through by -1 to make *x* positive. We have to remember, however, to reverse the inequality sign.

$$-x^2 + 16 < 0$$
$$(-1)x^2 + 16 < 0$$
$$(-1)(-1)x^2 + (-1)16 > (-1)0$$
$$x^2 - 16 > 0$$

Therefore, $x < -4$ or $x > 4$. When combining these two expressions into one expression, we write it as: $-4 > x > 4$.

67. Odd Man Out (♪ ♪)

Choice C
Classification: Prime Number Problem
Snapshot: This problem helps reveal the mathematical reason for why one number is a multiple of another number.

First let's visualize *P* as:

$$1 \times 2 \times 3 \times 4 \times 5 \times 6 \times 7 \times 8 \times 9 \times 10 \times 11 \times 12 \times 13.$$

This is also the equivalent of 13! (or 13 factorial)

Roman Numeral I is false. *P* is an even number. As long as we have a least one even number in our multiplication sequence, the entire product will be even. Remember an even number times an odd number or an even number times an even number is always an even number. For the record, *P* actually equals 6,227,020,800.

Roman Numeral II is false; Roman Numeral III is true. The key here is to look at the prime factors of *P*. These include: 2, 3, 5, 7, 11 and 13. For *P* to be a multiple of any number, that number must not contain any prime number that isn't already contained in *P*. What are the prime factors of 17?

Prime factorization:	Distinct prime factors:
17 = 1 x 17	17
24 = 2 x 2 x 2 x 3	2, 3

The number 17 has as one of its prime factors, the number 17. Since *P* does not contain this number it will not be a multiple of 17. It's as simple as that. Think of prime factors as the "DNA" of numbers. Any number *A* will not be a multiple of *B* if *B* contains any distinct prime number not included in *A*. Stated another way, *A* will be a multiple of *B* only if *A* contains, at a minimum, the same number of distinct prime factors as *B* does. For example, 6 is a multiple of 3 because 3 contains no prime numbers that aren't already included in 6 (i.e., 2, 3). 6 is not a multiple of 5 because 5 has a prime factor 5 which is not shared with the prime factors of the number 6.

P is a multiple of 24 because *P* contains all of the distinct prime numbers that 24 has.

68. Primed (♪)

Choice C
Classification: Prime Number Problem
Snapshot: To review prime numbers and prime factorization.

Number "x":	Factors:	Prime Factors:	"Primeness":
A) 10	1,2,5,10	2,5	5 - 2 = 3
B) 12	1,2,3,4,6,12	2,3	3 - 2 = 1
C) 14	1,2,7,14	2,7	7 - 2 = 5
D) 15	1,3,5,15	3,5	5 - 2 = 3
E) 18	1,2,3,6,9,18	2,3	3 - 2 = 1

69. Remainder (🜪 🜪)

Choice E

Classification: Remainder Problem

Snapshot: To review how to pick numbers for use in solving multiple and remainder problems.

A key step in this problem involves picking a number for *k* to work with based on the original information that *k* when divided by 7 leaves a remainder 5. This number is 12. We now substitute 12 for *k*.

I. 4k + 7	4k + 7 = 4(12) + 7 = 55
	55 ÷ 7 = 7, with a remainder of 6
II. 6k + 4	6k + 4 = 6(12) + 4 = 76
	76 ÷ 7 = 10, with a remainder of 6
III. 8k + 1	8k + 1 = 8(12) + 1 = 97
	97 ÷ 7 = 13, with a remainder of 6

70. Double Digits (🜪 🜪)

Choice D

Classification: Remainder Problem

Snapshot: When faced with multiple divisibility problems (*A* divided by *B* leaves *x* but *A* divided by *C* leaves *y*), find only those numbers which satisfy the first scenario then use this short-list of numbers to determine the solution to the next scenario.

The key to this problem is to do one part at a time rather than trying to combine the information. For example, list all two-digit numbers that when divided by 10 leave 3. These numbers include: 13, 23, 33, 43, 53, 63, 73, 83 and 93. Next, examine these numbers and determine which of these, when divided by 4, will leave a remainder of 3. These numbers include: 23, 43, 63 and 83.

Numbers:	Remainder:
13	1
23	3 ⇐
33	1
43	3 ⇐
53	1
63	3 ⇐
73	1
83	3 ⇐
93	1

71. Visualize (🌶️ 🌶️)

Choice A
Classification: Symbolism Problem
Snapshot: Learning to visualize the solution is the key to conquering symbolic or make-believe operations.

Set the problem up conceptually by first visualizing the solution:

$$v^* = v - \frac{v}{2}$$

$$(v^*)^* = v - \frac{v}{2} - \left(\frac{v - \frac{v}{2}}{2}\right)$$

$$3 = v - \frac{v}{2} - \left(\frac{v - \frac{v}{2}}{2}\right)$$

Multiply each term in the equation by "2."

$$(2)3 = (2)v - \cancel{(2)}\frac{v}{\cancel{2}} - (2)\left(\frac{v - \frac{v}{2}}{\cancel{2}}\right)$$

$$6 = 2v - v - \left(v - \frac{v}{2}\right)$$

$$6 = 2v - v - v + \frac{v}{2}$$

Calculate the outcome algebraically:

Multiply each term again by "2".

$$(2)6 = (2)2v - (2)v - (2)v + \cancel{(2)}\frac{v}{\cancel{2}}$$

$$12 = 4v - 2v - 2v + v$$

$$v = 12$$

72. Intercept (🌶️ 🌶️)

Choice A
Classification: Coordinate Geometry Problem
Snapshot: The slope formula is $y = mx + b$ where m is defined as the slope or gradient and b is defined as the y-intercept.

Start by visualizing the slope formula: $y = mx + b$. Let's determine the slope first. Slope "m" equals "rise over run."

$$\text{slope} = \frac{\text{rise}}{\text{run}} = \frac{\text{rise}_2 - \text{rise}_1}{\text{run}_2 - \text{run}_1} = \frac{3 - (-5)}{10 - (-6)} = \frac{8}{16} = \frac{1}{2}$$

$y = \frac{1}{2}x + b$. To find b let's put in the coordinates of the first point: $3 = \frac{1}{2}(10) + b$; $b = -2$. Now we have the complete slope formula: $y = \frac{1}{2}x - 2$.

To find the x-intercept, we set $y = 0$.

$$y = \frac{1}{2}x - 2$$

$$0 = \frac{1}{2}x - 2$$

$$-\frac{1}{2}x = -2$$

$$x = 4$$

73. Masquerade ( )

Choice D

Classification: Coordinate Geometry Problem

Snapshot: Positive lines slope upward ("forward slashes"); negative lines slope backward ("back slashes"). Graphs with slopes less than one (positive or negative fractions) are flat and closer to the x-axis. Graphs with slopes greater than one (coefficients > 1) are more upright and closer to the y-axis.

Take a minute and compare the general slope formula, $y = mx + b$, to the equation at hand.

$y = -2x + 2$

The slope is -2. It drops two units for every one unit it runs. A negative slope tells us that the graph is moving northwest-southeast.

The y-intercept is 2. This means that one point is (0, 2).

Lines A and B are out because they have positive slopes and we are looking for a negative slope. We are looking for a y-intercept of "2" so Line E (Choice E) is out. Focus on Lines C and D. Since the slope is -2, this means it drops two units for every one unit it runs and, because it is negative, it is moving northwest-southeast (note that if it had a positive slope, the graph would move southwest-northeast). You may be able to pick out Line D as the immediate winner. If not, test both the y-intercept and x-intercept to be absolutely sure. To test the y-intercept, which we already can see is (0,2), we set x equal to zero: Y = -2(0) + 2, and 2 is our answer. Line D intersects the y-axis at 2 as anticipated. To test the x-intercept, we set y equal to zero: 0 = -2x + 2, and 1 is our answer. Line D intersects the x-axis at (1,0). Thus, equation Line D is the clear winner based on its slope and its y-intercept and x-intercept.

Author's note: Additional proof? Whenever you know two points on a line, you can figure out the slope. Using the two points above, (0,2) and (1,0), we can find the slope of our line. Slope equals rise over run or algebraically (it doesn't matter which point is subtracted from the other):

$$\text{slope} = \frac{\text{rise}}{\text{run}} = \frac{\text{rise}_2 - \text{rise}_1}{\text{run}_2 - \text{run}_1} = \frac{2 - 0}{0 - 1} = \frac{2}{-1} = -2$$

Is -2 the slope that we are looking for? Yes.

74. Boxed In ( )

Choice D

Classification: Coordinate Geometry Problem

Snapshot: This problem highlights basic information regarding co-ordinate geometry. The slope of a horizontal line is $y = (..., -2, -1, 0, 1, 2, ...)$. The slope of a vertical line is $x = (..., -2, -1, 0, 1, 2, ...)$. The slope of the y-axis is $x = 0$; the slope of the x-axis is $y = 0$.

Go through each answer choice. Choices A, B, C and E represent boundary lines. Choice A, $x = 0$, is the y-axis. Choice B, $y = 0$, is the x-axis. Choice C, $x = 1$, forms the right boundary; the formula, $y = -\frac{1}{3}x + 1$, forms the top boundary. To test the inappropriateness of Choice D, $x - 3y = 0$, try placing various points into the equation. Any set of points on the line should be able to satisfy the equation. For example, take $(3,0)$. Now substitute $x = 3$ and $y = 0$ into the equation in Choice D, $x - 3y = 0$. You get $3 - 3(0) = 0$. This doesn't make sense and cannot be the correct equation. Try Choice E, $y + \frac{1}{3}x = 1$. Substitute $(3,0)$ and we get $0 + \frac{1}{3}(3) = 1$. This works—it is the proper equation and forms the roof, or top line, of the marked area.

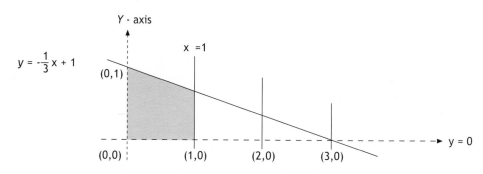

75. Magic ( )

Choice A

Classification: Plane Geometry Problem

Snapshot: This problem tests the simple definition of π.

Circumference = π x diameter. Since $c = \pi$ x d, the ratio of a circle's circumference to its diameter is: $\frac{\pi d}{d} = \pi$. This is the very definition of Pi; Pi is the ratio of the circumference of a circle to its diameter. The circumference of a circle is uniquely $\cong 3.14$ times as big as its diameter. This is always true. Choice D cannot be correct. A ratio is a ratio and, as such, does not vary with the size of the circle. For the record, the fractional equivalent of Pi is $\frac{22}{7}$.

76. Circuit ( )

Choice B

Classification: Plane Geometry Problem

Snapshot: To introduce geometry problems where the solution is expressed in algebraic terms.

Area = length x width
$a = l$ x w

Perimeter = 2(length) + 2(width)
$p = 2l + 2w$

(where a is area, l is length, w is width, and p is perimeter of a given rectangle)

Therefore, since none of the answer choices have reference to the variable of length, we substitute for the variable "*l*" as follows:

$$p = 2l + 2w \qquad \text{and} \qquad 1 = \frac{a}{w}$$

$$\text{so } p = 2\left(\frac{a}{w}\right) + 2w$$

Multiplying each term of the equation by *w*:

$$(w)p = (\cancel{w})2\left(\frac{a}{\cancel{w}}\right) + (w)2w$$
$$pw = 2a + 2w^2$$
$$2w^2 - pw + 2a = 0$$

77. Victorian (🐦 🐦)

Choice D
Classification: Plane Geometry Problem
Snapshot: The Pythagorean Theorem, $a^2 + b^2 = c^2$, can always be used to find the length of the sides of any right triangle. "Pythagorean triplets" are integers which satisfy the Pythagorean Theorem. The four common Pythagorean triplets that appear on the GMAT include: 3 : 4 : 5 ; 5 : 12 : 13 ; 8 : 15 : 17 ; and 7 : 24 : 25.

This is a classic problem that can be solved using the Pythagorean Theorem and formula: $a^2 + b^2 = c^2$ where *a*, *b* and *c* are sides of a triangle and *c* is the hypotenuse. In this problem, we concentrate on the first window and find the distance from the base of the house as follows: $(15)^2 + (x)^2 = (25)^2$ so x = 20. Then we concentrate on the second window and find the distance from the base of the house as follows: $(24)^2 + (x)^2 = (25)^2$ so x = 7. Don't forget that the ladder has been moved closer by 13 feet, not 7 feet.

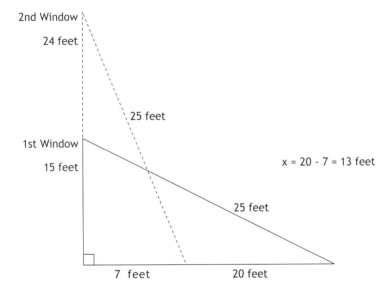

78. Kitty Corner ($\int$)

Choice B
Classification: Plane Geometry Problem
Snapshot: To review right-isosceles triangles and the relationships between their sides: $1 : 1 : \sqrt{2}$.

View the triangular wedge. The height is 2, the base is $2\sqrt{2}$ and the hypotenuse is *x*. Using the Pythagorean Theorem:

$a^2 + b^2 = c^2$
$(2)^2 + (2\sqrt{2})^2 = (x)^2$
$4 + 8 = x^2$
$x^2 = 12$
$x = \sqrt{12} = \sqrt{4 \times 3} = \sqrt{4} \times \sqrt{3} = 2\sqrt{3}$

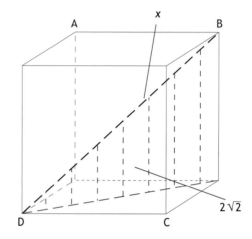

You may wonder, "How do we know the base is $2\sqrt{2}$." The base of the triangle is really the hypotenuse of the right isosceles triangle which is at the very bottom of the cube. Because all sides of the cube are 2 units in length, the hypotenuse of the bottom triangle is $2\sqrt{2}$. This information is critical to finding the hypotenuse of the triangle represented by *x*.

79. QR ($\int \int \int$)

Choice C
Classification: Plane Geometry Problem
Snapshot: This more difficult problem works in reverse of the previous one. Whereas the previous problem gave the measure of a side and asked us to calculate the "longest diagonal," this problem gives the measure the "longest diagonal" and asks us find the measure of a side, en-route to finding volume.

$a^2 + b^2 = c^2$
$x^2 + (x\sqrt{2})^2 = (4\sqrt{3})^2$
$x^2 + (x^2)(\sqrt{4}) = (16)(\sqrt{9})$
$x^2 + 2x^2 = 48$
$3x^2 = 48$
$x^2 = 16$
$x = 4$
$\therefore V = s^3 = (4)^3 = 64$

Note: The base of the cube forms a right isosceles triangle.

80. Diamond (𝄞 𝄞)

Choice A
Classification: Plane Geometry Problem
Snapshot: This problem tests an understanding of right-isosceles triangles and the ability to calculate the length of a single side when given the hypotenuse.

Either of the two dotted lines within the square serves to divide the square into two right-isosceles triangles. Since each dotted line has a length of 3 units, each side therefore has a length of $\frac{3}{\sqrt{2}}$. This calculation can be a bit tricky. Given that the ratios of the lengths of the sides of a right-isosceles triangle are $1 : 1 : \sqrt{2}$, we can use a ratio and proportion to calculate the length of the hypotenuse (the dotted line in the diagram that follows):

Standard ratio: $1 : 1 : \sqrt{2}$

Setup per this problem: $x : x : 3$

Ratio solved: $\frac{3}{\sqrt{2}} : \frac{3}{\sqrt{2}} : 3$

Calculation:

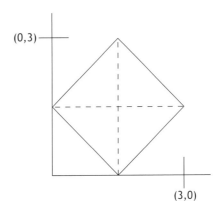

$$\frac{1}{\sqrt{2}} :: \frac{x}{3}$$

$$1(3) = x(\sqrt{2})$$

$$\frac{1(3)}{\sqrt{2}} = \frac{x(\sqrt{2})}{\sqrt{2}}$$

$$x = \frac{3}{\sqrt{2}}$$

Calculating Perimeter:

Perimeter = 4 x side = 4s

$$P = 4 \times \frac{3}{\sqrt{2}} = \frac{12}{\sqrt{2}} \text{ units}$$

We typically simplify radicals in order to eliminate having a radical in the denominator of a fraction. This is consistent with *Radical Rule #3* (see Chapter 3).

$$\frac{12}{\sqrt{2}} = \frac{12}{\sqrt{2}} \times \frac{\sqrt{2}}{\sqrt{2}} = \frac{12\sqrt{2}}{\sqrt{4}} = \frac{12\sqrt{2}}{2} = 6\sqrt{2} \text{ units}$$

81. Cornered (⌇ ⌇ ⌇)

Choice C

Classification: Plane Geometry Problem

Snapshot: This problem combines circle, square, and triangle geometry. Often the key to calculating the area of the odd-ball figures lies in subtracting one figure from another.

Here the solution to this problem lies in subtracting the area of the smaller (inner) circle from the area of the smaller (inner) square.

Area of Outer Square:

$$\text{Area} = \text{side}^2$$
$$A = s^2$$
$$2 = s^2$$
$$s = \sqrt{2}$$

Area of Inner Square:

$$A = s^2 = (1)^2 = 1 \text{ unit}^2$$

Note that above we pick the number "1" in so far as it is the simplest of integers.

Area of Inner Circle:

$$A = \pi r^2 = \pi \left(\frac{1}{2}\right)^2 = \frac{1}{4}\pi \text{ units}^2$$

Area of darkened corners equals:

$$\text{Area} = \text{Inner Square} - \text{Inner Circle}$$
$$A = 1 - \frac{1}{4}\pi \text{ units}^2$$

Explanation:

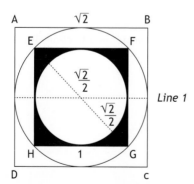

The key to this problem lies in first finding the length of one side of square ABCD. Obviously if the area of ABCD is 2 square units, the length of one side of square ABCD is calculated as the square root of 2 or $\sqrt{2}$. Line AB equals $\sqrt{2}$, and therefore *Line 1* is also $\sqrt{2}$. Line 1 may be viewed as the diameter of the outer circle. It is also the diagonal of square EFGH. EG also equals $\sqrt{2}$, and therefore EH and HG equal 1 unit (because the ratios of the length of the sides in an isosceles right triangle with angle measures of 45° : 45° : 90° is 1 - 1- $\sqrt{2}$. We can now calculate the measure of square EFGH (where each side equals 1 unit) and the area of the inner circle (with its radius of $\frac{1}{2}$ unit). That is, the length of a side of the inner square equals the diameter of the inner circle. Diameter is twice radius or, more directly, radius is one-half the diameter.

82. AC (🔥 🔥)

Choice E
Classification: Plane Geometry Problem
Snapshot: This problem merely requires that the candidate can calculate the height of a triangle but doing so requires viewing the triangle from different perspectives.

In the original diagram, the measure of BD is easy to calculate using the Pythagorean formula:

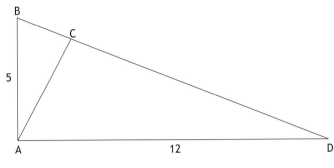

$c^2 = a^2 + b^2$
$c^2 = (12)^2 + (5)^2$
$c^2 = 144 + 25$
$c^2 = 169$
$c^2 = \sqrt{169}$
$c = 13$

Therefore the measure of BD is 13. As seen in the diagram below, we now know the measures of all sides of the triangle. We can also calculate the area of the triangle:

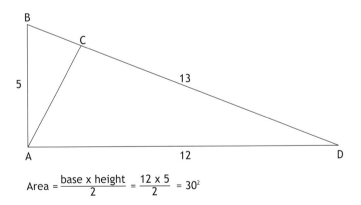

$$\text{Area} = \frac{\text{base x height}}{2} = \frac{12 \times 5}{2} = 30^2$$

When the diagram is flipped it is easy to calculate the *height* (AC) given that the area is 30 square units and the base is 13 units.

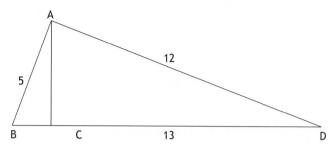

$$A = \frac{\text{base x height}}{2}$$

$$30 = \frac{\text{base x height}}{2}$$

$$30 = \frac{13 \times h}{2}$$

$$60 = 13 \times h$$

$$h = \frac{60}{13} \text{ units}$$

83. Woozy (𝄞 𝄞 𝄞)

Choice C

Classification: Plane Geometry Problem

Snapshot: This problem provides a review of both equilateral triangles and 30°- 60°- 90° triangles.

Conceptually, we want to subtract the area of smaller triangle PQT from the area of the larger equilateral triangle PRS. Note that in a 30°- 60°- 90° triangle, the ratios of the lengths of the sides are $1 : \sqrt{3} : 2$ units.

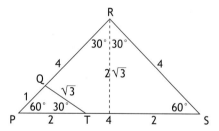

Area of triangle PRS equals:

$$\text{Area} = \frac{\text{base x height}}{2} = \frac{4 \times 2\sqrt{3}}{2} = \frac{8\sqrt{3}}{2} = 4\sqrt{3}$$

Area of triangle PQT equals:

$$\text{Area} = \frac{\text{base x height}}{2} = \frac{1 \times \sqrt{3}}{2} = \frac{\sqrt{3}}{2} = \frac{1}{2}\sqrt{3}$$

Therefore:

$$4\sqrt{3} - \frac{1}{2}\sqrt{3} = \frac{8}{2}\sqrt{3} - \frac{1}{2}\sqrt{3} = \frac{7}{2}\sqrt{3}$$

84. Lopsided ( )

Choice C
Classification: Plane Geometry Problem
Snapshot: To illustrate how to find the measures of angles indirectly.

Since m + n = 110 degrees; thus x = 70 degrees because a triangle n-m-x equals 180. Also triangle y-x-z also measures 180 degrees. The measure of o + p is found by setting the measures of y-x-z equal to 180 degrees. Thus, x = 70 ; y = 180 - o; z = 180 - p. Finally, 180 = 70 + (180 - o) + (180 - p)

o + p =250 degrees

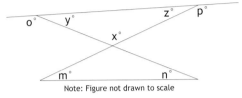

Note: Figure not drawn to scale

85. Sphere ( )

Choice D
Classification: Solid Geometry Problem
Snapshot: A number of very difficult geometry problems can be solved by picking small manageable numbers.

The best approach is to pick and substitute numbers. Say, for example, that the radius of the original sphere is 2 units, then:

Original Sphere:

$$\text{Volume} = \frac{4}{3}\pi r^3$$

$$\text{Ex: } V = \frac{4}{3}\pi(2)^3 = \frac{32}{3}\pi \text{ units}^3$$

New Sphere:

$$\text{New: Volume} = \frac{4}{3}\pi r^3$$

$$\text{Ex: } V = \frac{4}{3}\pi(4)^3 = \frac{256}{3}\pi \text{ units}^3$$

Final Calculation:

$$\frac{\text{new}}{\text{original}} = \frac{\frac{256}{3}\pi \text{ units}^3}{\frac{32}{3}\pi \text{ units}^3} = \frac{256^8}{3^1} \times \frac{3^1}{32^1} = 8 \text{ times}$$

86. Orange & Blue (ς ς)

Choice A
Classification: Probability
Snapshot: This problem introduces the *Complement Rule* of Probability (see *Part 3: The World of Numbers*).

The best way to view this problem is in terms of what you don't want. At least one orange means anything but "blue."

Probability of double blue:

$$\frac{3}{5} \times \frac{2}{4} = \frac{6}{20} = \frac{3}{10}$$

Therefore, probability of at least one orange:

$$P(A) = 1 - P(A)$$

$$1 - \frac{3}{10} = \frac{7}{10}$$

The "direct" method unfolds as follows:

Orange, Blue: $\quad \frac{2}{5} \times \frac{3}{4} = \frac{6}{20}$

Blue, Orange: $\quad \frac{3}{5} \times \frac{2}{4} = \frac{6}{20} \quad \left. \right\} \quad \frac{14}{20} \Rightarrow \frac{7}{10}$

Orange, Orange: $\quad \frac{2}{5} \times \frac{1}{4} = \frac{2}{20}$

Blue, Blue: $\quad \frac{3}{5} \times \frac{2}{4} = \frac{6}{20}$

Note that the total of all of the above possibilities equals "1" because there are no other possibilities other than the four presented here.

87. Exam Time (ς)

Choice E
Classification: Probability
Snapshot: The probability of two *non-mutually exclusive* events A or B occurring is calculated by adding the probability of the first event to the second event and then subtracting out the overlap between the two events. This is referred to in probability as the *General Addition Rule*.

$$\frac{9}{12} + \frac{8}{12} - \frac{6}{12} = \frac{11}{12}$$

P(A or B) = P(A) + P(B) - P(A and B). The probability of passing the first exam is added to the probability of passing the second exam, less the probability of passing both exams. If we don't make this subtraction, we will over count because we have overlap—the possibility that she will pass both exams. In this case, we can calculate the overlap as $\frac{3}{4} \times \frac{2}{3} = \frac{6}{12} = \frac{1}{2}$ because we assume the two events are independent.

Note that situations involving A or B do not necessarily preclude the possibility of both A and B. If we simply add probabilities we inadvertently double count the probability of A and B. We should only count it once and therefore we must subtract it once. See Group Problems, Problems #18-20).

One way to prove this result is to recognize that the probability of passing either exam is everything other than failing both exams. The probability of failing both exams is $\frac{1}{4}$ x $\frac{1}{3}$ = $\frac{1}{12}$. Therefore, the probability of passing either exam is $1 - \frac{1}{12} = \frac{11}{12}$.

88. Sixth Sense ( )

Choice D

Classification: Probability

Snapshot: This is a trickier problem. It is conceptually more difficult to see the overlap which is created whenever a double six occurs after two tosses of a fair dice.

$$\frac{1}{6} + \frac{1}{6} - \frac{1}{36} = \frac{12}{36} - \frac{1}{36} = \frac{11}{36}$$

P(A or B) = P(A) + P(B) - P(A and B). Formula: probability of one six *plus* probability of a second six *minus* probability of both sixes occurring *equals* probability of a six on either the first or second toss. Use the *Complement Rule* for proof: $1 - \left(\frac{5}{6} \times \frac{5}{6}\right) = \frac{11}{36}$. This translates to one minus the probability of rolling neither a six on the first roll nor the second roll of the dice.

One method of illustrating the solution is to write out the possibilities as depicted by the chart below. We could get a "6" on the first roll or a "6" on the second roll in which the corresponding outcomes would include: (6,1), (6,2), (6,3), (6,4), (6,5), (6,6) and (1,6), (2,6), (3,6), (4,6), (5,6), (6,6). There are twelve possibilities because (6,6) is represented twice. Therefore it must be subtracted out to arrive at the real probability of $\frac{11}{36}$.

	1	2	3	4	5	6
1						x
2						x
3						x
4						x
5						x
6	x	x	x	x	x	x

89. At Least One (💰 💰 💰)

Choice E

Classification: Probability

Snapshot: This problem involves three overlapping probabilities and is best solved using the *Complement Rule* of Probability. The direct mathematical approach is more cumbersome but parallels the solution to *German Cars* (see Problem #20).

"Short cut" Approach:

Using the *Complement Rule*, the probability of total failure is calculated as follows one minus the probability of failing all three exams:

The probability of not passing the first exam:

$$P(\text{not A}) = 1 - P(A) = 1 - \frac{3}{4} = \frac{1}{4}$$

Below is the probability of not passing the second exam:

$$P(\text{not B}) = 1 - P(B) = 1 - \frac{2}{3} = \frac{1}{3}$$

Below is the probability of not passing the third exam:

$$P(\text{not C}) = 1 - P(C) = 1 - \frac{1}{2} = \frac{1}{2}$$

The probability of failing all three exams:

$$\frac{1}{4} \times \frac{1}{3} \times \frac{1}{2} = \frac{1}{24}$$

The probability of passing at least one exam:

$$P(A) = 1 - P(\text{not A})$$

$$1 - \frac{1}{24} = \frac{23}{24}$$

"Direct" Approach:

The direct method is much more cumbersome. Mathematically it is solved by calculating the probability of passing only one of the three exams, two of the three exams, and all of the three exams.

Probability of passing exam one but not exams two or three:

$$1. \ P(A) \times P(\text{not B}) \times P(\text{not C}) = \frac{3}{4} \times \frac{1}{3} \times \frac{1}{2} = \frac{3}{24}$$

Probability of passing exam two but not exams one or three:

$$2. \ P(\text{not A}) \times P(B) \times P(\text{not B}) = \frac{1}{4} \times \frac{2}{3} \times \frac{1}{2} = \frac{2}{24}$$

Probability of passing exam three but not exams one or two:

$$3. \ P(\text{not A}) \times P(\text{not B}) \times P(C) = \frac{1}{4} \times \frac{1}{3} \times \frac{1}{2} = \frac{1}{24}$$

Probability of passing exams one and two but not exam three:

$$4. \text{ P(A) x P(B) x P(not C)} = \frac{3}{4} \times \frac{2}{3} \times \frac{1}{2} = \frac{6}{24}$$

Probability of passing exams one and three but not exam two:

$$5. \text{ P(A) x P(not B) x P(C)} = \frac{3}{4} \times \frac{1}{3} \times \frac{1}{2} = \frac{3}{24}$$

Probability of passing exams two and three but not exam one:

$$6. \text{ P(not A) x P(B) x P(C)} = \frac{1}{4} \times \frac{2}{3} \times \frac{1}{2} = \frac{2}{24}$$

Probability of passing all three exams:

$$7. \text{ P(A) x P(B) x P(C)} = \frac{3}{4} \times \frac{2}{3} \times \frac{1}{2} = \frac{6}{24}$$

Probability of not passing any of the three exams:

$$8. \text{ P(not A) x P(not B) x P(not C)} = \frac{1}{4} \times \frac{1}{3} \times \frac{1}{2} = \frac{1}{24}$$

The above are all the possibilities regarding the outcomes of one student taking three exams. Adding the first seven of eight possibilities above will result in the correct answer using the direct approach.

$$\text{Proof:} \frac{3}{24} + \frac{2}{24} + \frac{1}{24} + \frac{6}{24} + \frac{3}{24} + \frac{2}{24} + \frac{6}{24} = \frac{23}{24}$$

Note that the total of all eight outcomes above will total to 1, because 1 is the sum total of all probabilistic possibilities.

$$\text{Proof:} \frac{3}{24} + \frac{2}{24} + \frac{1}{24} + \frac{6}{24} + \frac{3}{24} + \frac{2}{24} + \frac{6}{24} + \frac{1}{24} = \frac{24}{24} = 1$$

90. Coin Toss (⟩⟩⟩)

Choice D
Classification: Probability
Snapshot: To highlight how the words "at most" also trigger the *Complement Rule* of Probability.

This easiest way to do this problem is to think in terms of what we don't want. At most three heads means that we want anything except *all heads* or *four heads*. This includes the following:

We don't want all heads: HHHHH $\rangle$ $\frac{1}{32}$

We don't want four heads: HHHHT
                                                  HHHTH
                                                  HHTHH $\Big\}$ $\frac{5}{32}$
                                                  HTHHH
                                                  THHHH

$$\text{Thus, } 1 - \left(\frac{1}{32} + \frac{5}{32}\right) = 1 - \frac{6}{32} = \frac{26}{32} = \frac{13}{16}$$

Author's note: This problem is the mirror opposite of the problem: "If a coin is tossed five times what is the probability of heads appearing at least two times?"

We don't want all tails: TTTTT $\rbrace \frac{1}{32}$

We don't want just one head:

$$\left.\begin{array}{l} \text{HTTTT} \\ \text{THTTT} \\ \text{TTHTT} \\ \text{TTTHT} \\ \text{TTTTH} \end{array}\right\rbrace \frac{5}{32}$$

Thus, $1 - \left(\frac{1}{32} + \frac{5}{32}\right) = 1 - \frac{6}{32} = \frac{26}{32} = \frac{13}{16}$

91. Antidote (🍴 🍴)

Choice D
Classification: Probability
Snapshot: This problem type may be called a "kill problem." The key is to solve the problem from the viewpoint of what fraction of the population is still alive. The number killed will be 1 minus the number that is alive.

How many people will be alive after three full days?

Answer: $\frac{2}{3} \times \frac{2}{3} \times \frac{2}{3} = \frac{8}{27}$.

P(A) = 1 - P (not A)

$1 - \frac{8}{27} = \frac{19}{27}$

The trap answer is: $\left(\frac{1}{3} \times \frac{1}{3} \times \frac{1}{3}\right) = \frac{1}{27}$. It is not possible to multiply by $\frac{1}{3}$ because this represents people killed. Everything must first be expressed in terms of how many people are alive. In "kill problems" we can never multiply "dead times dead."

92. Hiring (🍴 🍴)

Choice B
Classification: Permutation (Noted Exception)
Snapshot: This particular problem falls under neither the umbrella of probability nor permutation nor combination. It is included here because it is so frequently mistaken for a permutation problem.

7 x 4 x 10 = 280

The solution requires only that we multiply together all individual possibilities. Multiplying 7 (candidates for sales managers) by 4 (candidates for shipping clerk) by 10 (candidates for receptionist) would result in possibilities.

Author's note: This problem is about a series of choices. It utilizes the "multiplier principle" and falls within the Rule of Enumeration. The permutation formula cannot be used with this type of problem. This problem is concerned with "how many choices we have," not "how many arrangements are possible," as is the case with a permutation problem.

93. Fencing (🌶)

Choice C
Classification: Permutation
Snapshot: This problem is a permutation, not a combination, because order does matter. If Country A wins the tournament and Country B places second, it is a different outcome than if Country B wins and Country A places second.

$$_nP_r = \frac{n!}{(n-r)!}$$

$$_4P_2 = \frac{4!}{(4-2)!} = \frac{4 \times 3 \times \cancel{2} \times \cancel{1}}{\cancel{2!}} = 12$$

Author's note: Consider this follow-up problem. A teacher has four students in a special needs class. She must assign four awards at the end of the year: Math, English, History, and Creative Writing awards. How many ways could she do this assuming that a single student could win multiple awards?

$$n^r = 4^4 \qquad\qquad\qquad 4 \times 4 \times 4 \times 4 = 216$$

She has four ways she could give out the Math award, four ways she could give out the English award, four ways to give out the History award, and four ways to give out the Creative Writing award. Refer to Probability, Permutation & Combination, Rule #10, **(page 36)**.

94. Alternating (🌶 🌶)

Choice C
Classification: Permutations
Snapshot: This problem is foremost a joint permutation, in which we calculate two individual permutations and multiply those outcomes together. This problem also incorporates the "mirror image" rule of permutations.

$$2(3! \times 3!) = 2[(3 \times 2 \times 1) \times (3 \times 2 \times 1)] = 72$$

There are two possibilities with respect to how the girls and boys can sit for the make-up exam. A boy will sit in the first, third, and fifth seats and a girl will sit in the second, fourth, and sixth seats or a girl will sit in the first, third, and fifth seats and a boy will sit in the second, fourth, and sixth seats.

$$2(3! \times 3!) = 2[(3 \times 2 \times 1) \times (3 \times 2 \times 1)] = 72$$

$\underline{B} \times \underline{G} \times \underline{B} \times \underline{G} \times \underline{B} \times \underline{G}$

or:

$\underline{G} \times \underline{B} \times \underline{G} \times \underline{B} \times \underline{G} \times \underline{B}$

Author's note: There are two common variations stemming from this type of permutation problem:

Ex. Three boys and three girls are going to sit for a makeup exam. The girls are to sit in the first, second, and third seats while the boys must sit in the fourth, fifth and sixth seats. How many possibilities are there with respect to how the six students can be seated?

Answer: $(3! \times 3!) = 6 \times 6 = 36$ possibilities

Ex. Three boys and three girls are going to sit for a makeup exam. If there are no restrictions on how the students may be seated, how many possibilities are there with respect to how they can be seated?

Answer: $6! = 6 \times 5 \times 4 \times 3 \times 2 \times 1 = 720$ possibilities

95. Banana (ᔓ ᔓ)

Choice E

Classification: Permutations

Snapshot: This problem highlights the handling of "repeated letters" (or "repeated numbers"). The formula for calculating permutations with repeated numbers or letters is $\frac{n!}{x!\,y!\,z!}$, where x, y, and z are distinct but identical numbers or letters.

$$\frac{n!}{x!y!} = \frac{6!}{3! \times 2!} = \frac{6 \times 5 \times \cancel{4}^{2} \times \cancel{3 \times 2 \times 1}}{(\cancel{3 \times 2 \times 1}) \times (\cancel{2 \times 1})} = 60$$

The word "banana" has three "a's" and two "n's."

96. Table (ᔓ ᔓ)

Choice C

Classification: Permutations

Snapshot: This problem deals with the prickly issue of "empty seats."

$$\frac{5!}{2!} = \frac{5 \times 4 \times 3 \times \cancel{2!}}{\cancel{2!}} = 60$$

Author's note: The answer to this problem is the same as the previous problem *Code*. In theory, "empty seats" are analogous to "identical numbers" (or "identical letters") in permutation theory.

Also the geometric configuration of a table should not mislead. The solution to this problem would be identical had we been dealing with a row of five seats.

97. Singer (ᔓ ᔓ)

Choice C

Classification: Combinations

Snapshot: Joint Combinations are calculated by multiplying the results of two individual combinations.

First, break the combination into two calculations. First, the "old songs," and second, the "new songs."

$$_nC_r = \frac{n!}{r!(n-r)!}$$

$$_6C_4 = \frac{6!}{4!(6-4)!} = \frac{6!}{4!(2)!} = \frac{\cancel{6}^{3} \times 5 \times \cancel{4 \times 3 \times 2 \times 1}}{\cancel{4 \times 3 \times 2 \times 1} \times (\cancel{2 \times 1})} = 15$$

Thus, 15 represents the number of ways the singer can choose to sing four of six songs.

$$_nC_r = \frac{n!}{r!(n-r)!}$$

$$_5C_2 = \frac{5!}{2!(5-2)!} = \frac{5!}{2!(3)!} = \frac{5 \times \cancel{4}^{2} \times \cancel{3 \times 2 \times 1}}{2 \times \cancel{1}(\cancel{3 \times 2 \times 1})} = 10$$

Thus, 10 represents the number of ways the singer could chose to sing three of five old songs. Therefore, the joint combination equals 15 x 10 = 150.

In summary, the outcome of this joint combination is:

$$_nC_r \times {_nC_r} = \frac{n!}{r!(n-r)!} \times \frac{n!}{r!(n-r)!}$$

$$_6C_4 \times {}_5C_2 = \frac{6!}{4!(6-4)!} \times \frac{5!}{2!(5-2)!} = 15 \times 10 = 150$$

98. Reunion (🦢🦢🦢)

Choice D
Classification: Combinations
Snapshot: This problem *Reunion* is a rather complicated sounding problem but its solution is actually quite simple. We're essentially asking: How many groups of two can we create from eleven items where order doesn't matter? Or how many ways can we choose two items from eleven items where order doesn't matter?

$$_nC_r = \frac{n!}{r!(n-r)!}$$

$$_{11}C_2 = \frac{11!}{2!(11-2)!} = \frac{11 \times 10 \times 9!}{2!(9!)} = 55$$

99. Display (🦢🦢🦢)

Choice B
Classification: Combinations
Snapshot: This problem combines both the combination formula and probability theory.

First, the total number of ways she can choose 3 computers from 8 is represented by the following combination.

$$_nC_r = \frac{n!}{r!(n-r)!}$$

$$_8C_3 = \frac{8!}{3!(8-3)!} = \frac{8 \times 7 \times 6 \times 5!}{3!(5!)} = 56$$

Second, the total number of ways in which the two most expensive computers will be among the three computers is 6. For example, one way to visualize the situation is to think of the eight computers as A, B, C, D, E, F, G and H. If A and B are the most expensive computers, then there are six ways these two computers could be among the three computers chosen, namely ABC, ABD, ABE, ABF, ABG, and ABH. Yet another way of arriving at this figure is to visualize the two most expensive computers as fixed within any group of three. Therefore, "We ask how many ways can we choose a final computer from the group of eight, given that A and B are already in our group?" The answer to this part of the problem is derived by the following combination.

$$_6C_1 = \frac{6!}{1!(6-1)!} = \frac{6 \times 5!}{1!(5!)} = 6$$

The final answer: $\frac{6}{56} = \frac{3}{28}$

In summary, the following is perhaps the most succinct way to view this problem:

$$\frac{_nC_r}{_nC_r} = \frac{_6C_1}{_8C_3} = \frac{6}{56} = \frac{3}{28}$$

Below is an alternative solution:

$$\frac{1}{8} \times \frac{1}{7} \times 6 = \frac{6}{56} = \frac{3}{28}$$

100. Outcomes (🌶 🌶)

Choice A

Classification: Combinations

Snapshot: This bonus problem exists to test permutation and combination theory at a grassroots level. A two chili rating is assigned because it is meant to be completed within two minutes (the average time allocated for a GMAT math problem). A strong understanding of theory will allow the test-taker to avoid doing any calculations.

Roman Numeral I:

> True. $\qquad\qquad\qquad {}_5P_3 > {}_5P_2$

${}_5P_3 = 60$ while ${}_5P_2 = 20$. Order matters in permutations and more items in a permutation equals more possibilities.

Roman Numeral II:

> False. $\qquad\qquad\qquad {}_5C_3 > {}_5C_2$

${}_5C_3 = 10$ while ${}_5C_2 = 10$. Strange as it may seem, the outcomes are equal! "Complements in combinations" result in the same probability. Complements occur when the two inside numbers equal the same outside number. Here $3 + 2 + 5$. Note this phenomenon only occurs in combinations, not permutations.

Roman Numeral III:

> False. $\qquad\qquad\qquad {}_5C_2 > {}_5P_2$

${}_5C_2 = 10$ while ${}_5P_2 = 20$. Order matters in permutations and this creates more possibilities relative to combinations. Stated in the reverse, order doesn't matter in combinations and this results in fewer outcomes than permutations, all things being equal.

CHAPTER 6

DATA SUFFICIENCY

"Mathematics possesses not only truth, but supreme beauty —a beauty cold and austere, like that of sculpture."
(Lord Russell Bertrand)

ODDS AND EVENS

101. Even Odds ( )

If *x* and *y* are positive integers, is y(x - 3) odd?

> (1) *x* is an odd integer.
> (2) *y* is an even integer.

102. Consecutive ( )

If *p*, *q*, *r* are a series of three consecutive positive integers, is the sum of all the integers odd?

> (1) Two of the three numbers, *p,q,r* are odd numbers.
>
> (2) $\frac{p + q + r}{3}$ is an even integer.

AVERAGING

103. Vote ( )

Each person in a club with 100 members voted for exactly one of 3 candidates for president: A, B or C. Did candidate A receive the most votes?

> (1) No single candidate received more than 50% of the votes.
> (2) Candidate A received 32 votes.

POSITIVES AND NEGATIVES

104. ABC ( )

If *a*, *b*, and *c* are distinct nonzero numbers, is

$$\frac{(a - b)^3 (b - c)}{(a + b)^2 (b + c)^2} < 0?$$

> (1) a > b
> (2) a > c

INTEGERS AND NON-INTEGERS

105. Integers ( )

How many integers are greater than *x*, but less than *y*?

> (1) y = x + 5
> (2) x = $\sqrt{5}$

106. Between A and B (Ş Ş)

How many integers *n* are there such that *a* > *n* > *b*?

> (1) a - b = 4
> (2) *a* and *b* are not integers.

SQUARES AND CUBES

107. Units Digit (Ş Ş)

What is the units' digit of the non-negative integer *y*?

> (1) *y* is a multiple of 8.
> (2) The units' digit of y^2 is the same as the units' digit of y^3.

FACTORS AND MULTIPLES

108. Factors (Ş Ş)

How many distinct factors does positive integer *k* have?

> (1) *k* has more distinct factors than the integer 9 but less distinct factors than the integer 81.
> (2) *k* is the product of two distinct prime numbers.

109. Multiples (Ş)

If *x* and *y* are positive integers, is *2x* a multiple of *y*?

> (1) *x* is a multiple of *y*.
> (2) *y* is a multiple of *x*.

PRIME NUMBERS

110. Prime Time (Ş Ş)

If *n* is an integer, is *n* + 1 a prime number?

> (1) *n* is a prime number.
> (2) *n* + 2 is <u>not</u> a prime number.

111. Prime Time #2 (Ş Ş Ş)

If *x* and *y* are distinct integers, is *x* + *y* a prime number?

> (1) *x* and *y* are prime numbers.
> (2) *x* x *y* is odd.

FACTORING

112. F.O.I.L ($\int$)

What is the value of *a*?

(1) $a^2 - a = 2$
(2) $a^2 + a = 6$

113. X-Factor ($\int$)

Is x = 1?

(1) $x^2 - x = 0$
(2) $x^3 - x = 0$

INEQUALITIES

114. Reciprocal ($\int$)

If *x* and *y* cannot be equal to zero, is $\frac{x}{y} > \frac{y}{x}$?

(1) $x > y$
(2) $xy > 0$

115. Fraction ($\int \int$)

If *a* and *b* cannot be equal to zero is $0 < \frac{a}{b} < 1,$?

(1) $ab > 0$
(2) $a - b < 0$

116. Z-Ray ($\int$)

Is $z < 0$?

(1) $-z < z$
(2) $z^3 < z^2$

117. Ps and Qs ($\int \int$)

Is $pr > 0$?

(1) $pq > 0$
(2) $qr < 0$

118. Kookoo (⌇ ⌇)

Is $k + k < k$?

  (1) $k^2 > k^3$
  (2) $k^3 > k^2$

119. ABCD (⌇ ⌇)

Is $a + b > c + d$?

  (1) $a > c + d$
  (2) $b > c + d$

120. Upright (⌇ ⌇ ⌇)

If $\frac{a}{b} > \frac{c}{b}$, then is a greater than c?

  (1) a is positive
  (2) c is negative

STATISTICS

121. Central Measures (⌇ ⌇)

Students A and B each received 5 scores from science quizzes taken during their semester. Quizzes garner grades from 1.0 to 10.0, expressed in whole numbers. Did Student A receive a higher average (arithmetic mean) than did Student B?

  (1) The median of test quizzes for Student A is greater than the median of test quizzes for Student B.
  (2) The mode of test quizzes for Student A is greater than the mode of test quizzes for Student B.

122. Dispersion (⌇)

What is the Standard Deviation of the terms in set S?

  (1) Set S is composed of 7 consecutive even integers.
  (2) The average (arithmetic mean) of the terms in set S is 49.

ANSWERS AND EXPLANATIONS

The problems included in this section focus on number properties and statistics because these represent the majority of math problems found on the Data Sufficiency section of the GMAT. Words Problems and Geometry, for example, are tested in Data Sufficiency with far less frequency.

101. Even Odds (𝄞)

Choice D
Classification: Number Properties (Odds & Evens)
Snapshot: This problem highlights the basic concept that an even number times an odd number is always even (e.g., 2 x 2 = 4 ; 2 x 3 = 6). It also serves to remind the reviewer that "a negative answer to a yes/no Data Sufficiency question does not equal *insufficiency*; it equals *sufficiency*." The likely reason that this proves tricky for students who are first encountering GMAT Data Sufficiency is that it is intuitive to view positive and negative answers as extremes or polar opposites. In real life, the answer to the questions, "Is the light on or off?" or "Is the project complete or not?" can only result in an unambiguous "yes" or "no" answer and, as these answers are in opposite camps, we let this influence us in Data Sufficiency. However, in Data Sufficiency, a definitely "yes" or "no" answer results in sufficiency.

Statement (1) is sufficient. Knowing that x is odd tells us that the expression $(x - 3)$ is even because x is odd and an odd number subtracted from an odd number must be even. Once we know that the expression "$(x - 3)$" is even, we also know that an even number multiplied by y is an even number (it doesn't matter whether y is even or odd).

Statement (2) is also sufficient. Knowing that y is even tells us that the whole expression $y(x - 3)$ is even regardless of whether "$x - 3$" is odd or even. An even number (i.e., "y") multiplied by an even or odd number is always even.

So in answering the question, "Is $y(x - 3)$ odd?" the answer is definitely "no" because the whole expression is "even."

It might be interesting to point out that this problem does not include the words *distinct positive integers*. So it is possible that x and y could be the same number at the same time. Say, for example, y and x equal 2 such that $2(2 - 3) = -2$. This is still okay because -2, although negative, is still an even number. Also what if y and x were equal to 3 such that $3(3 - 3) = 0$. This is also okay because 0 is an even number! That's right—as strange as it may seem—the integer 0 is neither positive nor negative but it is considered an even integer.

102. Consecutive (𝄞)

Choice D
Classification: Number Properties (Odds & Evens)
Snapshot: When picking numbers for sets, try picking sets of three numbers. A set with only one number is too small and a set of four or five numbers will likely prove cumbersome.

Both statements are again sufficient. Pick some numbers. If two of the three numbers are odd numbers, their sum will always be <u>even</u>: 1, 2, 3 (sum to 6) and 3, 4, 5 (sum to 12). Therefore, based on Statement (1), the answer to the question, *Is the sum of all integers odd?* is "no" because the answer will always result in an even number. Statement (1) is sufficient, not insufficient.

Statement (2): Let's pick some groups of three consecutive numbers:

$$\frac{1 + 2 + 3}{3} = 2 \qquad \frac{2 + 3 + 4}{3} = 3 \qquad \frac{3 + 4 + 5}{3} = 4 \qquad \frac{4 + 5 + 6}{3} = 5$$

Since $\frac{a + b + c}{3}$ <u>must</u> be an even integer, it must also be true that two of the three numbers must be odd and this is exactly where we started with Statement (2). Therefore the sum of all integers will be even and the answer to the question will be "no"—the sum of all integers is not odd.

103. Vote (⟆)

Choice B
Classification: Number Properties (Average Problem)
Snapshot: Sometimes we don't know much about what is true, only what "can't be true."

Statement (1) does not tell you anything about the number of votes A received. Statement (2) tells us that Candidate A received 32 votes. Therefore, the other candidates received 100 - 32 = 68 votes. If we divide 68 by 2, we find that the other two candidates averaged 34 votes each: 2 more votes than A received. That means that there's no way that at least one of B or C did not get more votes than Candidate A. So Statement (2) allows us to answer 'No,' to the question in the stem, and is therefore sufficient.

104. ABC (⟆ ⟆)

Choice C
Classification: Number Properties (Positives & Negatives)
Snapshot: This problem highlights the value in picking from the following numbers: 2, -2, 1, -1, $\frac{1}{2}$, -$\frac{1}{2}$, and 0. In this problem, we need only try the numbers 1, 2 and -1, -2.

The first statement is insufficient. Here is a solution for the first statement:

$$a > b \qquad \text{Is } \frac{(a - b)^3 (b - c)}{(a + b)^2 (b + c)^2} < 0?$$

$$\text{Is } \frac{(+)(\pm)}{(+)(+)} < 0?$$

First of all, note that both of the expressions, $(a + b)^2$ and $(b + c)^2$, are always positive because a positive number squared or negative number squared is always positive. Looking at the numerators, if $a > b$, we know that $(a - b)^3$ is positive. Pick some numbers to prove this including: a = 2 and b = 1; a = -1 and b = -2 ; and a = 2 while b = -2.

Now for the hypothetical part. Here is the solution for the combined information. We don't know anything about *b* or *c*. But if $b > c$, then both expressions marked with b - c will be positive. If $b < c$, then the expression b - c in the numerator will be negative. Therefore, we can't tell whether the whole expression is less than 0.

Statement (2) is insufficient. Here is a solution to the second statement:

$$b > c \qquad \text{Is } \frac{(a - b)^3 (b - c)}{(a + b)^2 (b + c)^2} < 0?$$

$$\text{Is } \frac{(\pm)(+)}{(+)(+)} < 0?$$

If $b > c$, this tells us that the expression marked b - c is positive. Again, pick some numbers to prove this including: a = 2 when b = 1 ; a = -1 when b = -2 ; and a = 2 when b = -2. Now for the hypothetical part. We don't know anything about *a* or *b*. If $a > b$, then both a - b expressions will be positive; if $a < b$ then both a - b expressions will be negative. Therefore, we can't tell whether the whole expression is less than 0.

Now in terms of combining the statements. Knowing that $a > b$ and $b > c$ tells us that both expressions in the numerator are positive. Therefore the entire expression will always be positive. Strangely the trickiest part of this problem may not be the math—but rather how to interpret the result. Based on the information in Statements (1) and (2) combined, the answer to the original question is "no" because the whole expression is not less than 0; it is greater than or equal to zero. We must choose sufficiency!

105. Integers ($\int$)

Choice C
Classification: Number Properties (Integers & Non-Integers)
Snapshot: Do not assume all numbers are integers; think also in terms of non-integers.

The first statement is insufficient! This is tricky. Of course, we will want to pick some numbers. The key is to think not only in terms of integers but also in terms of non-integers (i.e., fractions and decimals).

	Pick Numbers:	Integers between x and y:
Statement (1)	$y = x + 5$	
	$6 = 1 + 5$	4 (ie., 2, 3, 4, 5)
	$5 = 0 + 5$	4 (ie., 1, 2, 3, 4)
	$4 = -1 + 5$	4 (ie., 0, 1, 2, 3)
	$5.5 = 0.5 + 5$	5 (ie., 1, 2, 3, 4, 5)

In short, there is either four or five integers between x and y. There are four integers between x and y if we assume x and y are integers and there are five integers between x and y if we assume x and y are non-integers.

The second statement is also insufficient. Knowing that $x = \sqrt{5}$ tells us nothing about y which could be any number—1 or 1,000,000. Let's put the statements together, approximating $\sqrt{5}$ as 2.2.

Using Statement (1) & (2):

$$y = x + 5$$
$$y = 2.2 + 5$$
$$7.2 = 2.2 + 5$$

∴ There are exactly 5 integers between x and y (i.e., between 2.2 and 7.2) and these include integers 3, 4, 5, 6, and 7.

106. Between A and B ($\int \int$)

Choice C
Classification: Number Properties (Integers & Non-Integers)
Snapshot: This follow-up problem is also included to reinforce the need to think in terms of non-integers, not just integers.

Statement (2) is the easiest statement to start with. Knowing just that a and b are not integers, leads to such a wide range of numerical possibilities that it is easy to see insufficiency. Try picking numbers such as: a = 2.5 while b = 0.5 or a = 1,000,000.5 while b = 0.5.

Statement (1) proves more difficult to catch. It looks to be sufficient but ends up being insufficient.

Pick Numbers:	Integers between x and y:
a - b = 4	
5 - 1 = 4	3 (ie., 2, 3, 4)
4 - 0 = 4	3 (ie., 1, 2, 3)
3 - (-1) = 4	3 (ie., 0, 1, 2)
4.5 - 0.5 = 4.0	4 (ie., 0, 1, 2, 3, 4)

107. Units Digit ($\int \int$)

Choice E
Classification: Number Properties (Multiples/Squares & Cubes)
Snapshot: The spotlight is on those numbers—0, 1, 5 and 6—which have the same units' digit whether squared or cubed. Don't forget the number "6"!

Statement (1) states that y is a multiple of 8. Potential numbers for become 8, 16, 24, 32, 40, etc. The units' digit of non-negative positive integer y could be 8, 6, 4, 2, 0, etc. So this stem is insufficient.

Statement (2) states that y^2 is the same as the units' digit of y^3. What non-negative integers satisfy this requirement? Such single digit integers include 0, 1, 5, and 6. This stem is also insufficient.

Integers:	Squaring:	Cubing:
0	$0^2 = \underline{0}$	$0^3 = \underline{0}$
1	$1^2 = \underline{1}$	$1^3 = \underline{1}$
5	$5^2 = 2\underline{5}$	$5^3 = 12\underline{5}$
6	$6^2 = 3\underline{6}$	$6^3 = 21\underline{6}$

Because both stems have multiple numbers that stratify them, they are individually insufficient. We can't tell what is the units' digit of non-negative integer y. Combining the information in both stems together, the overlap occurs on the numbers 0 and 6. This makes for Choice E. The trap answer is Choice C because many students will fail to see that numbers that end in 6 will have the same units' digit whether squared or cubed.

Author's note: For simplicity's sake, our four integers have included single digit integers, namely 0, 1, 5 and 6. Many other larger integers, which also end in 0, 1, 5, or 6, will also satisfy the precondition stipulated by Statement (2). These numbers include 10, 11, 15, 16, etc.

108. Factors ($\int\int$)

Choice D
Classification: Number Properties (Multiples & Factors)
Snapshot: This problem serves to review factors as well as prime number theory.

Statement (1) is sufficient because it tells us that *k* has 4 distinct factors; one more than 3, but one less than 5. That is, the integer 9 has three distinct factors: 1, 3 and 9. The integer 81 has five distinct factors: 1, 3, 9, 27 and 81. Therefore, by implication, *k* must have four distinct factors.

Statement (2) also tells us that *k* has four distinct factors. If *k* is the product of two distinct prime factors, its factors must be: 1, *x*, *y*, *xy*. Test this out. Take 2 x 3 = 6. Six is the product of two distinct prime factors. How many factors does 6 have? It has four factors: 1, 2, 3 and 6. How about 3 x 5 = 15? How many factors does 15 have? It has four factors: 1, 3, 5 and 15.

109. Multiples ($\int$)

Choice A
Classification: Number Properties (Multiples & Factors)
Snapshot: Pick "easy numbers" for problems involving multiples. Remember that multiples are always greater than or equal to a given number; factors are always less than or equal to a given number.

Pick numbers. For Statement (1), if *x* is a multiple of *y*, then the following are possibilities:

$\frac{x}{y}$	$\frac{1}{1}$	$\frac{2}{1}$	$\frac{4}{2}$	$\frac{8}{1}$

Statement (1) is sufficient. Obviously, if *x* is a multiple of *y* then 2*x* will also be a multiple of *y*.

Statement (2) however is insufficient. Let's pick the exact same numbers. For example, if *y* is 2 and *x* is 1 then 2*x* could be a multiple of *y*. Likewise if *y* is 2 and *x* is 2 then 2*x* is a multiple of *y*. But 2*x* might not be a multiple of *y*. For example, if *y* is 8 and *x* is 1, then 2*x* is not a multiple of *y* because 2 x 1 is not a multiple of 8.

$\frac{y}{x}$	$\frac{1}{1}$	$\frac{2}{1}$	$\frac{4}{2}$	$\frac{8}{1}$

110. Prime Time ($\int\int$)

Choice E
Classification: Number Properties (Prime Numbers)
Snapshot: Since the number 2 is the only even prime number, look for it to play a pivotal role in the solution to a prime number problem.

Statement (1) is insufficient. Knowing that *n* is a prime number does not tell us if n + 1 is a prime number. Ex. 2 + 1 = 3 (prime number) but 3 + 1 = 4 (non-prime number). Statement (2) is insufficient. Knowing that n + 2 is not a prime number does not tell us if n + 1 is a prime number. For example, the numbers which satisfy Statement (2) include 2, 4, 6, 7 and 8. Now using these numbers to answer the original question: Is n + 1 a prime number? we find: 2 + 1 = 3 (prime); 4 + 1 = 5 (prime); 6 + 1 = 7 (prime); 7 + 1 = 8 (non-prime); and 8 + 1 = 9 (non-prime).

Putting the stems together, we have (at least) two numbers which satisfy both stems. These include 2 and 7. So finally, "Is n + 1 a prime number?" It depends. Proof: 2 + 1 = 3 (prime) but 7 + 1 = 8 (non-prime).

111. Prime Time #2 (𝄞 𝄞 𝄞)

Choice C
Classification: Number Properties (Prime Numbers)
Snapshot: Just because the product of two numbers is odd, does not mean that both of the numbers are positive.

For Statement (1), let's pick from the prime numbers 2, 3, 5, 7. We can quickly see that 2 + 3 = 5 is a prime but that 3 + 5 = 8 is not a prime. So just knowing that x and y are prime doesn't give us a definite "yes" or "no" answer as to the question, "Is x + y a prime number?"

Let's also pick numbers for Statement (2): 3 x 1 = 3 and 3 x 5 = 15. Also, 3 x -1 = -3 and 5 x -1 = -5. This is particularly tricky because we will likely not think in terms of negative numbers. In short, Statement (2) is insufficient because 3 + 1 = 4 is not a prime number but 3 + (-1) = 2 is a prime number!

Putting the statements together, we must pick numbers which satisfy both statements—that is, numbers which are primes and which when multiplied together are odd. And we know that two odd numbers added together equal an even number. Therefore, the answer to the question, "Is x + y a prime number?" is most certainly "no", leading to an overall answer for this question of "sufficient."

112. F.O.I.L (𝄞)

Choice C
Classification: Number Properties (Factoring)
Snapshot: When both stems are insufficient in a "value" data sufficiency question, a single value in common between the sets will lead to Choice C (i.e., "overall sufficiency").

Since there are at least two answers for each stem, both stems are individually insufficient. But since there is a single value, and only one single value shared by both statements (i.e., the integer 2), both stems are together sufficient.

Factoring is a math process that seeks to find those numbers which would cause an equation to be equal to 0. For this reason, we typically set the equation equal to 0 to find these numbers.

Statement (1):

$$a^2 - a = 2$$
$$a^2 - a - 2 = 0$$
$$(a - 2)(a + 1) = 0 \qquad \text{Factors: } a \Rightarrow 2, -1$$

Statement (2):

$$a^2 + a = 6$$
$$a^2 + a - 6 = 0$$
$$(a - 2)(a + 3) = 0 \qquad \text{Factors: } a \Rightarrow 2, -3$$

113. X-Factor (⌇)

Choice E
Classification: Number Properties (Factoring)
Snapshot: When both stems are insufficient in a "value" Data Sufficiency question, two or more values in common between the sets will lead to Choice E.

Since there are at least two answers for each statement, both statements are individually insufficient. And since there are two (or more) values in common between the statements, namely 0 and 1, the statements together are insufficient.

$(1)\ x^2 - x = 0$
$\quad x(x - 1) = 0$ $\qquad\qquad$ Factors: $x \Rightarrow 0, 1$

$(2)\ x^3 - x = 0$
$\quad x(x^2 - 1) = 0$
$\quad x(x - 1)(x + 1) = 0$ $\qquad$ Factors: $x \Rightarrow 0, 1, -1$

Author's note: There are two situations to watch out for with respect to "two-variable, two-equation" scenarios on the Data Sufficiency section of the exam. The first occurs with respect to *non-distinct equations* and the second occurs with respect to *variables which cancel*.

What is the value of *x*?

$\quad$ (1) $3x + y = 7$
$\quad$ (2) $2y = 14 - 6x$

The above problem looks very much like a answer Choice C but, it in fact, answer Choice E, is correct. After all, each statement will by itself be insufficient but together they will prove sufficient. This would be true assuming that both equations are distinct equations (and we would simply substitute for one of the variables and solve for the other variable). However, they are not. In fact they are identical equations. Therefore the value of *x* cannot be determined.

What is the value of r?

$\quad$ (1) $4r + 3s = 5r + 2s$
$\quad$ (2) $3(r + s) = 9 + 3s$

The above problem also looks very much to be answer Choice C but it is in fact answer Choice B, which is correct. In the second statement, the variable *s* cancels and *r* is equal to 3. Although both equations are distinct equations, if a variable cancels in one of the equations, the value of the other variable will be determinable.

114. Reciprocal ($\int$)

Choice E
Classification: Number Properties (Inequalities)
Snapshot: This problem highlights the efficacy of picking from a small set of manageable numbers: 1, 2, -1, -2, $\frac{1}{2}$, -$\frac{1}{2}$ and 0.

Statement (1) is insufficient.
Since x >y, we try the following three pairs of numbers: 2, 1 and -1, -2 and 2, -2.

   i) When x = 2 and y = 1 then $\frac{2}{1} > \frac{1}{2} \Rightarrow$ yes!

   ii) When x = -1 and y = -2 then $\frac{-1}{-2} > \frac{-2}{-1} \Rightarrow$ no!

   iii) When x = 2 and y = -2 then $\frac{2}{-2} > \frac{-2}{2} \Rightarrow$ no!

Statement (2) is insufficient.
Since xy >0, we try 2, 1 and 1, 2 (simply reverse the order of the numbers).

   i) When x = 2 and y = 1 then $\frac{2}{1} > \frac{1}{2} \Rightarrow$ yes!

   ii) When x = 1 and y = 2 then $\frac{1}{2} > \frac{2}{1} \Rightarrow$ no!

Since we have already discovered insufficiency for the second statement, there is no need to try negative numbers. The mere juxtaposition of the positive numbers (i.e., 1, 2 and 2, 1) is enough to create insufficiency. However, when we have a double "I" situation (meaning both statements are individually insufficient), we put the statements together and ask: "Is there a pair of big seven numbers that satisfy both statements at the same time and yet lead to completely different answers (i.e., 'yes' or 'no')". The answer to this question is "yes." The numbers are 2, 1 and -1, -2. These are exactly the numbers we tested in Statement (1). Depending on whether we use a set of positive or negative numbers, we get two different answers to the question, "Is $\frac{x}{y} > \frac{y}{x}$?" One answer is "yes" and the second is "no." The answer is Choice E.

Author's note: When picking numbers for Data Sufficiency problems, particularly for "open-ended inequality problems," think first in terms of the "big seven" numbers. Open-ended inequality problems might be defined as problems in which virtually any number can be chosen for substitution. These include *Problems 102-108* in this section.

What are the "big seven" numbers? The "big seven" numbers are: 1, 2, -1, -2, $\frac{1}{2}$, -$\frac{1}{2}$ and 0. The words "big seven" appear in quotation marks because these numbers are obviously not big at all. They are small, manageable numbers.

Why do the "big seven" numbers work so well? Their secret lies in their *all-roundedness*. They offer a consistent, controlled base to work from when selecting numbers. They are representative of a large cross section of numbers, meaning that they embody the basic properties of all numbers. Review the number line below with the "big seven" numbers represented. Number properties are all about how numbers behave. For example, how do numbers behave when squared or cubed? Think of the "big seven" numbers as representatives. The way the number 2 behaves when squared or cubed is the same way any number greater than 1 behaves when squared or cubed. So the number 2 is our representative for numbers greater than 1 and it would make little sense to try other numbers such as 3 and 4. The way fractions such as $\frac{1}{2}$ behave when squared or cubed is similar to the way fractions between 0 and 1 behave when squared or cubed. In other words, it makes little sense to pick other fractions for substitution such as $\frac{1}{4}$ or $\frac{3}{4}$ because $\frac{1}{2}$ is our "big seven" representative for fractions between 0 and 1.

Why do the "big seven" numbers appear in the "egg" in pairs and on different levels? Answer—to indicate hierarchy. Try positive numbers first, then negatives, and then fractions. In other words, we should consider the positive numbers 1 and 2, before the negative numbers -1 and -2 and before the fractions $\frac{1}{2}$ and $-\frac{1}{2}$. If a statement can be proven insufficient using only positive numbers then there is no need to concern ourselves with negative numbers. Zero is a reserve number. Remember that 0 and 1 stay the same regardless of whether each is squared or cubed.

Question: "Should we have tried fractions in the problem above?"
Answer: No. There is no need. Fractions (i.e., $\frac{1}{2}, -\frac{1}{2}$) are used only when we have squares or cubes in the statements (stems) themselves.

115. Fraction (⚲ ⚲)

Choice E
Classification: Number Properties (Inequalities)
Snapshot: In terms of picking numbers, observe the importance of picking from both positive and negative integers.

Statement (1) is insufficient.
Since $ab>0$, we try 1, 2 and 2, 1 (in that order).

i) When $a = 1$ and $b = 2$ then $0<\frac{1}{2}<1 \Rightarrow$ yes!

ii) When $a = 2$ and $b = 1$ then $0<\frac{2}{1}<1 \Rightarrow$ no!

Statement (2) is insufficient.
Since $a - b<0$, we try 1, 2 and -2, -1.

i) When $a = 1$ and $b = 2$ then $0<\frac{1}{2}<1 \Rightarrow$ yes!

ii) When $a = -2$ and $b = -1$ then $0<\frac{-2}{-1}<1 \Rightarrow$ no!

So in putting the statements together, we ask the question: "Is there a pair of numbers that satisfy both stems simultaneously but which lead to different answers to the original question?" And the answer is "yes"; the numbers 1, 2 and -2, -1 in that order lead to one "yes" answer and one "no" answer. Overall, this results in *insufficiency* so answer Choice E is correct.

116. Z-Ray (⚲)

Choice A
Classification: Number Properties (Inequalities)
Snapshot: For problems in which the statements contain squares and cubes, we should instinctively try fractions (i.e., $\frac{1}{2}, -\frac{1}{2}$) in addition to positive and negative integers. All of these numbers are, of course, part of the "big seven" numbers.

Statement (1) is sufficient. If $-z<z$, then this tells us that z must be positive. Therefore in answering the question, "Is $z<0$?" the answer, according to Statement (1) is clearly "no." There is no need to substitute numbers to prove this.
Statement (2) is insufficient. Which of the "big seven" numbers satisfy the condition $z^3<z^2$? Answer: -2, -1, $-\frac{1}{2}$, and $\frac{1}{2}$. However,

upon substituting these numbers into the question "Is $z < 0$?" we find that three of these numbers, -2, -1, $-\frac{1}{2}$, allow us to answer "yes" but the positive fraction $\frac{1}{2}$ leads to a "no" answer. Note that, with respect to Statement (2), the numbers 1, 2, and 0 do not satisfy this pre-condition ($z^3 < z^3$) and therefore do not qualify.

117. Ps & Qs ( )

Choice C
Classification: Number Properties (Inequalities)
Snapshot: Although we could also substitute numbers into this problem, it is not necessary because conceptualization is always faster than substituting numbers. This is an example where there is no need to substitute numbers to achieve an outcome.

The first and second statements are clearly insufficient. The first stem contains no information about r while the second statement contains no information about p. Taken together, however, they are sufficient and we can answer the question with "no"; p x r is not greater than 0 because p x r is less than 0.

Conceptually, the stem $pq > 0$ tells us that both p and q are both either positive or negative (they have the same signs). The stem $qr < 0$ tells us that one of either q or r is negative while the other is positive. So combining this information: If p and q are positive then r is negative and that means p x r is less than 0. If p and q are negative then r is positive and that means p x r is negative.

118. Kookoo ( )

Choice B
Classification: Number Properties (Inequalities)
Snapshot: This is a very intimidating looking problem. The fractions $\frac{1}{2}$ and $-\frac{1}{2}$ become keys to solving it.

Statement (1) is insufficient. If $k^2 > k^3$ then k could only be one of -2, -1, $-\frac{1}{2}$, and $\frac{1}{2}$. The negative numbers just listed lead to a "yes" answer but the positive number $\frac{1}{2}$ leads to a "no" answer. In the second statement, If $k^3 > k^2$, then k must be a positive number greater than 1 and the answer to the question "Is $k < 0$?" is "no." (Note: The question, "Is $k + k < k$?" is also equivalent to "Is $k < 0$?" (add $-k$ to both sides) in so far as the only way for $k + k$ to be less than k is for k to be a negative number).

119. ABCD (♪ ♪)

Choice E
Classification: Number Properties (Inequalities)
Snapshot: Many candidates will pick Choice C for this problem. Force yourself to try negative numbers even if things look sufficient.

First of all, the two statements are individually insufficient. Statement (1) makes no mention of the variable b; Statement (2) makes no mention of the variable a. Therefore, neither statement is sufficient to answer the question of whether $a + b$ is greater than $c + d$.

The trap answer is Choice C. Many candidates will try positive numbers only, failing to try negative ones. Also, don't worry if every number is not strictly a "big seven" number. The solution below makes use of the number 3.

First try some positive numbers:

Statement (1):

$$a > c + d \qquad\qquad 3 > 1 + 1$$

Statement (2):

$$b > c + d \qquad\qquad 3 > 1 + 1$$

Conclusion:

$$a + b > c + d \qquad\qquad 3 + 3 > 1 + 1$$
Since 6 is greater than 2, the answer is "yes."

Next try some negative numbers:

Statement (1):

$$a > c + d \qquad\qquad -1 > -1 + -1$$

Statement (2):

$$b > c + d \qquad\qquad -1 > -1 + -1$$

Conclusion:

$$a + b > c + d \qquad\qquad -1 + -1 > -1 + -1$$
Since -2 is not greater than -2, the answer is "no."

And for the record:

Statement (1):

$$a > c + d \qquad\qquad -3 > -2 + -2$$

Statement (2):

$$b > c + d \qquad\qquad -3 > -2 + -2$$

Conclusion:

$$a + b > c + d \qquad\qquad -3 + -3 > -2 + -2$$
Since -6 is not greater than -4, the answer is also "no."

120. Upright (𝕊 𝕊 𝕊)

Choice C

Classification: Number Properties (Inequalities)

Snapshot: This problem provides the ultimate workout in terms of picking numbers. If we can quickly conceptualize all six scenarios below, we'll be able to tackle this type of question on the GMAT. Attack this problem using only four of the big seven numbers: 2, -2, 1 and -1.

Conceptual setup: Since we do not know whether b is positive or negative, we can assign b a value of +1 (per Scenarios 1, 2 and 3) and then b a value of -1 (per Scenarios 4, 5 and 6). Six possibilities unfold:

	Substitution:	Result:	Conclusion:
Scenario 1:	$\frac{2}{+1} > \frac{1}{+1}$	$2 > 1$	$a > c$
	(where $a = 2$, $c = 1$, $b = +1$)		
Scenario 2:	$\frac{-1}{+1} > \frac{-2}{+1}$	$-1 > -2$	$a > c$
	(where $a = -1$, $c = -2$, $b = +1$)		
Scenario 3:	$\frac{2}{+1} > \frac{-2}{+1}$	$2 > -2$	$a > c$
	(where $a = 2$, $c = -2$, $b = +1$)		

Note: As long as *b* is positive, *a* will be <u>greater</u> than c.

	Substitution:	Result:	Conclusion:
Scenario 4:	$\frac{1}{-1} > \frac{2}{-1}$	$-1 > -2$	$a < c$
	(where $a = 1$, $c = 2$, $b = -1$)		
Scenario 5:	$\frac{-2}{-1} > \frac{-1}{-1}$	$2 > 1$	$a < c$
	(where $a = -2$, $c = -1$, $b = -1$)		
Scenario 6:	$\frac{-2}{-1} > \frac{+2}{-1}$	$2 > -2$	$a < c$
	(where $a = -2$, $c = 2$, $b = -1$)		

Note: As long as *b* is negative, *a* will be <u>less</u> than c.

Statement (1) is insufficient. Given the precondition $\frac{a}{b} > \frac{c}{b}$, and the fact that *a* is positive, only Scenarios 1, 3 and 4 are possibilities. In Scenarios 1 and 3, *a* is greater than c, but in Scenario 4 *a* is less than c. We do not know whether $a > c$.

Statement (2) is insufficient. Given the precondition $\frac{a}{b} > \frac{c}{b}$, and the fact that c is negative, only Scenarios 2, 3 and 5 are possibilities. In Scenarios 2 and 3, *a* is greater than c, but in Scenario 5, *a* is less than c. We do not know whether $a > c$.

Summary: Given that both stems are insufficient, and the fact that *a* is positive and *c* is negative, the only scenario that is possible is Scenario 3, where $a > c$. We have a definitive answer to the question, "Is *a* greater than *c*?", and the answer rests with Choice C.

Don't fall into the trap of multiplying the original equation through by *b* to get $a > c$ and conclude, outright, that $a > c$. Because we do not know whether *b* is positive or negative, multiplying through by *-b* would change the inequality sign and reverse the result. That is, when we multiply or divide both sides of an inequality by a negative number, the inequality sign must be reversed.

If *b* is positive:

$$\cancel{b}\frac{a}{\cancel{b}} > \cancel{b}\frac{c}{\cancel{b}} = a > c$$

If *b* is negative:

$$-\cancel{b}\frac{a}{-\cancel{b}} > -\cancel{b}\frac{c}{-\cancel{b}} = a < c$$

121. Central Measures (𝄐 𝄐)

Choice E
Classification: Statistics (Measures of Central Tendency)
Snapshot: This problem highlights the need to understand the three measures of central tendency—mean, median, and mode.

Pick some numbers. These numbers prove that both Statements (1) and Statement (2) are insufficient. According to the data below, Set A has a higher median than Set B and yet it has a lower mean (arithmetic). We could easily arrange the data to prove that Set A could have a higher mean as well. Set A also has a higher mode than Set B but, as noted, it has a larger mean than Set A. And we could easily arrange the data to prove that Set A could have a higher mean as well.

	Median:	Mode:	Mean:
Set A: 1.0, 2.0, 6.0, 8.0, 8.0	6.0	8.0	$\frac{25}{5}$ = 5.0
Set B: 3.0, 3.0, 5.0, 9.0, 10.0	5.0	3.0	$\frac{30}{5}$ = 6.0

Author's note: The GMAT requires us to know how to calculate tendency—mean, median, and mode. Calculating the mean is easy; that's the way we typically calculate average. We add up all the items and divide by the number of items in a given set. Median is the "middle most" number. Mode is the most "frequently recurring" number. Something interesting happens when we have an even number of data in a set. Ex. 4.0, 4.0, 5.0, 6.0, 10.0 and 10.0. Here the median is $\frac{5.0 + 6.0}{2}$ = 5.5 and the mode is both 4.0 and 10.0. In an even set of data we will calculate the median by taking the average of the middle two terms but we never average modes.

122. Dispersion (〰 〰)

Choice A

Classification: Statistics (Standard Deviation)

Snapshot: We do not need to know the formula for standard deviation (nor are we required to know it for the GMAT). All we need to know is that "standard deviation is a measure of dispersion." The more dispersed data is, the higher the standard deviation; the less dispersed data is, the lower the standard deviation.

Pick two sets of seven consecutive even integers. For example: 2, 4, 6, 8, 10, 12, 14 and 94, 96, 98, 100, 102, 104 and 106. We can tell by looking that the arithmetic mean of these sets are 8 and 100 respectively. The relative distances that any of these numbers are from their respective arithmetic means are identical. That is, 2 is just as far from 8 as 94 is from 100 and 14 is just a far from 8 as 106 is from 100. What ever the standard deviation may be, it will be identical for both sets and, for that matter, for any seven consecutive even integers.

In Statement (2), let's pick two numbers which average to 49 but which are greatly different. For example, we could pick 1 and 97 or 48 and 50. However, even though their arithmetic means are identical, the standard deviation of these two sets would be drastically different.

Another term we need to know for the GMAT is "range." Range is the smallest item in a set subtracted from the largest item (or the positive difference between the largest and smallest numbers). The range for both of the above sets is 12; that is, 14 - 2 = 12 and 106 -94 = 12.

CHAPTER 7

SENTENCE CORRECTION

"Grammar and logic free language from being at the mercy of the tone of voice." (Resenstock-Huessy)

SUBJECT-VERB AGREEMENT

123. Leader (𝄞)

The activities of our current leader <u>have led to a significant increase in the number of issues relating to the role of the military in non-military, nation-building exercises.</u>

A) have led to a significant increase in the number of issues relating to the role of the military in non-military, nation-building exercises.

B) have been significant in the increase in the amount of issues relating to the role of the military in non-military, nation-building exercises.

C) has led to a significant increase in the number of issues relating to the role of the military in non-military, nation-building exercises.

D) has been significant in the increase in the number of issues relating to the role of the military in non-military, nation-building exercises.

E) has significantly increased the amount of issues relating to the role of the military in non-military, nation-building exercises.

124. Mammal (𝄞 𝄞)

According to scientists at the University of California, the pattern of changes that have occurred in human DNA over the millennia <u>indicate the possibility that every mammal alive today might be descended from a single female ancestor who</u> lived in Africa sometime between 750,000 and 1,000,000 years ago.

A) indicate the possibility that every mammal alive today might be a descendant from a single female ancestor who

B) indicate that every mammal alive today might possibly be a descendant of a single female ancestor who had

C) may indicate that every mammal alive today has descended from a single female ancestor who had

D) indicates that every mammal alive today might be a descendant of a single female ancestor who

E) indicates that every mammal alive today may be a descendant from a single female ancestor who

125. Critics' Choice (𝄞 𝄞)

<u>In this critically acclaimed film, there are a well-developed plot and an excellent cast of characters.</u>

A) In this critically acclaimed film, there are a well-developed plot and an excellent cast of characters.

B) In this critically acclaimed film, there is a well-developed plot and an excellent cast of characters.

C) In this film, which is critically acclaimed, there is a well-developed plot and an excellent cast of characters.

D) In this film, which has been critically acclaimed, there are a well-developed plot and an excellent cast of characters.

E) There is a well-developed plot and an excellent cast of characters in this critically acclaimed film.

126. Recommendations (⌇ ⌇)

Implementing the consultants' recommendations is expected to result in both increased productivity and decreased costs.

A) Implementing the consultants' recommendations is expected to result in

B) Implementing the consultants' recommendations are expected to result in

C) The expected result of enacting the consultants' recommendations are

D) The expected results of enacting the consultants' recommendations is

E) It is expected that enactment of the consultants' recommendations are to result in

127. Vacation (⌇)

Neither Martha or her sisters are going on vacation.

A) Neither Martha or her sisters are going on vacation.

B) Neither Martha or her sisters is going on vacation.

C) Neither any of her sisters nor Martha are going on vacation.

D) Neither Martha nor her sisters are going on vacation.

E) Neither Martha nor her sisters is going on vacation.

PRONOUN REFERENCE

128. Inland Taipan (⌇ ⌇)

The Inland Taipan or Fierce Snake of central Australia is widely regarded to be the world's most venomous snake; the poison from its bite invariably kills its victims unless treated within thirty minutes of an incident.

A) regarded to be the world's most venomous snake; the poison from its bite invariably kills its victims unless treated

B) regarded as the world's most venomous snake; the poison from its bite invariably kills its victims unless treated

C) regarded to be the world's most venomous snake; the poison from its bite invariably kills its victims unless it is treated

D) regarded as the world's most venomous snake; the poison from its bite invariably kills its victims unless they are treated

E) regarded to be the world's most venomous snake; the poison from its bite invariably kills its victims unless they are treated

129. Valuation (⸱ ⸱ ⸱ **)**

Financial formulas for valuing companies do not apply to Internet companies in the same way as they do to traditional businesses, because they are growing and seldom have ascertainable sales and cash flows.

A) Financial formulas for valuing companies do not apply to Internet companies in the same way as they do to traditional businesses, because they are growing and seldom have ascertainable sales and cash flows.

B) Internet companies are not subject to the same applicability of financial formulas for valuing these companies as compared with traditional businesses, because they are growing and seldom have ascertainable sales and cash flows.

C) Because they are growing and seldom have ascertainable sales and cash flows, financial formulas for valuing these companies do not apply to Internet companies in the same way as they do to traditional businesses.

D) Because they are growing and seldom have ascertainable sales and cash flows, Internet companies are not subject to the same applicability of financial valuation formulas as are traditional businesses.

E) Because Internet companies are growing and seldom have ascertainable sales and cash flows, financial formulas for valuing these companies do not apply to them in the same way as to traditional businesses.

MODIFICATION

130. Metal Detector (⸱ **)**

Using a metal detector, old coins and other valuables can be located by hobbyists even though they are buried in the sand and dirt.

A) Using a metal detector, old coins and other valuables can be located by hobbyists even though they are buried in the sand and dirt.

B) Old coins and other valuables can be located by hobbyists using a metal detector even though they are buried in the sand and dirt.

C) Using a metal detector, hobbyists can locate old coins and other valuables even though they are buried in the sand and dirt.

D) Buried in the sand and dirt, old coins and other valuables can be located by hobbyists using a metal detector.

E) A metal detector can be used to locate old coins and other valuables that are buried in the sand and dirt by a hobbyist.

131. Hungary (⸱ ⸱ **)**

With less than one percent of the world's population, Hungarians have contributed disproportionately to the fields of modern math and applied science.

A) With

B) Having

C) Despite having

D) Although constituting

E) In addition to accounting for

132. Management (♪ ♪)

<u>Based on their review of first quarter operating results, management's decision was</u> to forgo expansion plans and adopt a conservative marketing approach aimed at streamlining product offerings.

    A) Based on their review of first quarter operating results, management's decision was

    B) Based on a review of first quarter operating results, management made the decision

    C) Based on their review of first quarter operating results, management decided

    D) Based on first quarter operating results, management had decided

    E) Based on first quarter operating results, management decided

133. Natural Beauty (♪ ♪)

Plastic surgeons who perform surgery for non-medical reasons defend their practice on the basis of the free rights of their patients; many others in the health field, however, contend that plastic surgery degrades natural beauty, <u>which they liken to reconstructing a national park.</u>

    A) which they liken to reconstructing a national park.

    B) which they liken to a national park with reconstruction done to it.

    C) which they liken to reconstruction done on a national park.

    D) likening it to a national park with reconstruction done to it.

    E) likening it to reconstructing a national park.

PARALLELISM

134. Massage (♪ ♪)

Massage creates a relaxing, therapeutic, and rejuvenating experience both for <u>your body and your well-being.</u>

    A) both for your body and your well-being.

    B) for both your body and your well-being.

    C) both for your body and well-being.

    D) for both your body and well-being.

E) both for your body as well as your well-being.

135. Cannelloni ($\int$)

<u>Cannelloni has and always will be my favorite Italian dish.</u>

      A) Cannelloni has and always will be my favorite Italian dish.

      B) Cannelloni was, has, and always will be my favorite Italian dish.

      C) Cannelloni was and always will be my favorite Italian dish.

      D) Cannelloni has been and always will be my favorite Italian dish.

      E) Cannelloni is, has, and always will be my favorite Italian dish.

136. Europeans ($\int \int \int$)

<u>Italy is famous for its composers and musicians, France, for its chefs and philosophers, and Poland, for its mathematicians and logicians.</u>

      A) Italy is famous for its composers and musicians, France, for its chefs and philosophers, and Poland, for its mathematicians and logicians.

      B) Italy is famous for its composers and musicians, France for its chefs and philosophers, Poland for its mathematicians and logicians.

      C) Italy is famous for its composers and musicians; France for its chefs and philosophers; and Poland for its mathematicians and logicians.

      D) Italy is famous for its composers and musicians. France for its chefs and philosophers. Poland for its mathematicians and logicians.

      E) Italy, France, and Poland are famous for their composers and musicians, chefs and philosophers, and mathematicians and logicians.

COMPARISONS

137. Sweater ($\int$)

Although neither sweater is really the right size, <u>the smallest one fits best.</u>

      A) the smallest one fits best.

      B) the smallest one fits better.

      C) the smallest one is better fitting.

      D) the smaller of the two fits best.

E) the smaller one fits better.

138. Perceptions ( )

Because right-brained individuals do not employ convergent thinking processes, <u>like left-brained individuals</u>, they may not notice and remember the same level of detail as their counterparts.

     A) like left-brained individuals,

     B) unlike a left-brained individual,

     C) as left-brained individuals,

     D) as left-brained individuals do,

     E) as a left-brained individual can,

139. Bear ( )

<u>Like the Alaskan brown bear and most other members of the bear family, the diet of the grizzly bear consists</u> of both meat and vegetation.

     A) Like the Alaskan brown bear and most other members of the bear family, the diet of the grizzly bear consists

     B) Like those of the Alaskan brown bear and most other members of the bear family, the diets of a grizzly bear consist

     C) Like the Alaskan brown bear and most other members of the bear family, the grizzly bear has a diet consisting

     D) Just like the diet of the Alaskan brown bear and most other members of the bear family, the diets of the grizzly bear consist

     E) Similar to the diets of the Alaskan brown bear and most other members of the bear family, grizzly bears have a diet which consists

140. Angel ( )

<u>She sings like an angel sings.</u>

     A) She sings like an angel sings.

     B) She sings like an angel does.

     C) She sings as an angel sings.

     D) She sings as if an angel.

     E) She sings as if like an angel.

141. Testing (𝓢 𝓢 𝓢)

Unlike a college entrance exam, which follows a standardized format, <u>the formats for I.Q. tests vary considerably in both content and length.</u>

    A) the formats for I.Q. tests vary considerably in both content and length.

    B) the format for an I.Q. test varies considerably in both content and length.

    C) an I.Q. test follows a format that varies considerably in both content and length.

    D) an I.Q. test follows formats that vary considerably in both content and length.

    E) I.Q. tests follow formats that vary considerably in both content and length.

142. Assemblée Nationale (𝓢 𝓢)

<u>As Parliament is the legislative government body of Great Britain,</u> the Assemblée Nationale is the legislative government body of France.

    A) As Parliament is the legislative government body of Great Britain,

    B) As the legislative government body of Great Britain is Parliament,

    C) Just like the legislative government body of Great Britain, which is Parliament,

    D) Just as Parliament is the legislative government body of Great Britain, so

    E) Just as the Government of Britain's legislative branch is Parliament,

143. Geography (𝓢 𝓢)

Despite the fact that the United States is a superpower, <u>American high school students perform more poorly on tests of world geography and international affairs than do</u> their Canadian counterparts.

    A) American high school students perform more poorly on tests of world geography and international affairs than do

    B) American high school students perform more poorly on tests of world geography and international affairs as compared with

    C) American high school students perform more poorly on tests of world geography and international affairs as compared to

    D) the American high school student performs more poorly on tests of world geography and international affairs than does

    E) the American high school student performs more poorly on tests of world geography and international affairs as compared with

144. Sir Isaac Newton (⌇)

Within the scientific community, the accomplishments of Sir Isaac Newton are referred to more often <u>than any</u> scientist, living or dead.

A) than any

B) than any other

C) than those of any

D) than are those of any

E) than those of any other

145. Soya (⌇ ⌇)

In addition to having more protein than meat does, <u>the protein in Soya beans is higher in quality than that in meat.</u>

A) the protein in Soya beans is higher in quality than that in meat.

B) the protein in Soya beans is higher in quality than it is in meat.

C) Soya beans have protein of higher quality than that in meat.

D) Soya bean protein is higher in quality than it is in meat.

E) Soya beans have protein higher in quality than meat.

VERB TENSES

146. Trend (⌇ ⌇)

<u>The percentage of people remaining single in Holland increased abruptly between 1980 and 1990 and continued to rise more gradually over the next 10 years.</u>

A) The percentage of people remaining single in Holland increased abruptly between 1980 and 1990 and continued to rise more gradually over the next ten years.

B) The percentage of people remaining single in Holland increased abruptly between 1980 and 1990 and has continued to rise more gradually over the next ten years.

C) The percentage of people remaining single in Holland increased abruptly between 1980 and 1990 and had continued to rise more gradually over the next ten years.

D) There had been an abrupt increase in the percentage of people remaining single in Holland increased abruptly between 1980 and 1990 and it continued to rise more gradually over the next ten years.

E) There was an abrupt increase in the percentage of people remaining single in Holland increased abruptly between 1980 and 1990 which continued to rise more gradually over the next ten years.

147. Golden Years ( )

A recent study has found that within the past few years, many executives <u>had elected early retirement rather than face</u> the threats of job cuts and diminishing retirement benefits.

A) had elected early retirement rather than face

B) had elected early retirement instead of facing

C) have elected early retirement instead of facing

D) have elected early retirement rather than facing

E) have elected to retire early rather than face

148. Fire ( )

<u>Most houses that were destroyed and heavily damaged in residential fires last year were</u> built without adequate fire detection apparatus.

A) Most houses that were destroyed and heavily damaged in residential fires last year were

B) Most houses that were destroyed or heavily damaged in residential fires last year had been

C) Most houses that were destroyed and heavily damaged in residential fires last year had been

D) Most houses that were destroyed or heavily damaged in residential fires last year have been

E) Most houses that were destroyed and heavily damaged in residential fires last year have been

149. Politics ( )

Although he <u>disapproved of the political platform set forth by incumbent President George Bush during the 2004 US federal election, Senator John Kerry later conceded</u> that there must be a basis for a cooperative government and urged members of both parties to seek compromise.

A) disapproved of the political platform set forth by incumbent President George Bush during the 2004 US federal election, Senator John Kerry later conceded

B) disapproved of the political platform set forth by incumbent President George Bush during the 2004 US federal election, Senator John Kerry had later conceded

C) has disapproved of the political platform set forth by incumbent President George Bush during the 2004 US federal election, Senator John Kerry later conceded

D) had disapproved of the political platform set forth by incumbent President George Bush during the 2004 US federal election, Senator John Kerry later conceded

E) had disapproved of the political platform set forth by incumbent President George Bush during the 2004 US federal election, Senator John Kerry had later conceded

150. B-School (⌇ ⌇)

As graduate management programs become more competitive in the coming years in terms of their promotional and financial undertakings, schools have been becoming more and more dependent on alumni networks, corporate sponsorships, and philanthropists.

    A) As graduate management programs become more competitive in the coming years in terms of their promotional and financial undertakings, schools have been becoming

    B) As graduate management programs are becoming more competitive in the coming years in terms of their promotional and financial undertakings, schools have been becoming

    C) As graduate management programs become more competitive in the coming years in terms of their promotional and financial undertakings, schools have become

    D) As graduate management programs are becoming more competitive in the coming years in terms of their promotional and financial undertakings, schools have become

    E) As graduate management programs become more competitive in the coming years in terms of their promotional and financial undertakings, schools will become

151. Summer in Europe (⌇ ⌇)

By the time we have reached France, we will have been backpacking for 12 weeks.

    A) By the time we have reached France, we will have been backpacking for 12 weeks.

    B) By the time we have reached France, we will have backpacked for 12 weeks.

    C) By the time we reach France, we will have been backpacking for 12 weeks.

    D) By the time we will have reached France, we will have backpacked for 12 weeks.

    E) By the time we reached France, we will have been backpacking for 12 weeks.

ANSWERS AND EXPLANATIONS

123. Leader (⌇)

Answer: Choice A
Classification: Subject-Verb Agreement
Snapshot: This problem is included to show subject-verb agreement and to highlight the role of prepositional phrases in disguising the subject and verb.

The subject of a sentence determines the verb (i.e., singular subjects take singular verbs; plural subjects take plural verbs) and the subject of this sentence is "activities" (plural). The intervening phrase "of our current leader" is a prepositional phrase, and prepositional phrases can never contain the subject of a sentence. Visually cut out this phrase. The subject is "activities," the verb is "have," not "has." Another distinction that needs to be drawn relates to the difference between *number* and *amount*. "Number" is used for countable items and "amount" for non-countable items. Therefore, we have no problem choosing Choice A as the correct answer after applying only two rules—the first is a subject-verb agreement rule followed by the number vs. amount grammatical distinction. Also, per Choices B and D, the clause "has/have been significant in the increase" is not only awkward but also passive.

Author's note: Prepositional phrases (i.e., phrases introduced by a preposition) can never contain the subject of a sentence. Prepositions are informally said to be words that describe "directions a squirrel can go," which if you know something about squirrels, means every direction possible. Prepositions include words such as:

> after, against, at, before, between, by, concerning, despite, down, from, in, off, on, onto, out, over, through, under, until, up, with

The prepositions—*of, to, by, for, from*—are perhaps the most commonly encountered on the GMAT exam.

124. Mammal (🐦 🐦)

Answer: Choice D
Classification: Subject-Verb Agreement
Snapshot: This problem is also included to highlight the role of prepositional phrases within subject-verb agreements.

The subject of the sentence is "pattern" which is singular and a singular subject takes the singular verb "indicates." An additional way to eliminate Choices A and B is through the unnecessary use of the words "might" and "possibility" which express the same idea; either *possibility* or *might* is required. Also, the use of *might* in Choice D is better than *may* (Choice E) because *might* more clearly indicates "possibility" than does *may*. In choosing between Choices D and E, the idiom "descendant of" is superior to the unidiomatic "descendant from." Finally, note that in Choices B and C, *had*, the auxiliary of *lived*, should be deleted because the simple past tense is correct. The past perfect is not required; the past perfect tense, which employs "had," is used to refer to an action that precedes some other action also occurring in the past. *See Chapter 4: The World of Letters*, Verb Tenses, pages 44-50.

Author's note: This problem complements the previous one. The former problem contained a plural subject ("activities") and a single item in the prepositional phrase ("current leader"). This problem contains a singular subject ("pattern") and a plural item in the prepositional phrase ("changes").

125. Critics' Choice (🐦 🐦)

Answer: Choice A
Classification: Subject-Verb Agreement
Snapshot: This problem is included to highlight "there is/there are" constructions in which the subject of the sentence comes after, not before, the verb.

The compound subject is plural—well-developed plot <u>and</u> an excellent cast of characters—and therefore requires the plural verb, *are*. Choices B, C and E are out because of the incorrect verb "is." Choices C and D employ roundabout constructions which are inferior to *In this critically acclaimed film*. Choice D also employs the passive construction *which has been critically acclaimed*. Choice E rearranges the sentence but still incorrectly employs the verb "is."

Author's note: The normal order in English sentences is Subject-Verb-Object. *There is* and *there are* constructions represent special situations when the verb comes before the subject, not after the subject. This is tricky. Another related example is:

> Incorrect: "Here is the introduction and chapters one through five."

> Correct: "Here <u>are</u> the introduction and chapters one through five."

In the above example, the compound subject "introduction <u>and</u> chapters one through five" necessitates using the plural verb "are."

Correct: "Here is the introduction as well as chapters one through five."

The following is a list of "pseudo compound subjects": *as well as, along with, besides, in addition to,* and *together with*. In short, these connecting words do not create a plural subject. The only connecting word that can make a series of singular nouns into a plural subject is "and." In fact, "and" always creates a plural subject with one exception. If two items joined by "and" are so intimately linked together as to be considered a single unit, then the subject is considered singular and a singular verb is required. For example:

"Eggs and bacon is Tiffany's favorite breakfast."
"Cigarette and cigar smoke is prohibited."

126. Recommendations (𝄞 𝄞)

Answer: Choice A
Classification: Subject-Verb Agreement
Snapshot: This problem is included to highlight gerund phrases which, when acting as subjects of a sentence, are always singular.

The gerund phrase "Implementing the consultants' recommendations" is the subject of the sentence. As gerund phrases are always singular, the correct verb here is "is." In Choice C, "expected result" requires the verb "is" whereas in Choice D, "expected results" requires the verb "are." In Choice E, the "it is" construction creates an unnecessarily weak opener and an awkward sentence style.

Author's note: Remember that gerunds and infinitives are always singular and take singular verbs.

Gerunds: Gerunds end in "ing" and function as nouns. Informally they may be referred to as "nouns that look like verbs but function as nouns." As is the case here, they may also be the subject of a sentence.

Eating vegetables is good for you.

"Eating" is a gerund but "eating vegetables" is the gerund phrase that acts as the singular subject of the sentence.

Infinitives: Infinitives combine the basic form of a verb, generally preceded by "to" and may function as nouns, adjectives, or adverbs. Informally they may be referred to as "nouns (or adjectives or adverbs) that start with prepositions." When used as a noun, they may also serve as the subject of a sentence.

To err is human. To forgive is divine.

127. Vacation (𝄞)

Answer: Choice D
Classification: Subject-Verb Agreement
Snapshot: This problem is included to highlight the handling of correlative conjunctions such as "either/or" and "neither/nor" which may require a singular or plural verb.

The consistent appearance of "neither" indicates a "neither...nor" relationship. We can eliminate Choices A and B outright. The correct verb is said to match what comes after the *nor* construction. Since *her sisters* in D is plural, the plural verb "are" does the trick.

In summary, singular subjects following "or" or "nor" always take a singular verb; plural subjects following "or" or "nor" take a plural verb. Stated another way, when two items are connected by "or" or "nor", the verb agrees with the closer subject.

That is, the verb only needs to agree with the subject that comes after "or" or "nor."

There are two potentially correct answers:

> "Neither Martha nor her sisters <u>are</u> going on vacation."
>
> or
>
> "Neither her sisters nor Martha <u>is</u> going on vacation."

Note that only the first alternative above is presented by answer Choice D.

128. Inland Taipan (𝄞 𝄞)

Answer: Choice D
Classification: Ambiguous Pronoun Reference
Snapshot: This problem is included to highlight the occasional need to add personal pronouns in order to minimize ambiguity.

This form of ambiguous reference is subtle. The original sentence is missing "they" and without the pronoun—*they*—the word "treated" might refer to "poison" or "victims"; "treated" is only supposed to refer to "victims." In Choice C, the pronoun "it" logically but incorrectly refers to "bite". Technically it is not the bite that needs to be treated but the actual victims. Choices A, C and E erroneously employ the idiom "regarded to be" when the correct idiom is "regarded as." See *Chapter 4: The World of Letters, Grammatical Idioms*.

Author's note: The GMAT Verbal Section requires choosing the "best" answer, not the "right" answer as required in the Quantitative Section. There are two situations in GMAT Sentence Correction in which grammatically correct sentences may not end up being correct answer choices. The first occurs in passive sentences and the second with the use of pronouns.

Passive sentences:

> Weak: Errors were found in the report.

> Better: The report contained errors.

Neither of the above two sentences is grammatically incorrect. However, as a rule of style, an active sentence will always be chosen in favor of a passive sentence (all things being equal).

Pronoun reference:

> Weak: Sam never argues with his father when he is drunk.

> Better: Sam never argues with his father when Sam is drunk.
>
> or:
>
> Better: When he is drunk, Sam never argues with his father.

None of the above sentences are grammatically incorrect. However, as a rule of style, a sentence must be both grammatically correct and contextually clear. The sentence "Sam never argues with his father when he is drunk" is grammatically correct but contextually vague. Grammatically it is Sam's father who is drunk (a pronoun modifies the nearest noun that came before it; here the pronoun "he" modifies the noun "father"), even though we feel it is Sam who is drunk. Thus the sentence needs to be rephrased to clear up potential ambiguity.

129. Valuation (𝄟 𝄟 𝄟)

Answer: Choice E
Classification: Ambiguous Pronoun Reference
Snapshot: This problem is included to highlight ambiguity arising from the use of personal pronouns, and seeks to clear up such ambiguity, not by replacing pronouns, but by rearranging the sentence itself. Part of the reason it garners a three-chili rating is because the problem is long, and somewhat difficult to read and analyze in two minutes—the standard time allotted for completing any and all GMAT problems.

The problem with Choices A and B is that the word "they" refers to traditional businesses; this is illogical because traditional businesses are not growing, Internet companies are. Remember that a pronoun modifies the closest noun that precedes it. The structure in Choice C makes it seem as if "financial formulas" are growing and this, of course, is farcical.

Choices A and C use the awkward, "do not apply to X in the same way as they do to Y". A more succinct rendition is found in Choice E: "do not apply to X in the same way as to Y." In Choices A, C and E, the verb "apply" is more powerful and therefore superior to the noun form "applicability" (as used in Choices B and D). The note below provides additional insight into this rule of writing style.

Author's note: A general rule in grammar is that we shouldn't change verbs (or adjectives) into nouns. Verbs are considered more powerful than nouns. The technical name for this is no-no is "nominalization"; we shouldn't nominalize. Here are some examples:

Verbs:	Nouns:
reduce	reduction
develop	development
rely	reliability

Adjectives:	Nouns:
precise	precision
creative	creativity
reasonable	reasonableness

So "reduction of costs" is best written "reduce costs"; "development of a five-year plan" is best written "develop a five-year plan"; "reliability of the data" is best written "rely on the data"; "precision of instruments" is best written "precise instruments"; "creativity of individuals" is best written "creative individuals"; and "reasonableness of the working hours" is best written "reasonable working hours."

Question: Did you learn in high school that you shouldn't begin a sentence with the word "because?" If so, forget that "rule." According to the conventions of Standard Written English (SWE), which, incidentally, the GMAT abides by, the word "because" functions as a subordinating conjunction. Its use is effectively identical to that of "as" or "since" and we can think of these three words as substitutes. In short, there's actually no rule of grammar or style preventing us from beginning a sentence with the word "because."

130. Metal Detector (𝄟)

Answer: Choice C
Classification: Modification
Snapshot: This problem is included to highlight the case of misplaced modifiers. In particular, an introductory modifying phrase (a phrase that begins the sentence), always refers to the first noun or pronoun that follows it (and which is in the subjective

case). As a general rule: "modifying words or phrases should be kept close to the word(s) that they modify."

The only answer choice that is written in the active voice is Choice C. The other four answer choices are written in the passive voice (note the word "be," which signals the passive voices). In Choice A, coins and other valuables cannot *use* a metal detector; we must look for a person to act as the doer of the action. Choices E changes the meaning of the sentence, suggesting the hobbyists bury the coins themselves. Whereas Choices A and E are incorrect, Choices B, C and D are each grammatically correct. Choice C is the winner because, all things being equal, the active voice is deemed superior to the passive voice.

Author's note: As a mostly uninflected language, English depends heavily on word order to establish modifying relationships. Therefore, the position of words is important. Confusion occurs because most modifiers attach themselves to the first things they can "get their hands on" in the sentence, even if it isn't the right thing.

How can we recognize a passive sentence? Here's a quick list of six words that signal a passive sentence: *be, by, was, were, been,* and *being*. For the record, "by" is a preposition, not a verb form, but it frequently appears in sentences that are passive.

131. Hungary (∫ ∫)

Answer: Choice D
Classification: Modification
Snapshot: This problem is included to highlight a modification subtlety which necessitates the use of "account for" or "constitute."

Technically speaking, Hungarians don't *have* less than one percent of the world's population; they *account for* or *constitute* less than one percent of the world's population. This latter option is represented in Choice D. The logic of Choice E makes it incorrect. The transition words "in addition" are illogical because the sentence construction requires contrast, and the word "although" is consistent in this respect. For the record, another correct answer would have included: "Although accounting for less than one percent of the world's population, Hungarians have contributed disproportionately to the fields of modern math and applied sciences."

132. Management (∫ ∫)

Answer: Choice B
Classification: Modification
Snapshot: This problem is included to highlight a modification trap that can occur with phrases beginning with "based on."

Choice A is incorrect because the opening phrase, "Based on... operating results" cannot logically modify "management's decision"; it can only modify "management." Choice C is out because the pronoun "their" does not match its singular antecedent—"management"; the correct pronoun would be "its." In Choices D and E "management" cannot, technically speaking, be "based on first quarter operating results." Management could, however, "use" or "study" or "review" the operating results of the first quarter in order to make a decision.

Choice B, the only answer remaining, is correct. For the record, two additional correct answers would include:

"Based on a review of first quarter operating results, management decided..."
or:
"Based on its review of first quarter operating results, management decided..."

133. Natural Beauty (🜪 🜪)

Answer: Choice E
Classification: Modification
Snapshot: This problem is included to highlight another type of modification problem, known as "back sentence modification."

The final answer proves best—correct, logical, and succinct—in comparing *plastic surgery* to the act of *reconstructing a national park*. In short, the patient is like a national park while the act of plastic surgery is like the act of reconstructing a national park.

In Choices A, B and C, the relative pronoun "which" refers not to "plastic surgery" but to the noun immediately preceding it, "natural beauty." As a result, natural beauty is compared to "reconstructing a national park" (Choice A), to "a national park" (Choice B), and to "reconstruction" (Choice C). Choice D corrects this problem by eliminating the "which" construction and supplying the pronoun "it," thus referring clearly to "plastic surgery," but it illogically compares "plastic surgery" to "a national park."

134. Massage (🜪 🜪)

Answer: Choice B
Classification: Parallelism
Snapshot: This problem is included to highlight the use of parallelism in correlative conjunctions.

There are four common correlative conjunctions in English and as seen on the GMAT. These include: *either...or, neither...nor, not only...but also,* and *both...and.* The purpose of correlative conjunctions is to join things of equal weight. Therefore, things on both sides of each connector should be parallel in form and equal in weight.

The word pairing "both...as well as" is unidiomatic, so Choice E can be eliminated. Here the correlative conjunction is "both...and." The words that follow "both" and "and" must be parallel in structure. In Choice B, the correct answer, the words "your body" follow on both sides of "both" and "and" in perfect parallelism. Choices C and D are not parallel. For the record, there are effectively two possibilities:

> "Massage creates a relaxing, therapeutic, and rejuvenating experience for <u>both</u> your body <u>and</u> your well-being."
>
> *or:*
>
> "Massage creates a relaxing, therapeutic, and rejuvenating experience <u>both</u> for your body <u>and</u> for your well-being."

Here's another example:

Incorrect:	Jonathan <u>not only</u> likes tennis <u>but also</u> golf.
Correct:	Jonathan likes <u>not only</u> tennis <u>but also</u> golf.
	or:
Correct:	Jonathan <u>not only</u> likes tennis <u>but also</u> likes golf.

Two more correct versions would include:

Incorrect:	Sheila <u>both</u> likes to act <u>and</u> to sing.
Correct:	Sheila likes <u>both</u> to act <u>and</u> to sing.
	or:
Correct:	Sheila <u>both</u> likes to act <u>and</u> likes to sing.

135. Cannelloni (🌶)

Answer: Choice D
Classification: Parallelism
Snapshot: This problem is included to highlight an area of parallelism called ellipsis.

To test Choice D simply complete each component idea, making sure each makes sense. "Cannelloni <u>has been</u> my favorite dish...Cannelloni always <u>will be</u> my favorite dish." Now check this against the original: "Cannelloni <u>has</u> my favorite dish (doesn't work)...Cannelloni always <u>will be</u> my favorite dish." Choice E suffers the same fate as Choices A and B, erroneously omitting <u>has been</u>. Choices B and C are muddled; the word "was" illogically suggests that Cannelloni was once a favorite dish but no longer is.

Author's note: Ellipsis governs rules for when we can acceptably omit words in a sentence and still retain clear meaning. In the case of verbs (or verb forms), the rule is that it is okay to omit a second verb if it is the same as the first. Again, to check for faulty parallelism, complete each component idea in a sentence and make sure each part of the sentence can stand alone.

Correct	New York is a large and an exciting city.

There is no need to say: "New York is a large and <u>is</u> an exciting city," since the second verb "is" is the same as the first, and does not have to be written out.

Wrong	In my favorite Japanese restaurant, the food is fascinating and the drinks expensive.
Correct	In my favorite Japanese restaurant, the food <u>is</u> fascinating and the drinks <u>are</u> expensive.

Note that the verb in the second part of the sentence is different and <u>must</u> be written out.

Correct	*The Elements of Style* was written by William Strunk, Jr. and E.B. White.

Rules for ellipsis also govern other parts of speech such as prepositions as seen in the above example. There is no need to say: "*The Elements of Style* was written <u>by</u> William Strunk, Jr. and <u>by</u> E.B. White," since the second preposition 'by' is the same as the first, and does not have to be written out.

136. Europeans (🌶 🌶 🌶)

Answer: Choice A
Classification: Parallelism
Snapshot: This problem is included to highlight the use of parallelism with regard to ellipsis, and review the semi colons, omission commas, and sentence fragments.

In Choice A, the comma placed immediately after "France" and "Poland" is an *omission comma*—it takes the place of the missing words "is famous." The sentence effectively reads: "Italy is famous for its composers and musicians, France is famous for its chefs and philosophers, and Poland is famous for its mathematicians and logicians."

Choices B provides an example of a run-on sentence. There must be an "and" preceding the word "Poland." Also, an omissions comma is needed to take the place of the dual words "is famous." Choices C and D are sentence fragments. In Choice C, a semi colon can only be used if what follows is a grammatically complete sentence (independent clause). Neither "France for her chefs and philosophers" nor "Poland for her mathematicians and logicians" is an independent clause; they are fragments, a group of words which cannot stand on their own.

Choice E changes the meaning of the original sentence (that's a no-no in GMAT Sentence Correction). There's little doubt that France and Poland have composers, musicians, chefs, philosophers, mathematicians, and logicians, but the focus is on what each country is specifically famous for.

137. Sweater (𝄢)

Answer: Choice E
Classification: Comparisons
Snapshot: This problem is included to highlight the handling of the comparative and superlative adjective forms.

The words "neither one" indicates that we are dealing with two sweaters. When comparing two things, we use the comparative form of the adjective, not the superlative. Thus, the correct choice is "better," not "best." and "smaller," not "smallest." "Better" and "smaller" (comparatives) are used when comparing exactly two things; "best" and "smallest" (superlatives) are used when comparing three or more things.

Author's note: When two things are being compared, the *comparative* form of the adjective (or adverb) is used. The comparative is formed in one of two ways: (1) adding "er" to the adjective (for adjectives containing one syllable), or (2) placing "more" before the adjective (especially for adjectives with more than two syllables). Use one of the above methods, but never both: "Jeremy is wiser (or *more* wise) than we know, but never "Jeremy is more wiser than we know."

When three or more things are being compared, the *superlative* form of the adjective (or adverb) is used. The superlative is formed in one of two ways: (1) adding "est" to the adjective (for adjectives containing one syllable), or (2) placing "most" before the adjective (especially for adjectives with more than two syllables). Use one of the above methods, but never both: "He is the cleverest (or *most clever*) of my friends, but never "He is the most cleverest of my friends."

Some modifiers require internal changes in the words themselves. A few of these irregular comparisons are presented in the following chart:

Positive:	Comparative:	Superlative:
good	better	best
well	better	best
bad	worse	worst
far	farther, further	farthest, furthest
late	later, latter	latest, last
little	less, lesser	least
many, much	more	most

138. Perceptions (𝔖 𝔖)

Answer: Choice D
Classification: Comparisons
Snapshot: This problem is included to highlight the comparative idiom "as...do"/"as...does".

The problem pivots on the "like/as" distinction. If the underlined portion modifies "right-brained individuals," then "like" would be appropriate; however, if it parallels the clause "right-brained individuals do not organize," then "as" is appropriate. To modify "right-brained individuals," the underline should be next to the word, so choices A and B are not correct. Also, Choice A states that "right-brained individuals" and "left-brained individuals" are similar, whereas the rest of the sentence contrasts them. Choices C, D, and E use the correct connector, "as," but Choice E, like Choice B, uses the singular "adult," and Choices C and E employ phrases as opposed to clauses. Choice E provides the proper comparative clause.

Choice B is contextually sound but structurally awkward. Either of the following would be better:

Correct: Unlike left-brained individuals, right-brained individuals often do not organize their attention or perceptions systematically, and they may not notice and remember the same level of detail <u>as</u> their left-brained counterparts <u>do</u>.

Correct: Right-brained individuals often do not organize their attention or perceptions systematically and, unlike left-brained individuals, right-brain individuals may not notice and remember the same level of detail <u>as</u> their left-brained counterparts <u>do</u>.

139. Bear (𝔖 𝔖 𝔖)

Answer: Choice C
Classification: Comparisons
Snapshot: When making comparisons, the most basic rule is to make sure to compare like things. That is, compare apples with apples and oranges with oranges.

Here we want to compare *bears* with *bears* or *diets of bears* with *diets of bears*. The original, Choice A, compares animals with diets by erroneously comparing the "Alaskan brown bear and most other members" of the bear family to the "diet" of the grizzly bear. Choice B is structurally sound ("those" is a demonstrative pronoun that takes the place of "the diets") but unidiomatically refers to the "diets" of the grizzly bear. Idiomatic speech would require the use of "diet" to refer to a single bear species and "diets" to refer to more than one species of bear. Choice D uses the repetitious "Just like" (when "Like" alone is sufficient), as well as the unidiomatic "diets." Choice E commits the original error in reverse. Now "diets" of the Alaskan brown bear and most other members of the bear family are being compared directly to "grizzly bears."

All of the following provide potentially correct answers:

    (i)   Like the Alaskan brown bear and most other members of the bear family, the <u>grizzly bear</u> has a <u>diet</u> consisting of both meat and vegetation.

    (ii)   Like the Alaskan brown bear and most other members of the bear family, <u>grizzly bears</u> have a <u>diet</u> consisting of both meat and vegetation.

    (iii)   Like the <u>diets</u> of the Alaskan brown bear and most other members of the bear family, the <u>diet</u> of the grizzly bear consists of both meat and vegetation.

    (iv)   Like the <u>diets</u> of the Alaskan brown bear and most other members of the bear family, the <u>diet</u> of grizzly bears consists of both meat and vegetation.

140. Angel (💭 💭 **)**

Answer: Choice C
Classification: Comparisons
Snapshot: This problem is included to highlight proper comparisons involving "like" vs. "as."

The basic difference between "like" and "as" is that "like" is used for phrases and "as" is used for clauses. A phrase is a group of words that does not contain a verb; a clause is a group of words that does contain a verb. Choices D and E ungrammatically employ "as" in phrases, in addition to being awkwardly constructed.

There are three potentially correct versions:

      (1) She sings <u>like an angel</u>.
         "Like an angel" is a phrase (there is no verb) so "like" is the correct choice.

      (2) She sings <u>as an angel sings</u>.
         "As an angel sings" is a clause (contains the verb "sings") so "as" is the correct choice.

      (3) She sings <u>as an angel does</u>.
         "As an angel does" is a clause (contains the verb "does") so "as" is the correct choice.

Author note: Advertising is an arena where violations in English grammar may be turned to advantage. The American cigarette company Winston once adopted the infectious advertising slogan: "Winston tastes good like a cigarette should." The ungrammatical and somehow proactive use of "like" instead of "as" created a minor sensation, helping propel the brand to the top of the domestic cigarette market. A more recent advertising campaign by DHL in Asia also contains a grammatical violation: "No one knows Asia like we do." The correct version should read: "No one knows Asia as we do."

141. Testing (💭 💭 💭 **)**

Answer: Choice E
Classification: Comparisons
Snapshot: This problem is included as a type of oddball to highlight the reality that we do not always need to compare a singular item with singular item or plural item with plural item (e.g., college entrance exam vs. I.Q. tests). In context, a situation may necessitate comparing a singular item with a plural item or vice versa.

Choices A and B erroneously compare "a college entrance exam" with "the formats…." We want to compare "an exam with an exam" and "the format (or formats) of an exam" with "the format (or formats) of another exam." Although Choice C looks like the winning answer choice, upon closer examination we realize that a single format cannot itself vary considerably in terms of content and length. Choice D correctly employs "formats" but now the problem reverses itself: a single I.Q. test does not have "formats." Choice E correctly combines "I.Q. tests" in the plural with "formats" in the plural.

Here's a follow-up example:

    Incorrect   Unlike American college football, which is played on a standardized field, baseball is played on a field which varies considerably in shape and size.

    Correct   Unlike American college football, which is played on a standardized field, baseball is played on fields which vary considerably in shape and size.

142. Assemblée Nationale (⨔ ⨔)

Answer: Choice D
Classification: Comparisons
Snapshot: This problem is included to highlight the comparative idiom, "Just as...so (too)." Note that the brackets indicate the optional use of the word "too."

In Choices A and B, the use of "as" is incorrect. "As" functions as a subordinating conjunction and this means that the reader expects a logical connection between the fact that Britain has a Parliament and France has the Assemblée Nationale. Try substituting the subordinating conjunction "because" in either A or B and the illogical relationship becomes more apparent. "Because Parliament is the legislative government body of Great Britain, the Assemblée Nationale is the legislative government body of France."

The "just as...so (too)" idiom (Choice D) can be used to express this type of meaning. "Just as something, so something else." Choice D provides a standard comparison "the Parliament of Great Britain to the Assemblée Nationale of France." In Choice E, the comparison is awkward because we end up comparing the Government of Britain's Parliament with the Assemblée Nationale.

Choice C is not only awkward but "just like" is not correct; it is a redundancy where "like" would otherwise do the trick. "Like" is used for phrases whereas "as" is used for clauses. Clearly we are dealing with a clause. Remember that for GMAT purposes, you can have "Just as" but not "Just like."

Author's note: Savor this classic example.

Correct:	<u>Just as</u> birds have wings, <u>so too</u> do fish have fins.
Incorrect:	As birds have wings, fish have fins.
Incorrect:	As birds have wings, fish, therefore, have fins.

(Substituting "because" for "as" above, we can quickly see an illogical relationship; there is no connection between a bird having wings and a fish having fins.)

Incorrect:	Just like birds that have wings, fish have fins.

(We can't have "just like" on the GMAT. Besides, "like" is not used with clauses. "That have wings" is a clause.)

143. Geography (⨔ ⨔)

Answer: Choice A
Classification: Comparisons
Snapshot: This problem is included to highlight the correct use of the "more...than" idiom, used in comparing two things.

Make an initial note that we should ideally be comparing American high school students with Canadian high school students (plural with plural) because the non-underlined part of the sentence contains the words "counterparts." Be suspicious therefore of any of the answer choices which begin with "the American high school student." Check also that in all cases, verbs are correct. "Do" is a plural verb that matches the plural phrase "Canadian counterparts"; "does" is a singular verb that would be used to match the singular phrase, "Canadian counterpart."

The last piece of the puzzle is to eliminate the non-standard comparative constructions, namely "more...compared to" as well as "more...compared with." The correct idiom is "more...than" or "less...than." Thus Choices B, C and E cannot be correct.

144. Sir Isaac Newton (♪)

Answer: Choice E
Classification: Comparisons
Snapshot: This solution to this problem pivots on use of the demonstrative pronoun "those."

The words "those" and "other" must show up in the correct answer. Without the word "other," Choices A, C and D illogically compare Sir Isaac Newton to all scientists, living or dead, even though Sir Isaac Newton is one of those scientists. Without the word "those," Choices A and B illogically compare "the accomplishments of Sir Isaac Newton" to "other scientists." Obviously, we must compare "the accomplishment of Sir Isaac Newton" to "the accomplishments of other scientists." In Choice C, D and E, the word "those" exists to substitute for the phrase "the accomplishments."

Author's note: Faulty or improper comparisons often leave out key words, particularly demonstrative pronouns such as "those" and "that" which are essential to meaning.

Incorrect:	"Like many politicians, the senator's promises sounded good but ultimately led to nothing."
Correct:	"Like <u>those of</u> many politicians, the senator's promises sounded good but ultimately led to nothing."
Correct:	"Like <u>those of</u> many politicians, the promises of the senator sounded good but ultimately led to nothing."
Incorrect:	"Tokyo's population is greater than Beijing."
Correct:	"Tokyo's population is greater than the population of Beijing." or "Tokyo's population is greater than <u>that of</u> Beijing." or "Tokyo's population is greater than Beijing's."

145. Soya (♪ ♪)

Answer: Choice C
Classification: Comparisons
Snapshot: This problem highlights the use of the demonstrative pronoun "that."

Here, we must correctly compare "the protein in meat" to "the protein in Soya beans." The demonstrative pronoun "that" is very important because it substitutes for the words "the protein." Choice C creates a sentence which effectively reads: "In addition to having more protein than meat does, the protein in Soya beans is higher in quality than 'the protein' in meat."

Choices A and B are out because the word "meat" must come after the opening phrase "in addition to having more protein than meat does." Choice D correctly employs "Soya beans" but incorrectly uses "it" to make a comparison. "It" cannot stand for "the protein." Choice E incorrectly compares Soya bean protein to meat.

146. Trend (♪ ♪)

Answer: Choice A
Classification: Verb Tense
Snapshot: This problem is included to summarize the difference between the simple past tense versus the past perfect tense and the present perfect tense. The correct answer sides with the simple past tense.

Here, the simple past tense is all that is needed to refer clearly to the timeframe in the past (1980-1990). In Choice B, the present perfect tense "has continued" is inconsistent with the timing of an event that took place in the distant past. In Choice C, the past perfect tense "had continued" is not required because we are not making a distinction regarding the sequence of two past tense events.

In Choices D and E, the focus switches from a rise in the "percentage of people" to a rise in the "abrupt increase." This shift in meaning is unwarranted. The pronouns "it" (Choice D) and "which" (Choice E) are ambiguous and could refer to either the "percentage of people" or an "abrupt increase." Moreover, Choices D and E employ the passive constructions "there had been" and "there was"; these are considered weak sentence constructions and are best avoided.

147. Golden Years (𝄢)

Answer: Choice E
Classification: Verb Tense
Snapshot: This problem is included to highlight the difference between the present perfect tense versus the past perfect tense. The correct answer here sides with the present perfect tense.

Only Choice E uses the correct tense (present perfect), observes parallelism, and is idiomatic. Because the sentence describes a situation that continues into the present, Choices A and B are incorrect in using the past perfect "had elected," which denotes an action completed at a specific time in the past. Also, the dual expressions "x rather than y" and "x instead of y" are, according to Standard Written English, equivalent. However, the GMAT folks seem to side with the use of "rather than."

148. Fire (𝄢 𝄢)

Answer: Choice B
Classification: Verb Tense
Snapshot: This problem is included to highlight the difference between the past perfect tense versus the simple past tense and/or the present perfect tense. The correct answer sides with the past perfect tense. This problem also deals with the passive verb tense (had been/have been).

The solution to this problem is based on the same concept as the preceding problem. The past particle "had" must be used to refer to the first of two past tense events. In short, only Choice B uses the verb tenses correctly to indicate that houses were built or heavily damaged prior to their being destroyed by fire. Choices A, C, and E illogically state that some houses were both destroyed "and" heavily damaged; "or" is needed to indicate that each of the houses suffered either one fate or the other. In using only one verb tense, "were", Choice A fails to indicate that the houses were built before the fires occurred. Choices D and E erroneously employ the present perfect tense, saying in effect that the houses "have been constructed" after they were destroyed or heavily damaged last year.

149. Politics (𝄢 𝄢)

Answer: Choice D
Classification: Verb Tense
Snapshot: This problem is included to highlight the difference between the past perfect tense and the simple past tense. The correct answer sides with the past perfect tense.

The key phrase "he later conceded" triggers a sequence in tense. One past tense event is happening at an even earlier point in the past. This problem emphasizes an important distinction regarding the past perfect tense employing the particle "had." Had is used before the first of two past events. In this example, Senator John Kerry "disapproved" before he "conceded." Thus, the particle "had" must be placed before the first of the two past events: "had disapproved….later conceded."

Choices B erroneously proposes a reversal in sequence ("disapproved…had later conceded") while Choice E doubles the use of *had* to create a verbal muddle ("had disapproved...had later conceded"). Both of these choices result in illogical alternatives. Choice C incorrectly employs the present perfect tense (has) when the past perfect tense (had) is what is called for.

Another example: "Larry, who <u>had</u> studied Russian for five years, went to work in Moscow." This implies that Larry completed his studies before he went to Moscow.

150. B-School (𝄐 𝄐)

Answer: Choice E
Classification: Verb Tense
Snapshot: This problem is included to highlight the difference between the simple future tense versus the present perfect tense (both simple and progressive verb forms). This problem sides with the use of the simple future tense. A review of the simple and progressive verb forms is included.

Since all answer choices contain the words "in the coming years," we definitely know we are dealing with the future, and Choice E complements our search for a simply future tense.

In Choices A and B, the tense "have been becoming" (present perfect progressive tense in the passive voice) just doesn't work. In Choices C and D, the present perfect tense is also out. The present perfect tense is only useful for events that began in the past but touch the present. Here we need a tense that takes us into the future.

In summary, what is it that we need to make this problem work? The answer is that we need either a present tense verb to indicate concurrent changes in business schools or a future tense (2nd verb) to indicate what will happen in the future. In other words, in addition to Choice E, the following are also correct possibilities:

"As graduate management programs (become/are becoming) more competitive in the coming years in terms of their promotional and financial undertakings, schools (will become/are becoming) more and more dependent on alumni networks, corporate sponsorships, and philanthropists."

151. Summer in Europe (𝄐 𝄐)

Answer: Choice C
Classification: Verb Tense
Snapshot: This problem encapsulates the correct use of the future perfect tense.

This problem requires the use of the future perfect tense. Choices A and B present incorrect versions of the present perfect tense, employing the construction "have reached." Choices D and E create erroneous alternatives by commingling past tense constructions with future tenses. Choice D presents an incorrect version which doubles up the present perfect tense "have reached" with the future perfect tense "will have backpacked."

Choice E mixes the simple past tense "reached" with the future perfect tense (in the progressive form). For the record, an equally correct answer would have been: "By the time we reached France, we had been backpacking for 12 weeks." This would represent the correct use of the past perfect tense (in the passive voice). Of course, the original sentence clearly indicates that the travelers are looking into the future—they still have not yet arrived in France.

CHAPTER 8

CRITICAL REASONING

"I can stand brute force, but brute reason is quite unbearable. There is something unfair about its use. It is hitting below the intellect."
(Oscar Wilde)

COMPARISON AND ANALOGY ASSUMPTIONS

152. Crime ($\int$)

According to an article in the *Life and Times* section of the Sunday newspaper, crime is on the downturn in our city. Police initiatives, neighborhood watches, stiff fines, and lengthened prison terms have all played a significant role in reducing the number of reported crimes by twenty percent.

Which of the following would most weaken the belief that crime has decreased in our city?

A) A neighboring city has also reported a decrease in crime in its Sunday newspaper.

B) Police officers were among those citizens who voted for a bill to support police initiatives to reduce crime in our city.

C) Most of the recent police arrests were repeat offenders.

D) The author of the article includes white-collar crime in his definition of crime, thus increasing the chance of reported crime.

E) It is possible for reported crime to have gone down while actual crime has remained the same or actually gone up.

153. Banff National Park ($\int \int \int$)

A recent report determined that although only 8 percent of drivers entering Banff National Park possessed yearly entry permits, as opposed to day passes, these drivers represented fifteen percent of all vehicles entering the Park. Clearly, drivers who possess yearly entry permits are more likely to enter Banff National Park on a regular basis than are drivers who do not.

The conclusion drawn above depends on which of the following assumptions?

A) The number of entries to Banff National Park by drivers with yearly entry permits does not exceed the number of yearly entry permits issued by the Park.

B) Drivers who possess yearly entry permits to Banff National Park are more likely to stay longer in the Park than drivers who do not.

C) All drivers with yearly entry permits to Banff National Park entered the Park at least once during the period of the report.

D) Drivers possessing yearly entry permits to Banff National Park are more likely to enter the Park regularly than are drivers who do not.

E) Drivers who entered Banff National Park with yearly permits during the period of the report were representative of the types of drivers who have entered other national parks with similar yearly permits.

154. Hyperactivity (⌇ ⌇)

Viewing children as more hyperactive today than they were 10 years ago, many adults place the blame squarely on the popularity of video games and multi-media entertainment.

Which of the following revelations would most undermine the argument above?

A) Even if children today are more hyperactive than they were 10 years ago, they are widely viewed as more spontaneous and creative.

B) The claim that children are more aggressive today is a more serious charge than their being considered more hyperactive.

C) Children's books published in recent years contain on average more pictures than do children's books published in the past.

D) There are more types of behavior deemed hyperactive today than there were 10 years ago.

E) Incidences of ailments such as Attention Deficit Hyperactivity Disorder (ADHD) are reported to be on the increase in recent years.

CAUSE AND EFFECT ASSUMPTIONS

155. Cyclists (⌇ ⌇)

Touring professional cyclists have been shown to have between 4 and 11 percent body fat. If we could all decrease our body fat to that level, we could all cycle at a world-class level.

Which statement(s) below accurately describe the flaw in the method of reasoning used in the above argument?

I. It assumes a causal relationship between two highly correlated events.

II. It suggests that low body fat is a sufficient condition rather than a necessary condition for becoming a world-class cyclist.

III.Its conclusion is based on evidence which, in turn, is based on its conclusion.

A) I only   B) II only   C) I & II only   D) II & III only   E) All of the above

156. SAT Scores ($\int$)

Parents are too easily impressed with the recent rise in average SAT scores at the top American undergraduate universities and colleges. Unfortunately, this encouraging statistic is misleading. Scores have risen not because students possess better math, English, and writing skills but because students are better at taking tests. For those students accepted at the top undergraduate universities and colleges, studies confirm that skills in the basics of reading, writing, and mathematics have been on the gradual decline over the past twenty years.

The author argues primarily by

      A) denying the accuracy of his opponents' figures.

      B) finding an alternative explanation for his opponent's evidence.

      C) introducing irrelevant information to draw attention away from the main issue.

      D) employing circular reasoning.

      E) suggesting that his opponent's evidence may be flawed.

157. Valdez ($\int \int$)

Since Ana Valdez was installed as President of the Zipco Corporation, profits have averaged 15 percent each year. During the tenure of her predecessor, the corporation's profits averaged only 8 percent per year. Obviously Ms. Valdez's aggressive international marketing efforts have caused the acceleration in the growth of Zipco's profits.

Which of the following, if true, would most weaken the conclusion drawn above?

      A) During the tenure of Ms. Valdez's predecessor, the corporation began an advertising campaign aimed at capturing consumers in developing countries between the ages of 19 and 25.

      B) The corporation's new manufacturing plant, constructed in the past year, has a 35 percent greater production capacity.

      C) Since Ms. Valdez became President, the corporation has switched the primary focus of its advertising from print ads to radio and television commercials.

      D) Ms. Valdez hired a well-known headhunting firm which found talented vice-presidents for two of the corporation's five divisions.

      E) Just before Ms. Valdez took over as President, her predecessor, Mr. Jones, directed the acquisition of a rival corporation, which has nearly doubled the corporation's yearly revenues.

158. Headline (﹩ ﹩)

The headline of the *Daily College Inquirer* read: "Obesity Linked to Depression."

Which of the following, if true, would most weaken the implied conclusion drawn between becoming overweight and falling into depression?

   A) An obese person may not understand why he or she is depressed or how to escape from the grips of depression.

   B) Depression can result from things other than obesity.

   C) Low self-esteem is frequently cited as the cause of both obesity and depression.

   D) A person twice as overweight as another person is not likely to be twice as depressed.

   E) Depression has been further linked to desperation and suicide.

159. TV Viewing (﹩ ﹩)

An investigator divided 128 adults into two distinct groups (high-TV viewers and low-TV viewers) based on the number of hours of violent TV programming watched per day. A significantly larger percentage of the high-viewing group than of the low-viewing group demonstrated a high level of aggression. The investigator concluded that it was greater TV viewing particularly of violent programming that resulted in higher aggression levels.

Which of the following, if true, most seriously weakens the conclusion above?

   A) Some subjects in the high-viewing group experienced lower levels of aggression than did other subjects in the high-viewing group.

   B) Some subjects in the low-viewing group did not experience any aggression.

   C) Fear of aggressive tendencies as a result of watching large amounts of TV was the reason some subjects restricted their viewing of TV.

   D) Some subjects watched live programming whereas other viewers watched pre-recorded TV programs.

   E) High levels of aggression caused some subjects to increase their viewing, particularly of violent TV programs.

160. Shark (🖋 🖋)

In a marine reserve off the south coast of Australia, people are sometimes attacked by sharks. Here, it is believed that the sharks will only attack people who are mistaken for seals, which occurs when surfers wear entirely black body suits. So for the past few years, surfers have started wearing bright metallic body suits. While many area residents remain skeptical, no surfer wearing a metallic body suit has yet been attacked by a shark.

Which of the statements below, if true, would best support the argument of those who advocate the use of metallic body suits?

A) Surfers at other surf areas who wear metallic body suits have not been attacked recently by sharks.

B) A number of surfers in this marine area wearing black body suits have been attacked recently by sharks.

C) No sharks have been spotted in this marine reserve off the south coast of Australia in recent months.

D) Some of the surfers who wear metallic suits also wear wristbands that contain metal bells in order to frighten away any sharks.

E) Underwater divers have observed sharks attacking tuna and other ocean fish, some of them black in color.

REPRESENTATIVE SAMPLE ASSUMPTIONS

161. Movie Buffs (🖋)

According to a recent survey, any sequel to the movie *Victim's Revenge* will not fare well. Respondents to a recent survey of movie goers leaving the Sunday matinees around the country indicated that movies based on serial killers with psychopathic tendencies have fallen out of vogue with current movie buffs. Therefore, if movie studios want to produce films that are financially successful, they should avoid producing such films.

Which of the following would most weaken the idea that film studios should stop production of stories and dramas based on serial killers with psychopathic tendencies?

A) Movie stars have a significant following of individuals who see their every film.

B) People who attend Sunday matinees are not representative of the views of the movie going population as a whole.

C) The film *Psycho*, originally directed by Alfred Hitchcock, was a big hit in 1960, and was later remade as a movie in 1998.

D) Both student enrollment in college criminology courses and book sales based on the lives of real-life serial killers are up.

E) The cost of making such movies requires skillful actors who can portray emotional conflict and intellectualism and these actors demand high salaries.

162. Putting (🐧 🐧)

Are you having trouble getting the golf score you deserve? Is putting your pariah? The new Sweet Spot Putter is designed to improve your golf game overnight without intensive lessons. Even rank amateurs can dramatically increase their putting accuracy by 25 percent. You too can achieve a low golf score with the new Sweet Spot Putter.

Someone who accepted the reasoning in the advertisement above would be making which one of the following assumptions?

   A) Without quality equipment, a golf player cannot improve his or her game.

   B) The new Sweet Spot Putter will improve an amateur's game more than it will improve a professional's game.

   C) The quality of a person's golf game is largely determined by the accuracy of his or her putting.

   D) The new Sweet Spot Putter is superior to any other putter currently on the market.

   E) Lessons are not as effective at improving the accuracy of a player's putting as is the use of quality equipment.

163. Critic's Choice (🐧 🐧)

In a newly released book, *Decline of the Novelist*, the author argues that novelists today lack technical skills that were common among novelists during the past century. In this regard, the book might be right, since its analysis of 200 novels—100 contemporary and 100 non-contemporary—demonstrates convincingly that few contemporary novelists exhibit the same skill level as that of non-contemporary novelists.

Which of the following points to the most serious logical flaw in the critic's argument?

   A) The title of the author's book could cause readers to accept the book's thesis even before they read the literary analysis of those novels that support it.

   B) There could be criteria other than the technical skills of the novelist by which to evaluate a novel.

   C) Those novels chosen by the critic for analysis could be those that most support the book's thesis.

   D) The particular methods currently used by novelists may require even more literary skill than do methods used by writers of screenplays.

   E) A reader who was not familiar with the language of literary criticism might not be convinced by the book's analysis of its 200 novels.

164. Temperament (𝄂 𝄂 𝄂)

Steve: "Rick and Harriet, two of my red-haired friends, are irritable. It seems true that red-haired people have bad tempers."

John: "That's ridiculous, red-haired people are actually quite docile. Jeff, Muriel, and Betsy—three of my red-haired friends—all have placid demeanors."

Which of the statements below provides the most likely explanation for the two seemingly contradictory statements above?

A) The number of people who are red-haired that Steve knows may be different from the number of people who are red-haired that John knows.

B) The number of red-haired people that both Steve and John know may not be greater in total than the number of non red-haired people that both Steve and John know.

C) It is likely that Steve or John has incorrectly assessed the temperament of one or more of his red-haired friends.

D) It is likely that both Steve and John know of friends who are not red haired and yet also have bad tempers.

E) The examples that Steve uses to support his conclusion and the examples that John uses to support his conclusion are likely both valid.

165. Questionnaire (𝄂 𝄂)

President: "I'm worried about the recent turnover in MegaCorp. If employees leave our company disgruntled, such negative feelings can hurt our reputation in the marketplace."

Human Resources Manager: "Your concerns are unfounded. As part of our post-employment follow-up process, we send questionnaires to each employee within thirty days of his or her leaving the company. These questionnaires seek honest answers and remind employees that all responses will be kept confidential. Of the last 100 employees who left our company, 25 have responded, and only five people have mentioned having had any negative employment experience.

The Human Resource Manager's argument is most vulnerable to criticism on the grounds that it fails to acknowledge the possibility that

A) opinions expressed in such questionnaires are not always indicative of how employees actually felt.

B) many of those who harbored truly negative feelings about their employment experience at MegaCorp did not respond to the questionnaire.

C) the Public Relations firm, Quantum, recently hired by MegaCorp. has successfully designed several programs specially aimed at boosting the company's public image.

D) questions asking about negative employment experiences have been placed at the end, not at the beginning, of the questionnaire.

E) the response rate in general for questionnaires is 10%, meaning that only 1 in 10 questionnaires can be expected to be completed and returned.

IMPLEMENTATION ASSUMPTIONS

166. Classics (⌇ ⌇ ⌇)

Any literate person who is not lazy can read the classics. Since few literate persons have read the classics, it is clear that most literate persons are lazy.

Which of the following is an assumption on which the argument above is based?

A) Only literate persons can understand the classics.

B) Any literate person should read the classics.

C) Any literate person who is lazy has no chance of reading the classics.

D) Any literate person who will not read the classics is lazy.

E) Any literate person who can read the classics will choose to do so.

167. Public Transportation (⌇ ⌇)

People should switch from driving their cars to work on the weekdays to taking public transportation such as buses and subways. In major cities such as New York, London, or Tokyo, for example, cars are an expensive and inefficient means of transportation and fossil fuel emissions are the major source of the city's pollution.

All of the following are assumptions in the argument above EXCEPT:

A) There may be easier ways to combat pollution in large cities than by having people switch to taking public transportation.

B) There are enough people who actually own cars, which are currently being used to drive to work, to make this plan realistically feasible.

C) Public transportation is both available and accessible should someone wish to switch.

D) Current public transportation systems can accommodate all the people who decide to switch.

E) The city can afford to pay public transport drivers and related personnel who may otherwise remain idle once the morning and evening rush hour periods are over.

168. Rainbow Corp (𝄪)

"Tina obviously cares little about the environment. She continues to use Purple Rider Felt Pens even though the company that makes these pens, Rainbow Corp, has been the focus of several recent newspaper articles as a result of its indictment for several violations involving dumping toxic wastes in the harbor."

Which of the following would serve to most weaken the claim that Tina cares little about the environment?

A) Although the Rainbow Corp has been the subject of several newspaper articles, it has been praised by consumers for its high quality products.

B) Tina is not aware of the recent newspaper articles which feature Rainbow Corp and its indictment for several violations involving dumping toxic wastes in the harbor.

C) The newspaper which ran the articles of Rainbow's indictments also owns a "gossip magazine" called the *Regional Inquirer.*

D) The public relations department of Rainbow Corp never issued a statement denying that the company had violated the law.

E) Tina was a member of an environmental protection organization during her freshman and sophomore years in college.

NUMBER-BASED ASSUMPTIONS

169. Med School (𝄪 𝄪)

A student activist group has released a report that suggests that female students have more difficulties in earning admittance to medical school. The facts in the report speak for themselves: seventy-five percent of all students in medical school are male, but fewer than half of all female applicants reach their goal of being admitted to medical school.

Which of the following data would be most helpful in evaluating the argument above?

A) The portion of all admissions officers who are male versus female.

B) The percentage of eligible female students admitted to medical school who accept a particular school's offer of admission and the percentage of eligible male students admitted to medical school who also accept that particular school's offer of admission.

C) The percentage of eligible female students admitted to medical school and the percentage of eligible male students admitted to medical school.

D) Comparative records on acceptance rates of male and female applicants in other graduate programs such as business, law, and the sciences.

E) The dropout rate for female and male students while in medical school.

170. Military Expenditures (𝔖 𝔖)

Proponents of greater military spending for the Reno Republic argue that the portion of their national budget devoted to military programs has been steadily declining for a number of years, largely because of rising domestic infrastructure development costs. Yet groups opposed to increasing military expenditure point out that the military budget of Reno Republic, even when measured in constant or inflation-adjusted dollars, has increased every year for the past two decades. Which of the following, if true, best resolves the apparent contradiction presented above?

A) Countries in the same region as the Reno Republic have increased the annual portion of their national budgets devoted to military spending.

B) The advocates of greater military spending have overestimated the amount needed for adequate defense of the country.

C) Domestic infrastructure development costs have indeed risen as sharply as the advocates of greater military spending claim they have.

D) Military expenditures have risen at a rate higher than the rate of inflation.

E) The total national budget has increased faster than military expenditure has increased.

171. Fiction Books (𝔖 𝔖 𝔖)

A major publishing conglomerate released a survey concerning the relationship between a household's level of education and the kind of books found in its library. Specifically, members of higher-education-level households had more books in their libraries. The survey also indicated that higher-education-level households had a greater percentage of books that were fiction versus non-fiction in their libraries as compared with lower-education-level households.

Which of the following can be properly inferred from the survey results cited above?

A) People with the highest levels of education buy more fiction books than non-fiction books.

B) Households with higher education levels have more fiction books than non-fiction books.

C) Households with lower education levels have more non-fiction books than fiction books.

D) Households with lower education levels have more non-fiction books than do households with higher education levels.

E) Households with higher education levels have more fiction books than do households with lower education levels.

172. Nova vs. Rebound (∫ ∫)

Jill: In our survey 53 percent of those questioned said they used Nova Running Shoes for jogging and 47 percent said they used Rebound Running Shoes for jogging.

Jack: In that case everyone questioned used one product or the other.

Jill: No, 24 percent said they didn't use either one.

Jill's statements imply that

    A) not all of those questioned liked to go jogging.

    B) some of those who said they used either Nova or Rebound Running Shoes for jogging were lying.

    C) some of those who used Nova Running Shoes for jogging were among those who also used Rebound Running Shoes for jogging.

    D) some of those who used neither product were nevertheless familiar with Nova and Rebound Running Shoes.

    E) many Nova and Rebound Running Shoes are actually made in the same factory in various international locations.

173. Grapes (∫ ∫)

It costs much less to grow an acre of grapes in California than it costs to grow an acre of watermelons in Oklahoma. This fact should be obvious to anyone who reads last year's annual farm report, which clearly shows that many millions of dollars more were spent last year growing watermelons in Oklahoma than were spent growing grapes in California.

Which of the following, if true, would most seriously call the reasoning above into question?

    A) Profits on the sale of Californian grapes are much higher than the profits derived from the sales of Oklahoma watermelons.

    B) There were far fewer total acres of grapes grown in California last year than total acres of watermelons in Oklahoma.

    C) An acre of grapes in Oklahoma costs much more to grow than an acre of watermelons in California.

    D) Part of Californian grown grapes were used to feed livestock whereas all of the watermelons grown in Oklahoma were used for human consumption.

    E) State subsidies accounted for a larger percentage of the amount spent growing watermelons in Oklahoma than of the amount spent growing grapes in California last year.

174. Act-Fast (⚲ ⚲)

One Act-Fast tablet contains twice the pain reliever found in a tablet of regular Aspirin. A consumer will have to take two Aspirin tablets in order to get the relief provided by one Act-Fast tablet. And since a bottle of Act-Fast costs the same as a bottle of regular Aspirin, consumers can be expected to switch to Act-Fast.

Which of the following, if true, would most weaken the argument that consumers will be discontinuing the use of regular Aspirin and switching to Act-Fast?

    A) A regular Aspirin tablet is twice as large as an Act-Fast tablet.

    B) Neither regular Aspirin nor Act-Fast is as effective in relief of serious pain as are drugs available only by prescriptions.

    C) Some headache sufferers experience a brief period of nausea shortly after taking Act-Fast but not after taking regular Aspirin.

    D) A regular bottle of Aspirin contains more than twice as many tablets as does a bottle of Act-Fast.

    E) The pain reliever in Act-Fast is essentially the same pain reliever found in regular Aspirin.

LOGIC-BASED ASSUMPTIONS

175. Intricate Plots (⚲)

The ability to create intricate plots is one of the essential gifts of the scriptwriter. Strong plot development ensures that eventual movie goers will be intellectually and emotionally satisfied by the story. If scriptwriting is to remain a significant art form, its practitioners must continue to craft intricate plots.

The author of the argument above would most probably agree with which one of the following statements?

    A) If a script has an intricate plot, it must necessarily be a significant art form.

    B) A script without an intricate plot will never become a blockbuster movie.

    C) If a script does not have an intricate plot, it will probably not be a significant art form.

    D) Scriptwriting is the most likely art form to become a significant art form.

    E) A scriptwriter must craft multiple plots within his or her scripts.

176. Pub (𝄐 𝄐)

"During final exam week, our local pub sells a lot of beer; but it isn't final exam week, so our local pub must not be selling much beer."

Which of the following is logically most similar to the argument above?

    A) When people are happy, they smile, but no one is smiling, so it must be that no one is happy.

    B) When people are happy, they smile; our family members are happy, so they must be smiling.

    C) When people are happy, they smile, but one can smile and not be happy.

    D) When people are happy, they smile, but no one is happy, so no one is smiling.

    E) When people are not happy, they do not smile; our family members are smiling, so they must not be unhappy.

177. Balcony (𝄐 𝄐)

If your apartment is above the fifth floor, it has a balcony.

The statement above can be logically deduced from which of the following statements?

    A) No apartments on the fifth floor have balconies.

    B) An apartment does not have a balcony unless the apartment is above the fifth floor.

    C) All apartments above the fifth floor have balconies.

    D) All balconies are built for apartments above the fifth floor.

    E) Balconies are not built for apartments below the fifth floor.

178. Global Warming (𝄐 𝄐 𝄐)

Jacques: If we want to stop global warming, we must pass legislation to reduce fossil fuel emissions.

Pierre: That's not true. It will take a lot more than passing legislation aimed at reducing fossil fuel emissions in order to stop global warming.

Pierre's response is inaccurate because he mistakenly believes that what Jacques has said is that

    A) passing legislation to reduce fossil fuel emissions is necessary to reduce global warming.

    B) only the passing of legislation to reduce fossil fuel emissions is capable of stopping global warming.

    C) if global warming is to be stopped, legislation to reduce fossil fuel emissions must be passed.

    D) passing legislation to reduce fossil fuel emissions is enough to stop the global warming.

    E) global warming will not be stopped by passing legislation to reduce fossil fuel emissions.

179. Sales (⌇ ⌇)

Debra: To be a good salesperson, one must be friendly.

Tom: That's not so. It takes much more than friendliness to make a good salesperson.

Tom has understood Debra's statement to mean that

A) being friendly is the most important characteristic of being a good salesperson.

B) if a person is a good salesperson, he or she will be friendly.

C) a salesperson only needs to be friendly in order to be a good salesperson.

D) most good salespersons are friendly people but only some friendly people are good salespersons.

E) if a person isn't friendly, he or she will not make a good salesperson.

180. Football (⌇ ⌇)

Marie: Every person on the Brazilian World Cup Football Team is a great player.

Beth: What! The Italian World Cup Football Team has some of the best players in the world.

Beth's reply suggests that she has misunderstood Marie's remark to mean that

A) only Brazilian World Cup Team players are great players.

B) Marie believes that the Brazilian World Cup Football Team is the best overall football team.

C) the Italian World Cup Football Team consists of less than great players.

D) the Brazilian World Cup Football Team is likely to defeat the Italian World Cup Football Team should they meet in match play.

E) individual Brazilian World Cup Team players will play as well as a unit as will the Italian World Cup Team players.

BOLDED-STATEMENT PROBLEM

181. Smoking (🎺 🎺)

The dangers of smoking, although well documented, are often ignored even today. According to numerous published accounts, a person who smokes habitually has a thirty percent greater chance of developing cancer or heart disease than someone who does not smoke. Many individuals residing outside the health and wellness fields either find research on the ill effects of smoking to be uncompelling or choose to ignore such evidence altogether. **They are likely to point to instances of individuals who smoke regularly despite living well into their nineties.** What these people fail to realize is that there is a difference between a highly correlated event and a causally related event. The absence of a causally related event does not negate the validity of a highly correlated event.

Which of the following best describes the purpose of the bolded statement?

A) It is evidence used to support a conclusion that follows.

B) It is a counter argument used as a persuasive device.

C) It is evidence used to support a counterclaim.

D) It is an assumption challenged through rebuttal.

E) It is an unstated premise, linking the argument's evidence to its broader conclusion.

ANSWERS AND EXPLANATIONS

152. Crime (🎺)

Answer: Choice E
Classification: Comparison and Analogy Assumptions
Snapshot: Watch for "scope shifts" that occur when one term is inadvertently substituted for another as an argument unfolds.

The key to understanding this problem is to see the scope shift that occurs as a result of switching terms from "crime" to "reported crime." Obviously, reported crime is not the same thing as actual crime. As answer Choice E states: "It is possible for reported crime to have gone down while actual crime has remained the same or actually gone up." In order to make comparisons we need to stick to terms that are of equivalent meaning.

Choice A is incorrect. This answer choice slightly strengthens, not weakens, the original argument. In Choice B, it does not matter whether police officers, as citizens themselves, voted for a bill on initiatives to reduce crime in the city. It also does not matter as in Choice C whether most arrests were repeat offenders. First-time offenders or repeat offenders, crime is crime.

The fact that crime has come to include white-collar crime (Choice D) actually strengthens the argument. It suggests that there could be more incidences of crime (or cases of reported crime), which makes a decrease in crime (or cases of reported crime) potentially that much more significant.

153. Banff National Park (⸮ ⸮ ⸮)

Answer: Choice D
Classification: Comparison and Analogy Assumptions
Snapshot: This is an even more subtle "scope shift" which occurs with the addition of the words "on a regular basis." Without these words, the argument is otherwise sound.

From a content standpoint, this problem is similar to an allocation or distribution scenario within number-based assumptions. Just because a driver with a yearly pass enters the Park more often than does a driver with a day pass, this does not technically mean that a driver enters the Park on a more regular or consistent basis. Case in point: a driver with a yearly pass might enter the Park ten times a month but do so at the beginning and end of the month only, or even with multiple frequency on given days. Such "concentrated entries" would not constitute regular entries—"more" does not necessarily mean "more regularly."

The argument does not depend on Choice A, B, C or E. In fact, it is virtually certain that the number of entries made by drivers with yearly permits does exceed the number of yearly entry permits issued by the Park. After all, almost all drivers with yearly permits will likely enter the Park more than once during the year (that's why they have yearly permits). The argument does not depend on drivers with yearly permits staying longer in the Park (Choice B); it is an "entry" that counts, not the duration of the stay. It is also not necessary for *all* drivers to have entered the Park at least once during the period of the report (Choice C). Some of the drivers with yearly passes might not have entered the Park once. The only thing that is important is that the 8 percent of drivers possessing yearly permits do in fact constitute 15 percent of the vehicles entering the Park during the period of the report. In Choice E, there is no need to compare drivers in this report to those who entered *other* national parks.

Here is another problem which is structurally similar in design and which makes the scope shift—"regular basis"—even easier to spot. Again the answer is Choice D.

> A recent report by the Press Club determined that although only 8 percent of those members entering the Club were in fact correspondent members as opposed to non-correspondent members, these members represented 15 percent of all the members entering the club. Clearly, correspondent members are more likely to enter the Press Club on a regular basis than are non-correspondent members.
>
> The conclusion drawn above depends on which of the following assumptions?
>
> A) The number of times individual correspondent members enter the Press Club does not exceed the number of entries by non-correspondent members.
>
> B) Correspondent members are more likely to stay for longer periods of time per visit at the Press Club than non-correspondent members.
>
> C) All members with correspondent memberships entered the Press Club at least once during the period of the report.
>
> D) Correspondent members are more likely to enter the Press Club regularly than are non-correspondent members.
>
> E) Correspondent members who entered the Press Club during the period of the report were representative of the types of members who frequent other affiliated press clubs.

154. Hyperactivity (⌇ ⌇)

Answer: Choice D
Classification: Comparison and Analogy Assumptions
Snapshot: Changes in definition destroy the ability to make comparisons. Check to see that the way terms are defined remains consistent.

The idea that there are more types of behavior deemed hyperactive indeed weakens the claim that children today are more hyperactive than they were 10 years ago. In short, there are more ways to "check off" and confirm hyperactive behavior. In order to compare the hyperactively of children today versus 10 years ago, we need an even playing field in terms of the comparability of terms: the definition of hyperactivity or the criterion for hyperactive behavior must remain consistent over time. Choices A and B are effectively out of the argument's scope. We are not talking about creativity and spontaneity nor are we primarily concerned about other potentially more serious issues beyond hyperactivity. The impact of having more or less pictures in children's books remains unclear (Choice C) as does an increase in ailments such as Attention Deficit Hyperactivity Disorder (ADHD) per Choice E.

155. Cyclists (⌇ ⌇)

Answer: Choice C
Classification: Cause and Effect Assumptions
Snapshot: This problem is included to review "correlation vs. causation" and "necessary vs. sufficient" conditions.

Roman Numeral I is true. Correlation does not equal causation. This argument assumes a causal relationship is responsible for a correlation. There is likely a high correlation between low body fat and being a world-class (or touring professional) cyclist. But there may well be a high correlation among other variables as well. For example, a likely high correlation exists among muscular strength and world-class cycling, technical skills (maneuvering a bike) and world-class cycling, and mental toughness and being a world-class cyclist.

Roman Numeral II is also true. Having low body fat is a necessary but not sufficient condition for one being a world-class cyclist. In other words, having a low body fat does not make a person a world-class cyclist of and by itself. One needs other attributes too.

This problem can also be solved as an, "if...then" type problem. The original reads, "If one is a world-class cyclist, then one has 4 to 11 percent body fat." When the "if...then" statement is erroneously reversed (as it is in the conclusion of this argument), the argument becomes, "If one has four to eleven percent body fat, then one can be a world-class cyclist." It is also true to say that when an "if...then" statement is reversed, a necessary condition is erroneously turned into a sufficient condition. See *Chapter 4: The World of Letters*, **(Pages 60-61)**.

Roman Numeral III is false. The argument is not flawed due to circular reasoning. In circular reasoning, a conclusion is based on evidence and that evidence is, in turn, based on the conclusion.

156. SAT Scores ($\int$)

Answer: Choice B

Classification: Cause and Effect Assumptions

Snapshot: This question was chosen as a classic example of an alternative explanation which serves to weaken cause and effect type arguments. When tackling "cause and effect" scenarios, think first in terms of alternative explanations.

The argument basically says that SAT scores have gone up because students are better test-takers, not because students possess better academic skills. Are students smarter or just better test-takers?

Choices A and E may appear tricky. Actually the author doesn't deny his opponent's figures or suggest his evidence is flawed. In fact, the author agrees with his opponent's facts (test scores are getting higher). What the author is saying is that his opponent's evidence is incomplete, not flawed.

Cause and effect fallacies exist when there is confusion as to the causal relationship between two events. See if the argument is set up in terms of some situation A causing some situation "B". Ask, "Is A really causing event B?" Show that A does not necessarily lead to B and the argument is weakened or falls apart.

Here is a summary of how both arguments unfold:

Opponent's argument:

Conclusion:	Students are better skilled.
Assumption:	There is a correlation between higher test scores and better skills.
Evidence:	Test scores are getting higher.

Author's argument:

Conclusion:	Students are better test-takers, not better skilled academically.
Assumption:	There exists no strong correlation between higher test scores and better skills.
Evidence:	Studies confirm students are weaker in the basics.
Evidence:	Test scores are getting higher.

Author's note: Consider the person who says: "No wonder Todd chose to attend a good university. He set himself up for the good job when he graduated." We cannot assume that Todd went to university for the purpose of getting a good job afterward. He may have gone to university to play on a varsity sports team with the hope of playing professional sports. He may have gone purely for the academic experience with no vocational thoughts at all, and then again, he may have gone just to get away from home, meet new friends, and enjoy himself socially.

Let's flow this example in terms of alternative causal explanations. Focus on the assumption of each argument.

Author's original argument:

Conclusion:	The reason Todd chose to go to a good university was to get a good job upon graduation.
Assumption:	Going to a good university caused Todd to get a good job upon graduation.

Evidence:	Todd went to a good university. He got a good job upon graduation.

To weaken this argument, we concentrate on finding an alternative explanation. There are at least three as suggested below.

Ex. "The sports person"

Conclusion:	Todd went to a good university with a nationally recognized sports team because he wanted to play on that varsity sports team.
Assumption:	A person would not go to a good university and play on a well-known varsity sports team unless that was his or her primary motivation for doing so.
Evidence:	Todd went to a good university. He played on a nationally recognized varsity sports team.

Ex. "The academic"

Conclusion:	Todd went to university for the academic challenge.
Assumption:	A person would not go to university and excel academically unless that was his or her primary objective for going to university.
Evidence:	Todd went to a good university. He excelled academically.

Ex. "The all-rounded person"

Conclusion:	Todd went to a good university to all-round himself socially.
Assumption:	A person would not go to university and join several well-known clubs unless motivated to do so for social reasons.
Evidence:	Todd went to a good university. He joined several well-known clubs on campus and met many new friends.

157. Valdez (♪ ♪)

Answer: Choice E
Classification: Cause and Effect Assumptions
Snapshot: This follow-up problem reinforces the need to think in terms of alternative *causal* explanations. If an argument suggests that A is causing B, check to see that another cause, namely C, is not instead causing B.

Choice E would most weaken the original argument. By citing a plausible alternative explanation, it serves to undermine the idea that Ms. Valdez's international marketing program was the reason for the jump in profits from 8 percent to 15 percent. The alternative explanation suggests that the increase in profits is due to a corporate acquisition prior to Ms. Valdez's appointment to president which doubled Zipco's annual revenues. We do have to assume in Choice E that revenues and profits are linked proportionately; nonetheless it is still the best choice.

In Choices A through D, none of these choices brings us close enough to increased revenues or profits. They all mention potentially positive things, but we don't have a clear assurance that they brought in the bucks (dollars). Choice B, perhaps the best wrong answer choice, simply says that production capacity has increased. We do not know whether an increase in production *capacity* equals an actual increase in production, or if such an increase in production has resulted in more profits.

158. Headline ( ))

Answer: Choice C
Classification: Cause and Effect Assumptions
Snapshot: A more complex form of alternative explanation occurs when two effects result from a single cause. Thus, if the argument suggests that A is causing B, then consider the possibility that another cause, namely C, could be causing *both* A and B.

The idea that low self-esteem may be the cause of both obesity and depression most weakens this argument. Here, obesity and depression are deemed the joint *effects* of another single cause—low self-esteem.

Per Choice A, it is not essential to the argument that one understands why he or she is depressed or how to escape from the grips of depression. It is only essential that obesity be the cause of depression. In Choice B, it is not necessary for obesity to be the only cause of depression; there could be many ways to become depressed besides becoming obese. In Choice D, it is not necessary that obesity and depression be linked proportionally, even if causally related. Depression could occur whenever one is declared "overweight" even though it would be logical to assume that one who is more overweight is also to some degree more depressed. Per Choice E, the terms "desperation and suicide" even if linked to depression are outside the scope of the claim—"obesity is linked to depression."

159. TV Viewing ( ))

Answer: Choice E
Classification: Cause and Effect Assumptions
Snapshot: This problem highlights the phenomenon of reverse causation. If A is thought to be causing B, the idea that B is causing A is called reverse causation and casts serious doubt on the notion that A is really causing B.

One way to destroy or seriously damage a causal relationship (e.g., A causes B) is to show that it is not A that causes B but B that causes A. This is what Choice E does by suggesting reverse causation. It suggests that aggressive people go looking for violent TV programming, not that violent TV programming makes people aggressive.

Choice A may weaken things a bit but not drastically. The fact that some viewers in the high-viewing group experienced lower levels of aggression than did other subjects in the high-viewing group is not an improbable result. What matters is that more high-viewers experienced more aggression overall relative to low-viewers. Ditto for Choice B. Choice C is incorrect because it is irrelevant whether fear did or did not cause some viewers to restrict their viewing. If it did, it will only mean that these viewers should show less signs of aggression because they weren't viewing as much. The reason why they are not viewing is effectively irrelevant. Choice D is also irrelevant; what matters is that people actually viewed the programs, not whether the programs were live or pre-recorded.

160. Shark ( ))

Answer: Choice B
Classification: Cause and Effect Assumptions
Snapshot: Test the "other side"—if you hear that a full moon causes the crime rate to rise, always ask what the crime rate is like when the moon is not full.

First, let's go to the incorrect answer choices. Answer A is the closest correct answer because it generally supports the idea that surfers in other areas are also not being attacked. Choice A slightly strengthens the original argument. Choice C weakens the argument suggesting that there are no sharks left in the reserve. Choice D also weakens the argument by suggesting that an alternative explanation (i.e., wristbands with metal bells) may be key to understanding why sharks are not attacking surfers. Choice E is essentially irrelevant; we are talking about surfers, not divers or tuna fish. In Choice B (correct answer), what we really want to know is whether sharks attack surfers wearing black suits while avoiding surfers wearing metallic suits.

What do you need in order to prove that metallic suits really work? The framework for setting this problem up is the basis for experimental design problems, as seen in real-life research.

	Shark Attacks	No Shark Attacks	Total Number of Surfers
Black Suits	(a)	(b)	xx
Metallic Suits	(c)	(d)	xx
	Xx	xx	xxx

This problem highlights the trap of "proof by selected instances." People trying to prove the efficacy of wearing metallic suits cite examples from categories (a) and (d). That is, they cite instances of surfers wearing black suits and getting attacked by sharks (see a) and also cite instances of surfers in metallic wetsuits who do not get attacked by sharks (see d). People trying to prove the efficacy of wearing traditional black suits cite examples from categories (b) and (c). That is, they cite instances of surfers wearing metallic suits and getting attacked by sharks (see c) while citing instances of surfers wearing black suits and not getting attacked by sharks (see b).

Actually what we *really* want to know is a percentage comparison—the number of surfers wearing black suits who are attacked by sharks divided by the total number of surfers wearing black suits vs. the number of surfers wearing metallic suits who are attacked by sharks divided by the number of surfers wearing metallic suits.

161. Movie Buffs (∫)

Answer: Choice B
Classification: Representative Sample Assumptions
Snapshot: The word "survey" is a strong signal that a representative sample assumption is on the horizon.

This is a classic representative sample assumption question. The argument assumes that a sample based on people attending Sunday matinees (afternoon) is representative of the whole country of movie goers. The question, "How representative is the opinion of those attending Sunday matinees?" For example, Sunday matinee movie goers might consist of a disproportionate number of family viewers (i.e., people with children) who prefer not to watch bizarre or violent movies during their Sunday afternoons. For this sample to be representative, we need to survey at least some Saturday night movie goers, Saturday matinee movie goers, and weekday movie goers.

Choice A does weaken the argument somewhat by suggesting that people will see a movie regardless of its genre just so long as their star actor (or actress) appears. Choice C is incorrect because we are concerned about the *current* tastes of movie goers (based on a recent survey) and not the movie hits of yesteryear.

Choice D is incorrect. We cannot assume that increased book sales and college enrollment in criminology courses is necessarily linked to trends among movie goers. As far as we know, the moderate increase in course enrollments is the result of many other factors.

Choice E is incorrect because it notionally strengthens the idea that movie producers should stop producing these types of movies because they are financially unsound. If actor salaries are high, then movie production costs will be higher, putting pressure on the bottom line.

162. Putting (𝄞 𝄞)

Answer: Choice C
Classification: Representative Sample Assumption
Snapshot: Representative sample assumptions are based on the idea that some smaller "thing" is representative of a larger whole.

The argument assumes that the ability to putt is the pivotal factor in determining whether a person can achieve a low golf score. There are many ingredients to a good golf game including putting, driving, iron shots, chipping, sand-trap shots, judging weather, pacing, strategy, temperament, experience, physical fitness, and competitiveness. This passage assumes that it all happens on the putting green. Although it would be impossible to argue that putting is not an important component to achieving a low score in golf, it is certainly not the only factor.

Choice A is incorrect. We cannot assume that there is no way to improve a golf game other than with quality equipment. Practice itself might be enough to simply improve a golf game. The argument does suggest that if a person wants to make great improvements in his or her golf game then he or she needs to make improvements in putting and, ideally, purchase a new Sweet Spot Putter.

Choice B is incorrect because it forms an unwarranted comparison that is not assumed in the argument. We do not know whether a new Sweet Spot Putter will improve an amateur's game more than it will improve a professional's game or vice-versa. Likewise, Choice D is incorrect because we do not know whether the new Sweet Spot Putter is superior to any other putter currently on the market. For all we know, Sweet Spot Putter is just one of three new miracle putters.

Per Choice E, we also have no way of knowing whether lessons are, or are not, as effective at improving the accuracy of a player's putting as is the use of quality equipment.

163. Critic's Choice (𝄞 𝄞)

Answer: Choice C
Classification: Representative Sample Assumptions
Snapshot: Check to see if evidence has been "hand-picked" to support a claim being made.

Since there are certainly far more than 100 contemporary novels and 100 non-contemporary novels to choose from, a question arises as to whether those novels chosen are representative of the entire population of contemporary versus non-contemporary novels. It is possible that the author of *Decline of the Novelist* chose novels which best supported his/her thesis—that today's novelists are not as skillful as the novelists of yesteryear. Choice A might weaken the argument slightly but certainly wouldn't weaken it seriously. Choice B, while highly plausible, is irrelevant to the argument because the author focuses his/her argument on technical skill. Choice D is simply out-of-scope since we don't know anything about the literary skill required to do screenplays. Choice E is irrelevant; it doesn't matter whether the average reader is familiar with the terms of literary criticism; it only matters that the book's author is familiar with these terms.

164. Temperament (𝄞 𝄞)

Answer: Choice E
Classification: Representative Sample Assumptions
Snapshot: "Evidence omitted" may hold the key to understanding the validity of an argument.

This is an example of "proof by selected instances." Each person—Steve and John—will simply choose examples which support his intended claim. Steve picks red-haired people who have bad tempers to support his claim that red-haired people are bad tempered. John picks red-haired people who have good tempers to support his claim that red-haired people are not bad tempered. The fact that the number of red-haired people (Choice A) that one person knows is more or less than the number of red-haired people that the other person knows has no clear effect on reconciling the two statements. In fact, it is quite possible that the percentage of red-haired people that each knows is quite close, say 5 percent; after all that's the magic of percentages as opposed to numbers—they express things in relative terms. In Choice B, it is only plausible that the number of red-haired people both Steve and John know would be, in aggregate, less than the total non-red-haired people both know. Confirmation of this likely reality will not reconcile the two seemingly contradictory statements.

It is also unclear whether Choice C has any effect. Any mis-assessments may prove net positive or net negative or may have a counter-balancing effect. It is almost axiomatic that both Steve and John know of friends who are not red-haired and have bad tempers but this will do nothing to reconcile the contradictory statements, so Choice D is out. Note that the procedure for actually proving whether or not red-hair is correlated with bad temper falls within the context of experimental design. Refer to Problem #160, *Shark*, **(page 235)**.

165. Questionnaire (⌇⌇)

Answer: Choice B
Classification: Representative Sample Assumptions
Snapshot: Surveys or questionnaires completed and returned may not be representative of respondents' viewpoints in general if surveys or questionnaires not returned would have otherwise yielded conflicting information.

If those former employees of Mega Corp who harbor very negative feelings about the company remain silent (i.e., they don't respond to the questionnaire) then such views have been ostensibly omitted from inclusion. Choice A, may also be a concern, but it is impossible to tell whether it refers to employees who felt much better about their employment experience or much worse (we can't assume employees necessarily felt worse!). In Choice C, we can't assume that the public relations efforts of Quantum have any affect on the employees who have left the company; besides, designing programs and implementing programs are two different things. The placement of questions within the questionnaire (Choice D) is likely irrelevant or its impact, inconclusive. Choice E serves to strengthen the Human Resource Manager's claim because the response rate achieved by Mega Corp (i.e., 25/100 or 25%) is greater than the general response rate of 10 percent; of course, the higher the response rate the better.

166. Classics (⌇⌇⌇)

Answer: Choice E
Classification: Implementation Assumptions
Snapshot: The capability or ability to do something should not imply application of those abilities, whether due to choice or neglect.

In order for a plan to work, desire or motivation on the part of the individual or organization must be present. Here, the operative word is "can" and the ability to do something does not necessarily translate to the "will" to do something. "Can" does not equal "will."

Perhaps the easiest way to summarize the problem is to say that just because most literate people have not read the classics does not mean that they are necessarily lazy. Most literate people may simply choose not to spend their time doing so. Also, even if a person is lazy he or she may still be able to read the classics. For example, the literate but lazy person may just read very slow or in fits and starts but still arrive at the finish line. All we do know is that some people have likely read the classics. For all we know, some of these people might be motivated and some might be lazy. We cannot assume that all of the people who have read the classics belong to the motivated group.

Choice D is not correct because the original statement is not a true "if...then" statement and the contrapositive is not a valid inference as it would otherwise be. The original statement only states that, based on a precondition, a person "can" read the classics.

Choice D is not correct because the original statement is not a true "if...then" statement, meaning that the contrapositive is not a valid inference (as it would otherwise be). The original statement only states that a person who is literate and not lazy "can" read the classics.

Here is an example which illustrates how Choice D might have been a correct choice. Say the original statement was a true "if...then" statement as follows:

Hypothetical: "If a person is literate and is not lazy *then* he or she will read the classics."

Here, the contrapositive leads to a correct inference (see *Chapter 4, World of Letters*, and the discussion on Critical Reasoning).

Statement: "If a person has not read the classics then he or she is a literate person who is lazy!"

167. Public Transportation (♪ ♪)

Answer: Choice A
Classification: Implementation Assumptions
Snapshot: One way to uncover implementation assumptions is to anticipate bottlenecks. This problem is also chosen to highlight the "all of the following would weaken/strengthen the argument EXCEPT" question format in which the correct answer is very often an *irrelevant* answer choice.

The fact that there may be better or easier ways to lower pollution levels in most large cities falls outside the scope of this argument. The argument only concerns itself with the idea that people should leave their cars at home and take public transportation to combat pollution.

This question was chosen to highlight implementation assumptions that can occur in Critical Reasoning problems. Choices B, C, D, and E are all valid implementation assumptions. Choice B questions whether there are enough people who actually own cars or who actually use cars to drive to work. In the most basic sense, if people do not own cars the argument is irrelevant. Choice C highlights a lack of required opportunity to make a plan work. Public transportation must be both available and accessible should someone decide to switch. Choices D and E highlight unanticipated bottlenecks, namely that the current public transportation system can accommodate all the people who decide to switch, as well as meet financial requirements.

Author's note: Here's a quick review problem written with a light-hearted tone:

People who often wear green shirts tend to score high on standardized exams because wearing green shirts makes you feel smarter and more optimistic.

All of the following would weaken the argument above EXCEPT:

A) Many people who regularly wear green shirts have a tendency to read questions on standardized exams too quickly, thereby failing to grasp critical nuances within problems.

B) People who often wear green shirts are rarely among the best prepared students in terms of those sitting for a standardized exam.

C) Many people who frequently wear green shirts are especially unlucky on days when they sit for standardized exams.

D) The frequency with which green shirts are worn has been scientifically proven to have absolutely no effect on a person's performance on standardized exams.

E) People who often wear green shirts also like chocolate mint ice cream.

Choice E is correct in so far as it does not weaken the argument. This statement is simply irrelevant to the argument at hand.

168. Rainbow Corp (§)

Answer: Choice B
Classification: Implementation Assumptions
Snapshot: An argument may depend on the assumption that a person or organization is aware of a pre-existing fact, situation, or condition.

If Tina is not aware of the recent newspaper articles featuring Rainbow Corp as an environmental culprit, it does not make real sense to conclude that she does not care about the environment. Choices A and C are irrelevant. In Choice D, even if the company's public relations department didn't issue a statement denying that the company violated the law, this doesn't mean that the company is guilty of any wrong doing. The actual guilt or innocence of Rainbow Corp has no impact on the issue at hand because Tina has no idea of the indictment. In Choice D, the fact that Tina was a member of an environmental protection organization during her freshman and sophomore years in college weakens the claim a little but not substantially so.

Author's note: Let's review another example. Suppose that a certain global think tank is reviewing national anthems and their historical themes. It concludes that most national anthems have militaristic themes due in part to their creation during times of war, conflict, or strife. Therefore, the think tank recommends that in the context of preserving global peace and stability, countries should consider changing their national anthem to rid them of any militaristic references. What would weaken this claim? Any explanation that suggests that citizens today are unaware of such militaristic themes present in their countries' national anthems.

169. Medical School (§ §)

Answer: Choice C
Classification: Number-based Assumptions
Snapshot: Beware of comparing numbers directly with percents.

Percents and numbers do not always mix. Seventy-five percent cannot be compared with "half of all females applicants." This question only makes sense if we know the percentage of females accepted to medical school and compare this figure with the percentage of males accepted to medical school. A likely scenario is that 75 percent of all students in medical school are male because 75 percent of all applicants are male; 25 percent of all students accepted to medical school are female because 25 percent of the total applicants are female—little surprise.

Let's take a hypothetical example. Say that 10,000 applicants apply for a spot at a top medical school. What if 25 percent of the applicant pool is female while 75 percent is male? This means that 2,500 females will apply for admission and 7,500 males will apply for admission.

The opening class will consist of 500 students and only 1 in 20 applicants or 5 percent (500/10,000) of the applicants is accepted. Common sense tells us that with rules of fair selection in place, the opening class should be 75 percent male and 25 percent female, which directly reflects the applicant pool. Thus, the number of females in the opening class should be 125 (500 x 25%) while the number of males in the opening class should be 375 (500 x 75%).

Now, relate these facts to the scenario presented in the original passage. "The facts in the report speak for themselves: seventy-five percent of all students in medical school are male, but fewer than half of all the 2,500 female applicants reach their goal of being admitted to medical school." Of course less than half of all females are admitted; only 1 in 20 students overall is accepted!

Choices A, B, D, and E are all irrelevant to the issue at hand. In Choice B there is no reason to suspect that the yield rates (percentage of offers given by medical schools that are accepted by students) would in any significant way be affected by gender. So although it might warrant some consideration, it is by no means a close contender with Choice C.

170. Military Expenditures ($\int \int$)

Answer: Choice E
Classification: Number-based Assumptions
Snapshot: This problem presents a classic case where one or more items increase in dollar or absolute terms but decrease in percentage terms relative to a larger pie.

This problem highlights the concept of the "growing pie." The apparent inconsistency is resolved if it is true that the portion or percentage of the national budget represented by military expenditures has increased by a greater amount than actual expenditures. If, for example, the national budget has increased ten-fold during the past two decades and the amount of actual expenditures (inflation adjusted) has increased by 1 percent per year, then the portion devoted to military expenditure has likely shrunk. Even if actual dollars spent on military expenditures is increasing each year, as long as overall (or total) expenditures is increasing more, the amount of military expenditures, in percentage terms, is falling.

The opposite of growing pies is shrinking pies. If this problem were a shrinking pie, actual dollars spent on military expenditures would be decreasing each year, but as long as overall expenditures were shrinking faster, the amount of military expenditures, in percentage terms, would be rising.

Author's note: "Growing pies" or "shrinking pies" also present examples of the tangling of numbers and percents. Here are two examples from everyday living. Growing Pie—You may spend *more money* on personal phone calls this year compared with last year, but this does not mean that the percentage of your disposable income that you spend on phone calls has gone up. It is quite possible, for example, that you have enjoyed a significant increase in your disposable income. Therefore, although the actual money that you spend on personal phones calls has gone up, the percentage of your disposable income that you spend on phone calls has gone down. In short, a growing pie often results in an increase in dollar expenditures despite a corresponding decrease in the percentage of money being spent.

Shrinking Pie—You may spend *less hours* dining out than you used to, but this does not mean that you spend less of your free time dining out. What if you have a lot less free time these days? This would imply that an equal (or even fewer) number of hours dining out would mean that a greater portion (percentage) of your free time is spent dining out. In short, a shrinking pie often results in a decrease in dollar expenditures despite a corresponding increase in the percentage of money being spent.

171. Fiction Books ($\int \int \int$)

Answer: Choice E
Classification: Number-based Assumptions
Snapshot: If Student A spends a greater percentage of his or her disposable income on beer than coffee as compared with Student B, then this does not mean that Student A spends more money on beer than coffee.

This problem illustrates the ultimate tangling of numbers with percents. Choice A is out of scope because we don't know about people with the highest levels of education; we only know about high levels of education (HEL) households and low level of education (LEL) households. Also, we do not know whether people really *buy* these books, are *given* these books, or *inherit* these books. Choices B, C, and D are out because we do not know for sure whether HEL households or LEL households have more or less fiction vs. non-fiction books. We also do not know whether members of HEL households have more or less non-fiction books as compared with LEL households. The only thing we do know for sure is that if HEL households have more books in total than LEL households and a higher percentage of fiction vs. non-fiction, then it must be true that HEL households contain a greater *number* of fiction books than LEL households.

All of the following are significant possibilities based on hypothetical numbers of books and percentages. Again, upon examination, the only thing that must be true is that for any given scenario the number of fiction books in HEL households must be greater than the number of fiction books in LEL households. Let's use 100 books and 50 books to test things out. The number of fiction books for HEL households, Column (1), will always be greater than the number of fiction books for LEL households, Column (3).

Scenario #1 – HEL households have 80 percent fiction books and 20 percent non-fiction books while LEL households have 50 percent fiction books and 50 percent non-fiction books.

HEL Households		LEL Households	
100 books		50 books	
[	]	[	]
(1)	(2)	(3)	(4)
(fiction)	(non fiction)	(fiction)	(non fiction)
80 books	20 books	25 books	25 books

Scenario #2 – HEL households have 70 percent fiction books and 30 percent non-fiction books while LEL households have 50 percent fiction books and 50 percent non-fiction books.

HEL Households		LEL Households	
100 books		50 books	
[	]	[	]
(1)	(2)	(3)	(4)
(fiction)	(non fiction)	(fiction)	(non fiction)
70 books	30 books	25 books	25 books

Scenario #3 – Get ready for this! HEL households could have 40 percent fiction books and 60 percent non-fiction books while LEL households have 20 percent fiction books and 80 percent non-fiction books. Note that this is possible because the percentage of fiction books for HEL households is still greater—40 percent—than the percentage of fiction books for LEL households—20 percent.

HEL Households		LEL Households	
100 books		50 books	
[	]	[	]
(1)	(2)	(3)	(4)
(fiction)	(non fiction)	(fiction)	(non fiction)
40 books	60 books	10 books	40 books

Author's note: Here's a problem which combines the concepts tested in the two previous problems: *Military Expenditures* and *Fiction Books*. Ponder the following statement:

> "The percentage of white wine bottled to red wine bottled in Germany is greater than the percentage of white wine bottled in France."

Does this mean that there is more white wine bottled in Germany than white wine bottled in France? Answer—No. Why? Because the size of the wine industry in France is so much bigger than the wine industry in Germany. The French "pie," so to speak, is much bigger than the German "pie"; five times in fact.

Does the original statement mean that Germany bottles more white wine than it does red wine or that France bottles more white wine than it does red wine? The answer is "no" on both accounts.

Let's draw upon some plausible numbers in line with real statistics. France produces five times as much wine as Germany does. Of all the wine produced by Germany, 75 percent is white wine and 25 percent is red wine. Of all the wine produced by France,

25 percent is white wine and 75 percent is red wine. Even though the percentage of white wine bottled to red wine bottled in Germany is greater than the percentage of white wine bottled in France, France still produces more white wine than Germany does. Here are simple numbers to prove our point. Let's say that France produces 500 bottles of wine each year and Germany produces 100 bottles of wine each year. Therefore, France produces 125 bottles of white wine whereas Germany produces 75 bottles of white wine.

<table>
<tr><td>French Wine Production
500 bottles</td><td>German Wine Production
100 bottles</td></tr>
<tr><td>[   ]</td><td>[   ]</td></tr>
<tr><td>(1)   (2)</td><td>(3)   (4)</td></tr>
<tr><td>(White Wine) (Red Wine)</td><td>(White Wine) (Red Wine)</td></tr>
<tr><td>125 bottles 375 bottles</td><td>75 bottles 25 bottles</td></tr>
</table>

172. Nova vs. Rebound (𝄞 𝄞)

Answer: Choice C
Classification: Number-based Assumptions
Snapshot: Overlap occurs when the number of "items" add up to more than 100 percent. Situations involving either A or B do not necessarily preclude the possibility of both A and B.

We cannot assume that a person liked either Nova or Rebound without taking into account the possibility that a person liked both name brand shoes at the same time. This situation results in overlap and accounts for the fact that the percentage appears to be greater than 100%. That is: 53% + 47% + 24% = 124%.

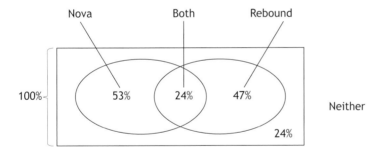

For the record, the following is the mathematical solution.

General Formula:	*Applied to this problem:*
+ Item #1	+ 53%
+ Item #2	+ 47%
- Both	- x%
+ Neither	+ 24%
100%	100%

The number who liked *both* is calculated as 53% + 47% - x% (both) + 24% (neither) = 100%. Therefore, the number of people liking both Nova and Rebound was 24 percent. This problem is both strange and tricky because 24 percent is the identical figure for the "both" and "neither" components in the calculation. See *Chapter 5: Problem Solving*, Problem #18, **(page 118).**

173. Grapes (🍷 🍷)

Answer: Choice B
Classification: Number-based Assumptions
Snapshot: Total costs must be distinguished from per unit costs.

The assumption is that both crops were grown on the same number of acres. Of course, per acre costs in each U.S. state are determined as follows:

$$\frac{Costs}{Acres} = \text{Cost per acre}$$

In Choice B, we cannot make an assessment on the cost per acre basis without knowing the total costs *and* the total acres. Despite the greater total costs to grow watermelons in Oklahoma (compared with California), if many more acres of watermelons were grown in Oklahoma (as compared with grapes in California), then the cost per acre to grow watermelons in Oklahoma might very well be lower.

Answer Choices A and C fall outside the scope of the argument. In Choice A, we are talking about "costs to grow," not profits on the sale. Choice C switches terms around. In the original, we are only talking about watermelons in Oklahoma and grapes in California. We must stick with the information as presented. In Choice D, how the crops are being *used* is irrelevant. In Choice E, the source of money used to grow crops is also irrelevant. It does not matter who pays for the cost of growing the crops—farmers, the government (or state subsidies), or Aunt Jessie—costs are costs.

174. Act-Fast (🍷 🍷)

Answer: Choice D
Classification: Number-based Assumptions
Snapshot: Efficiency is calculated by dividing output by total hours (or units). Cost efficiency is calculated by dividing cost by total hours (or units).

This problem is built on the assumption that the number of tablets per bottle is equal. Therefore if a bottle of Aspirin contains more than twice as many tablets as does a bottle of Act-Fast, then logic dictates that a bottle of Aspirin provides a greater amount of pain reliever. And since the cost per bottle is the same, it stands to reason that *cost efficiency* of Aspirin is greater than that of Act-Fast.

What we really want to determine is how much pain reliever we're getting and how much it is costing us. In Choice A, there is no mention of the number of tablets per bottle so we cannot determine how much pain reliever in aggregate we're getting for our money. Furthermore, implied logic dictates that if one Act-Fast tablet contains twice the pain reliever found in a tablet of regular Aspirin then an Act-Fast tablet should be twice the size of a regular Aspirin tablet (or an Aspirin tablet should be one-half the size of an Act-Fast tablet). Whereas Choice B is beyond the scope of the argument, Choice C weakens the argument but not nearly to the extent Choice D does. There is also no need for the pain reliever to be of a different type or strength as suggested by Choice E.

175. Intricate Plots (🍷)

Answer: Choice C
Classification: Logic-based Assumptions
Snapshot: This problem highlights the valid use of the contrapositive. Formulaically, "If A then B" is logically equivalent to "If not B then not A."

The last line of the introductory blurb gives us an "if…then" statement which serves as the conclusion of the passage. "If scriptwriting is to remain a significant art form, its practitioners must continue to craft intricate plots." In determining what the author would most probably agree with, we need to look for logically deducible statements. Choice C, the correct answer, forms the contrapositive. "If a script does not have an intricate plot, it will probably not be a significant art form."

Choice A is an example of the fallacy of affirming the consequence. There are likely other factors that go into the making of a significant art form other than intricate plots. Choice B is the fallacy of denying the antecedent. Choice D is outside the scope of the argument; we do not know whether scriptwriting is the most likely art form to become a significant art form. Choice E is out; there is no reason to believe that more is better; perhaps one intricate plot per script is enough.

176. Pub (☙ ☙)

Answer: Choice D
Classification: Logic-based Assumptions
Snapshot: This is known as the fallacy of denying the antecedent: "If A then B" does not equal "If <u>not</u> A, then <u>not</u> B."

Looking back at the original, we find that just because it is not final exam week does not necessarily mean that the pub is not selling a lot of beer. For all we know the pub sells a lot of beer each and every week because it is a popular pub. It is certainly likely that the pub does sell a lot of beer during final exam week when students relieve stress. There could also be other lucrative weeks particularly when sports matches are being played such as football and basketball games.

In Choice D, just because no one is happy doesn't necessarily mean some people won't smile. There could always be those people who smile regardless of whether they are happy or sad. Look at the original statement and concentrate on finding a similar structure.

Original Argument (albeit fallacious!):

If final exam week ⟶ sell lots beer
≠ final exam week ⟶ ≠sell lots beer

Now match this structure with correct Choice D:

If happy ⟶ smile
≠ happy ⟶ ≠ smile

177. Balcony (☙ ☙)

Answer: Choice C
Classification: Logic-based Assumptions
Snapshot: One way to think about an "If...then" statement in the form of "If A, then B", is that just because A leads to B does not mean that C, D, or E could not also lead to B.

We are told that all apartments above the fifth floor have balconies. We cannot, however, logically infer that apartments on or below the fifth floor do not have balconies. Answer Choices B and E provide tempting traps. For all we know, every apartment from the first floor on up has a balcony.

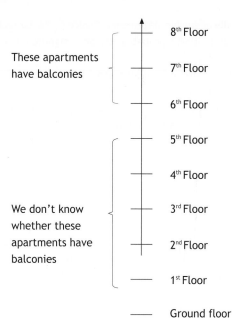

8th Floor

7th Floor

These apartments have balconies

6th Floor

5th Floor

4th Floor

We don't know whether these apartments have balconies

3rd Floor

2nd Floor

1st Floor

Ground floor

Author's note: The statement, "If a person is rich, then he or she will vote in favor of a tax cut," does not mean that if a person is poor he or she will not also vote in favor of a tax cut. Let's take another example from the world of advertising: The fact that increased expenditures on advertising has led to an increase in company sales does not mean that an increase in company sales could not have been achieved through other means—hiring more salespersons, lowering retail price, or hiring a famous, talented manager.

178. Global Warming (〄 〄 〄)

Answer: Choice D

Classification: Logic-based Assumptions

Snapshot: "If...then" statements may be viewed in terms of necessary conditions versus sufficient conditions. If a person needs water to remain healthy, this does not mean that water alone is enough to keep a person healthy. "If healthy then water" does not mean "If water then healthy". This is because water is a necessary but not a sufficient condition for good health.

If we want to stop global warming then we must pass legislation. Or: If stop global warming ⟶ pass legislation. Distinguish between necessary and sufficient conditions. It is necessary to pass legislation to stop global warming but it is not a sufficient condition for doing so. It is not a sufficient condition because there are likely several other factors necessary to stop global warming. For starters, we may in all cases need more than just legislation; we may need legal enforcement of approved laws. Moreover, other factors may need to be present as well such as the need to legislate to preserve forested areas. Furthermore, Choice C is a near identical restatement of the original statement. Answer Choices A and B are all correct interpretations of Jacques" original "if...then" statement. However, since Pierre believes Jacques' statement is not true, we must look for an erroneous answer choice.

Choice E is an opposite answer choice. Pierre's mistake consists in believing that legislation is the sole causal agent in stopping global warming (as opposed to one of several factors); his misunderstanding does not lie in the belief that legislation is an ineffective step toward stopping global warming.

Here's a related but simpler example:

Jacques: If you want to keep your pet dog alive, you must give it water every day.

Pierre: That's not true. It takes a lot more than water to keep your pet dog alive.

Pierre's response is inaccurate because he mistakenly believes that what Jacques has said is that

A) the giving of water is necessary for keeping your pet dog alive.

B) only the giving of water will keep your pet dog alive.

C) if your pet dog is to be kept alive, it must be given water.

D) the giving of water is enough to keep your pet dog alive.

E) your pet dog will not be kept alive by giving it water.

179. Sales (⌡ ⌡)

Answer: Choice C
Classification: Logic-based Assumptions
Snapshot: The statement "If A then B" does not equal "Only A's are B's." For example, the statement "If one wants to make a good salad, one should use tomatoes," should not be interpreted to mean that "tomatoes are the only thing necessary to make a good salad" or that "a good salad can be made merely by including tomatoes."

Let's summarize what Debra said:

1a.   "If a person is a good salesperson, then he or she must be friendly."

What Debra said is also equivalent to the following:

1b.   Only friendly persons are good salespersons.

Now let's summarize what Tom thought Debra said:

2a.   "If a person is friendly, then he or she will make a good salesperson."

Tom's statement is also equivalent to the following:

2b.   Only good salespersons are friendly persons.

Tom has effectively reversed the original "if...then" statement (per 1a above) and erroneously committed the fallacy of affirming the consequence. Tom would have been correct had he instead responded, "Oh, what you mean is that only friendly people are capable of making good salespersons," or "I agree, a good salesperson must be friendly," or "Sounds about right. If you're not friendly, then you're not going to make a good salesperson." Although these statements sound tricky to the ear, they are simply a matter of logic. "If A then B statements" must be translated as "Only B's are A's" in order to be correct. See *Chapter 4: The World of Letters,* Exhibit 4-8: Logical Equivalency Statements, **(page 64).**

Choice B is a restatement of Debra's original statement. It cannot be correct because Tom disagrees with her. Choice E is a logical inference based on Debra's original statement (it is the contrapositive!). Choices A and D are not correct because regardless of whether the statements are true in themselves they do not lie at the crux of Tom's misunderstanding.

Author's note: The following provides a snapshot of logical equivalency statements:

Logical equivalency statements:	Examples:
If A, then B	If it is a cat, then it is a mammal.
If not B, then not A	If it is not a mammal, then it is not a cat.
All As are Bs	All cats are mammals.
Every A is a B.	Every cat is a mammal.
Only Bs are As	Only mammals are cats.

180. Football (𝄎 𝄎)

Answer: Choice A
Classification: Logic-based Assumptions
Snapshot: The statement "Every A is a B" does not equal "Only A's are B's." For example, the statement, "Every cat is a mammal," should not be interpreted to mean that "only cats are mammals."

According to the rules of logical equivalency, the statement, "<u>Every</u> person on the Brazilian World Cup Football Team is a great player," may be translated as, "<u>If</u> a person is on the Brazilian World Cup Football Team, <u>then</u> he is a great player." And this may be further translated as, "Only great players are Brazilian World Cup Football players."

Choice A cannot be true. The statement, "Only Brazilian World Cup Football players are great players," is exactly what Beth has misunderstood Marie's remark to mean. Beth thinks Marie has said, "Brazil has all the great World Cup Football players."

Choices B, C, D and E are all unwarranted inferences.

181. Smoking (𝄎 𝄎)

Answer: Choice C
Classification: Bolded-Statement Problems
Snapshot: Bolded statement questions now appear as regular guests on the GMAT exam.

The structure of the passage can be summarized as follows: An argument (consisting of two sentences) is put forth and a counter argument (consisting of two sentences) ensues followed, in turn, with a final rebuttal (consisting of one sentence).

Conclusion: The dangers of smoking, although well documented, are often ignored even today.

Evidence: According to numerous published accounts, a person who smokes habitually has a 30-percent greater chance of developing cancer or heart disease than someone who does not smoke.

Conclusion: Many individuals residing outside the health and wellness fields either find research on the ill effects of smoking to be uncompelling or choose to ignore such evidence altogether.

Evidence: **They are likely to point to instances of individuals who smoke regularly despite living well into their nineties.**

Rebuttal: What these people fail to realize is that there is a difference between a highly correlated event and a causally related event. The absence of a causally related event does not negate the validity of a highly correlated event.

Choices D and E are immediately out. It is impossible for any assumption to appear as a statement in the passage; assumptions are by definition implicit while conclusions and evidence are explicit. This bolded statement is also not a counter argument (Choice B). An argument is a claim supported by evidence. What appears in this sentence just evidence—no claim. In Choice A, what follows is not the conclusion but a rebuttal. The main conclusion appeared as the opening sentence.

CHAPTER 9

READING COMPREHENSION

"I took a speed reading course and read *War and Peace* in twenty minutes. It involves Russia."
(Woody Allen)

SOCIAL SCIENCE PASSAGES

Passage 1 ( ) (569 words)
Read the passage below before answering the five questions that follow.

For more than 40 years, a controlling insight in my educational philosophy has been the recognition that no one has ever been—no one can ever be—educated in school or college. That would be the case if our schools and colleges were at their very best, which they certainly are not, and even if the students were among the best and the brightest, as well as conscientious in the application of their powers. The reason is simply that youth itself—immaturity—is an insuperable

5   obstacle to becoming educated. Schooling is for the young. Education comes later, usually much later. The very best thing for our schools to do is to prepare the young for continued learning in later life by giving them the skills of learning and the love of it. Our schools and colleges are not doing that now, but that is what they should be doing.

To speak of an educated young person or of a wise young person, rich in the understanding of basic ideas and issues, is as much a contradiction in terms as to speak of a round square. The young can be prepared for education in the years

10   to come, but only mature men and women can become educated, beginning the process in their forties and fifties and reaching some modicum of genuine insight, sound judgment and practical wisdom after they have turned 60. This is what no high school or college graduate knows or can understand. As a matter of fact, most of their teachers do not seem to know it. In their obsession with covering ground and in the way in which they test or examine their students, they certainly do not act as if they understood that they were only preparing their students for education in later life rather than trying

15   to complete it within the precincts of their institutions.

Those who take this prescription seriously would, of course, be better off if their schooling had given them the intellectual discipline and skill they need to carry it out, and if it also had introduced them to the world of learning with some appreciation of its basic ideas and issues. But even the individual who is fortunate enough to leave school or college with a mind so disciplined, and with an abiding love of learning, would still have a long road to travel before he or she

20   became an educated person. If our schools and colleges were doing their part and adults were doing theirs, all would be well. However, our schools and colleges are not doing their part because they are trying to do everything else. And adults are not doing their part because most are under the illusion that they had completed their education when they finished their schooling.

Only the person who realizes that mature life is the time to get the education that no young person can ever acquire

25   is at last on the high road to learning. The road is steep and rocky, but it is the high road, open to anyone who has skill in learning and the ultimate goal of all learning in view—understanding the nature of things and man's place in the total scheme. An educated person is one who through the travail of his own life has assimilated the ideas that make him representative of his culture, that make him a bearer of its traditions and enable him to contribute to its improvement.

The above passage was written by Mortimer J. Adler, author and former chairman of the board of directors of Encyclopedia Britannica.

The first passage above and the accompanying questions below are presented to highlight analytical techniques for use in answering Reading Comprehension questions. This Passage 1 exceeds 500 words in length and contains five questions. Reading Comprehension passages on the GMAT are usually not longer than 450 words in length and contain no more than four questions.

Questions – Choose the best answer based on the previous passage.

182. The author's primary purpose in writing this passage is to

    A) highlight major tenets in educational philosophy in the last 40 years.

    B) raise public awareness for the need of teachers with training in the liberal arts.

    C) contrast the words schooling and education.

    D) suggest that youth stands in the way of one becoming educated.

E) cite the importance of reading with active discussion.

183. According to the passage, the best thing that our schools can do is to

A) improve academic instruction at the grassroots level.

B) advocate using the word "education" in place of the word "schooling" to better convey to adults the goal of teaching.

C) convey to students that only through high scholastic achievement can one become truly educated.

D) implement closely the opinions of adults who have already been through the educational process.

E) help students acquire the skills for learning.

184. It can be inferred from the passage that the educated person must

A) possess more maturity than passion.

B) not be less than 40 years of age.

C) be at least a university graduate.

D) have read classic works of literature.

E) have traveled widely in order to understand his or her own culture.

185. Which of the following pairs of words most closely describe the author's attitude towards *adults* as mentioned in the passage?

A) uninformed participants

B) unfortunate victims

C) conscientious citizens

D) invaluable partners

E) disdainful culprits

186. How is the previous passage organized?

A) An objective analysis is put forth supported by factual examples.

B) A single idea is presented with which the author does not agree.

C) A thesis is presented and support given for it.

D) Two ideas are contrasted and a conciliatory viewpoint emerges.

E) A popular viewpoint is criticized from a number of perspectives.

Passage 2 (⨕ ⨕ ⨕) (450 words)

How does ritual affect relationships between groups and entities external to them? According to traditional cultural anthropology, aggregates of individuals who regard their collective well-being as dependent upon a common body of ritual performances use such rituals to give their members confidence, to dispel their anxieties, and to discipline their social organization. Conventional theories hold that rituals come into play when people feel they are unable to control events and processes in their environment that are of crucial importance to them. However, recent studies of the Tsembaga, a society of nomadic agriculturalists in New Guinea, suggest that rituals do more than just give symbolic expression to the relationships between a cultural group and components of its environments; they influence those relationships in measurable ways.

Perhaps the most significant finding of the studies was that, among the Tsembaga, ritual operates as a regulating mechanism in a system of a set of interlocking systems that include such variables as the area of available land, necessary length of fallow periods, size of the human and pig populations, nutritional requirements of pigs and people, energy expended in various activities, and frequency of misfortune. In one sense, the Tsembaga constitute an ecological population in an ecosystem that also includes the other living organisms and nonliving substances found within the Tsembaga territory. By collating measurable data (such as average monthly rainfall, average garden yield, energy expenditure per cultivated acre, and nutritive values of common foods) with the collective decision to celebrate certain rituals, anthropologists have been able to show how Tsembaga rituals allocate energy and important materials. Studies have described how Tsembaga rituals regulate those relationships among people, their pigs, and their gardens that are critical to survival; control meat consumption; conserve marsupial fauna; redistribute land among territorial groups; and limit the frequency of warfare. These studies have important methodological and theoretical implications, for they enable cultural anthropologists to see that rituals can in fact produce measurable results in an external world.

By focusing on Tsembaga rituals as part of the interaction within an ecosystem, newer quantitative studies permit anthropologists to analyze how ritual operates as a mechanism regulating survival. In the language of sociology, regulation is a "latent function" of Tsembaga ritual, since the Tsembaga themselves see their rituals as pertaining less to their material relations with the ecosystem than to their spiritual relations with their ancestors. In the past, cultural anthropologists might have centered on the Tsembaga's own interpretations of their rituals in order to elucidate those rituals; but since tools now exist for examining the adaptive aspects of rituals, these anthropologists are in a far better position to appreciate fully the ecological sophistication of rituals, both among the Tsembaga and in other societies.

187. The primary purpose of the passage is to

A) Propose that the complex functions of ritual have been best analyzed when anthropologists and ecologists have collaborated in order to study human populations as measurable units.

B) criticize anthropologists' use of an ecological approach that ignores the symbolic, psychological, and socially cohesive effects of ritual.

C) evaluate theories of culture that view ritual as an expression of a society's understanding of its relationship to its environment.

D) point out the ecological sophistication of Tsembaga ritual and suggest the value of quantitative methods in assessing this sophistication.

E) argue that the studies showing that the effects of Tsembaga ritual on the environment can be measured prove that the effects of ritual on other environments can also be measured.

188. On the basis of the information in the passage, one might expect to find all of the following in the recent anthropological studies of the Tsembaga except

    A) an examination of the caloric and nutritive value of the Tsembaga diet.

    B) a study of the relationship between the number of Tsembaga rituals and the number of pigs owned by the Tsembaga.

    C) an analysis of the influence of Tsembaga forms of worship on the traditions of neighboring populations.

    D) a catalog of the ways in which Tsembaga rituals influence planting and harvest cycles.

    E) a matrix summarizing the seasonality of Tsembaga rituals and the type and function of weapons made.

189. Which of the following best expresses the author's view of ritual?

    A) Rituals symbolize the relationships between cultural groups and their environments.

    B) As a cultural phenomenon, ritual is multifaceted and performs diverse functions.

    C) Rituals imbue the events of the material world with spiritual significance.

    D) A society's view of its rituals yields the most useful information concerning the rituals' functions.

    E) The spiritual significance of ritual is deemed greater than the material benefits of ritual.

190. The author of the passage uses the term "latent function" (third paragraph) in order to suggest that

    A) the ability of ritual to regulate the environment is more a matter of study for sociologists than for anthropologists.

    B) sociological terms describe ritual as precisely as anthropological terms.

    C) anthropologists and sociologists should work together to understand the symbolic or psychological importance of rituals.

    D) anthropologists are more interested in the regulatory function of rituals of the Tsembaga than they are the psychological function of rituals.

    E) the Tsembaga are primarily interested in the spiritual values that are embodied in their rituals.

SCIENCE PASSAGE

Passage 3 (♪ ♪ ♪) (315 words)

Supernovas result in the complete disruption of stars at the end of their lives and are among the most energetic events in the universe. Originally, the distinction between Type I and Type II supernovas was based solely on the presence or absence of hydrogen atoms (hydrogen lines). Supernovas without hydrogen lines were called Type I, while those with hydrogen lines were Type II. Subsequent analysis of many of these events revealed that this empirical classification scheme in fact reflected two different mechanisms for the supernova explosion.

Type I supernovas happen in binary stars—two stars that orbit closely each other—when one of the two binary stars is a small, dense, white dwarf star. If the companion star ranges too close to the white dwarf that it is orbiting, the white dwarf's gravitational pull will draw matter from the other star. When the white dwarf acquires enough matter to become at least 1.4 times as big as the Sun, it collapses and explodes in a supernova.

Type II supernovas occur when a star, much more massive than the Sun, ends its life. When such a star begins burning out, the core of the star quickly collapses releasing amazing energy in the form of neutrinos, a kind of particle smaller than an atom. Electromagnetic radiation—energy that is electric and magnetic—causes the star to explode in a supernova. Whereas Type I supernovas typically destroy their parent stars, Type II explosions usually leave behind the stellar core.

The classification scheme regarding the mechanism for supernova explosions helps to more succinctly answer the question: Is the Sun in danger of becoming a supernova? Neither is our Sun orbiting a white dwarf nor does our Sun have the mass necessary to become a supernova. Furthermore, it will be another billion years until the Sun runs out of fuel and swells into a red giant star before going into a white dwarf form.

191. How is this passage organized?

A) A single phenomenon is introduced and two overlapping classification schema are described.

B) An original theory is mentioned before being overturned as a result of new findings.

C) Two complementary mechanisms for describing a single phenomenon are discussed and a conclusion is offered.

D) A new classification scheme is described and an example of how it works is provided.

E) Two different classification systems are outlined and a question posed to help reconcile both.

192. Which of the following best summarizes the author's answer to the question: Is the Sun in danger of becoming a supernova?

A) The Sun is too large to have a white dwarf as a partner and lacks the physical size required to become a red giant.

B) Even if the Sun were paired with a white dwarf, the Sun does not have the mass necessary to create sufficient electromagnetic radiation.

C) The Sun is not in danger of being absorbed by a white dwarf, nor does it have the size to qualify as a Type II supernova.

D) Without a white dwarf orbiting the Sun, the Sun has no obvious way to increase its size to become a Type II supernova.

E) The Sun will inevitably become a supernova once it passes from a red giant to white dwarf but not for at least a billion years.

193. It can be inferred from the passage that

A) Before a star such as the Sun can become a white dwarf, it must first become a red giant star.

B) A dense white dwarf's gravitational pull on its companion star causes the companion star to collapse and explode as a supernova.

C) Subsequent analysis of the mechanism by which supernovas explode has led to the distinction between Type I and Type II supernovas.

D) In a Type II supernova, energy and electromagnetic radiation causes a star to collapse and explode.

E) Supernovas are rare events in our universe.

194. According to the passage, which statement or statements below are true?

I. The energy created from a Type II explosion is greater than the energy created by a Type I explosion.

II. The sun is not a binary star.

III. Both Type I and Type II supernovas result in the complete destruction of the exploding star.

A) I only

B) II only

C) I and III only

D) II and III only

E) I, II and III

ANSWERS AND EXPLANATIONS

Passage 1 ( )

Question 182 - Choice D
Classification: Overview question
Snapshot: When attacking an Overview question, look for the words of the *topic* and avoid overly detailed, factually correct answer choices.

Choice A is too general because a discussion of educational philosophy in the last 40 years would likely incorporate the viewpoints of many individuals, not just the author's viewpoint. Choice B is outside the scope. We do not necessarily know whether teachers should or should not receive more liberal arts training. The author only states that he believes that teachers are covering too much ground (2nd paragraph). Choice C is a correct statement within the context of the passage. However, it is too detailed to satisfy the primary purpose as demanded by this *overview* question.

For an *overview* question, there are effectively five reasons why wrong answers are wrong. An answer choice will either be out of a passage's scope, opposite in meaning, distorted in meaning, too general or too detailed. Whereas Choice C was *too detailed*, Choice A is an example of an overly *general* answer choice. It is very useful to be on the look out for *out-of-scope* answer choices. This was the fate of answer Choices B and E. Note that *opposites* or *distortions* are <u>not</u> common wrong answer choices with regard to overview-type questions.

A time-honored tip for answering *overview* questions involves performing a T-S-P drill (see Reading Comprehension, Chapter 4). That is, we seek to identify the passage's topic, scope, and purpose. *Topic* is defined as the broad subject matter of the passage. It's an "article on education." The topic is therefore "education." *Scope* is defined as the specific aspect of the topic that the author is interested in. The scope here is "schooling vs. education." Lastly, *purpose* is defined as the reason the author sat down to write the article. His purpose is to say, "Colleges or universities can't educate; they exist to prepare students for later learning because youth itself makes real education impossible."

Knowing the topic, scope, and purpose is enough to answer directly the question at hand. And knowing the author's purpose will likely set us up for another right answer on at least one of the remaining questions. Note that identifying the topic alone can help get us halfway to a right answer. The correct answer to an *overview* question almost always contains the words of the topic. In this case, the word "education" (or its derivative "educated") does not appear in answer Choices B or E. We can feel fairly confident eliminating both of these choices.

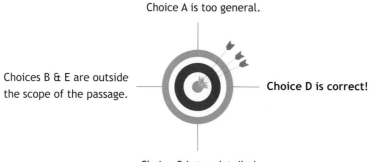

Choice A is too general.

Choices B & E are outside the scope of the passage.

Choice D is correct!

Choice C is too detailed, although factually correct.

Question 183 - Choice E
Classification: Explicit-detail question
Snapshot: Look for a literal answer—an Explicit-detail question enables the reader to go back into the passage and "underline" the correct answer.

Where is the correct answer to be found? Look back at **line 6**, "...prepare the young for continued learning in later life by giving them the skills of learning..." and **line 16**, "...better off if their schooling had given them the intellectual discipline and skill...." The word *skill* surfaces both times that the author talks about what schools should be doing.

Choices A is outside the scope of the passage. The passage does not talk about improving academic instructions or anything to do with grassroots levels of education. Nor does the passage talk about the opinions of adults.

Choice B is essentially opposite in meaning. To be correct, the answer choice should read, "redefine 'education' as 'schooling' so to better convey to parents the goals of teaching". The author feels that adults have missed the point in thinking that finishing school is the same as finishing one's education; in fact, schools exist to school and education comes later. Choice D may also be classified as *opposite* in meaning if we stick to the general spirit of the passage. The author believes that adults are very much uninformed and have missed the major point of education **(lines 24-26)**; therefore closely implementing their opinions is essentially opposite the author's intended meaning.

Choice C is a *distortion*. Distortions are most often created by the use of extreme words or the use of categorical or absolute-type wordings. Here the word "only" signals a potential distortion. The author would likely agree that high scholastic achievement is a possible requirement for becoming educated but not a sufficient condition in and of itself. In fact, the author really doesn't mention scholastic achievement, so we might choose *out-of-scope* if we did not happen to focus initially on the absolute-type wording.

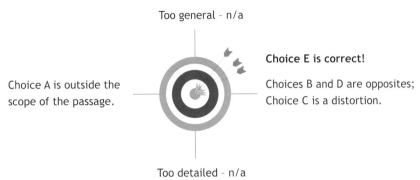

Too general – n/a

Choice A is outside the scope of the passage.

Choice E is correct!

Choices B and D are opposites; Choice C is a distortion.

Too detailed – n/a

Question 184 – Choice B
Classification: Inference question
Snapshot: The challenge with *inference* questions is to find an answer that isn't explicitly mentioned in the passage but one which can be logically inferred.

Although the author does not give an exact "education formula", he effectively says that a number of factors are necessary to travel the "high road" to becoming educated. These include: passion, a knack for learning, discipline, and maturity. In terms of maturity, he clearly states, "The young can be prepared for education in the years to come, but only mature men and women can become educated, beginning the process in their forties and fifties and reaching some modicum of genuine insight, sound judgment and practical wisdom after they have turned 60." Obviously, according to the author, if maturity begins in a person's forties and takes another 10 to 20 years, then an individual could not be less than 40 years of age and still be considered educated.

Wrong answer choices in *inference* questions often fall outside the scope of the passage. Choice A is *out-of-scope* and is specifically referred to as an unwarranted comparison. The author does not say whether he believes becoming educated takes more passion than maturity or more maturity than passion.

Choice C is perhaps the trickiest wrong answer choice. The author doesn't imply that one has to be a university graduate. In fact, he mentions "school and college" (lines 1, 6 and 24) which suggests that he may well lump high school in with college and/or university. A high school graduate might have enough schooling to get onto the road of education. Moreover, the author doesn't claim one must be a four-year college or university graduate or even whether one has to attend college or university.

There is no mention of classic works of literature, so Choice D is out of scope; we cannot answer this question based on information presented in the passage. Choice E is wrong because the author never mentions travel. Don't mistake the word "travail," (line 27, meaning "struggle") for "travel." Moreover, it is possible, without evidence to the contrary, that a person could never have left his or her own country and still understand those ideas that make him or her representative of his or her particular culture.

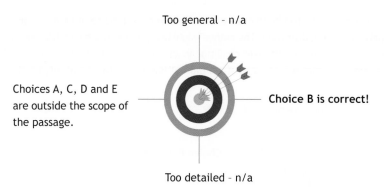

Too general – n/a

Choices A, C, D and E are outside the scope of the passage.

Choice B is correct!

Too detailed – n/a

Question 185 – Choice A

Classification: Tone question

Snapshot: *Tone* questions ask about the author's feeling or attitude toward someone or something in the passage. Basically, the author will be either positive, negative, or neutral. In most cases, especially with respect to Social Sciences passages (versus Science passages), the fact that the author would sit down to write something hints that he or she has some opinion about the topic at hand. Therefore, the neutral answer choice is not usually correct, even if available. For this question, we have, on the positive and supportive side, the word pairs: "invaluable partners," "conscientious citizens," or "unfortunate victims." On the negative side, we have "uninformed participants," or "disdainful culprits."

The author's attitude toward adults is somewhat negative but not excessively so. The feeling is more like frustration. The author believes that adults are essentially clueless, incapable of making the distinction between schooling and education (lines 22 -23). Therefore, positive sounding Choices C and D are out. Choice B, "unfortunate victims," is sympathetic but the author thinks that adults are not victims, just mis-focused. Choice E, "disdainful culprits," is too negative.

Question 186 – Choice C

Classification: Passage organization question type.

Snapshot: Think in terms of the number of viewpoints and the relationship of these viewpoints.

The author introduces his thesis or summary in the very first sentence, "...a controlling insight in my educational philosophy...", then he goes on to support it with his personal observations, experiences, and opinions. Thus, Choice A is not correct. No objective analysis is put forth; if there were, we would expect to see some surveys, statistics, or alternative viewpoints introduced. Choice B is wrong because there is a single idea presented but the author agrees with it because it is his own idea. Choice D is incorrect as there are not two viewpoints presented, just one. Choice E suggests a popular viewpoint but it is highly unlikely that many people have adopted this viewpoint because, according to the author, even teachers and adults haven't really caught on. Lastly, a number of perspectives are not drawn upon. The author chooses to spend the entire article developing his single viewpoint, "no one has ever been—no one could ever be—educated in school or college."

Passage 2 (𝕊 𝕊 𝕊)

Question 187 – Choice D

Classification: Overview question

Snapshot: Make sure to read "the first sentence of the passage first but the last sentence of the passage next." Sometimes the author concludes at the bottom of the passage.

The major theme in this passage is that rituals are not only used by the Tsembaga society in a symbolic sense (that is, religiously, psychologically, or socially) but also in a practical or material sense. Furthermore, these impacts or influences can be measured. Measurement is a key theme. Case in point: "they influence those relationships in measurable ways" (first paragraph); "they enable cultural anthropologists to see that rituals can in fact produce measurable results in the external world" (second paragraph); and "newer quantitative studies permit anthropologists to analyze how ritual operates" (third paragraph). Choice D is a succinct rendition.

The passage does not suggest that anthropologists and ecologists collaborate for best results (Choice A), even though the passage does suggest that anthropologists analyze ecological factors. Choice B is incorrect because the author does not criticize the symbolic role of rituals; he or she instead extends the discussion of rituals to include regulatory functions or mechanisms. The last sentence of the first paragraph makes this point: "However, recent studies of the Tsembaga, a society of nomadic agriculturalists in New Guinea, suggest that rituals do more than give symbolic expression to the relationships between a cultural group and components of its environment…."

The author does not evaluate theories of culture as indicated by Choice C. His or her sole example is limited to the Tsembaga people. The author therefore does not prove that these studies show the measurable effects of rituals on other environments (per Choice E).

Question 188 - Choice C
Classification: Inference question
Snapshot: This INFERENCE question serves to introduce the "all of the following except" phraseology.

The effects of rituals on neighboring populations is not described in the second paragraph so Choice C would be the most unlikely candidate for inclusion in an anthropological study in support of the author's thesis. The influence of rituals on "the Tsembaga diet" (Choice A), "the number of pigs owned" (Choice B), "planting and harvest cycles" (Choice D), or "type and function of weapons made" (Choice E), all would be likely candidates for *inclusion* in such a report.

Question 189 - Choice B
Classification: Inference question.
Snapshot: This question is similar to an *overview* question but one which focuses on a specific subtopic within the passage.

The first sentence of the second paragraph lists many ways that rituals act as regulating mechanisms. It is obvious therefore that "ritual is multifaceted and performs diverse functions." Choice A is not incorrect per se, but rather it is incomplete. The author's view that ritual does more than symbolize relationships appears in the last sentence of the first paragraph: "However, recent studies of the Tsembaga, a society of nomadic agriculturalists in New Guinea, suggest that rituals do more than give symbolic expression to the relationships between a cultural group and components of its environment; they influence those relationships in measurable ways." Choice C is essentially opposite the author's view. The choice would have better read: "Rituals imbue the events of the spiritual (symbolic) world with material significance." Choice D is also opposite in meaning. According the last sentence of the passage (it's a long one), the author implies that anthropologists are in a better position to understand a society's culture than is the society itself. In Choice E, we cannot confirm or negate this answer choice based on information presented in the passage. It is not clear whether the spiritual significance of ritual is deemed greater than the material benefits of ritual or whether the material benefits of ritual are deemed greater than the spiritual benefits of ritual.

Question 190 - Choice E
Classification: Explicit-detail/Inference question
Snapshot: This is essentially a "vocabulary" question and one which requires some verbal interpretation.

The terms "latent function" and "hidden function" are worthy substitutes. Although the author states that "the Tsembaga themselves see their rituals as pertaining less to their material relations with the ecosystem than to their spiritual relations with their ancestors", this does not mean that such rituals do not for them perform other essential roles. The author brings up "latent function" to suggest there is "hidden benefit" in the use of ritual for the Tsembaga; these additional benefits are practical, not symbolic.

In Choices A and B, the author is not pitting anthropologists and sociologists against one another, or for that matter, the study of anthropology and sociology. Nor is the author suggesting that the two sides work together as suggested by Choice C. The author is also not concluding that anthropologists are more interested in the regulatory function of rituals than the psychological or symbolic importance of rituals (Choice D), even though the former—regulatory functions of ritual—was the focus of this passage. Note that the use of the comparative word "more" (Choices A and D) often create *out-of-scope* answer choices.

Passage 3 (🎵 🎵 🎵)

Question 191 - Choice D
Classification: Passage Organization question
Snapshot: Science passages typically exist to "describe" (as opposed to Social Science passages which typically exist to "argue") and such passages frequently incorporate two theories, hypotheses, or explanations.

The new scheme is based on the distinction between Type I and Type II supernovas; the original scheme is one based on the absence of hydrogen (Type I) or the presence of hydrogen (Type II). The example of the Sun is provided as support for how the classification system works. Choice D best summarizes this structure.

In Choice A, the schema do not overlap; they are distinct. A supernova is classified either as Type I or Type II, but never both. In Choice B, it is inaccurate to describe the original theory as being overturned. The new theory is very much an "extension" of the old theory rather than a "replacement." In Choice C, no conclusion is offered. For example, the author does not state that Type I is "better or worse" than Type II, or that Type I is easier to use in describing or explaining the occurrence of supernovas than Type II. No reconciliation between the two different classification systems is provided per Choice E. The two different systems are very much distinct and do not lend themselves to reconciliation.

Question 192 - Choice C
Classification: Explicit-Detail/Inference question
Snapshot: This question links two parts of the passage, namely the last paragraph with paragraphs two and three.

Answer Choice C describes accurately and completely the author's view in the final paragraph. The Sun does not have a white dwarf orbiting it, so it can't qualify as a Type I supernova. Nor does the Sun have the size necessary to become a Type II supernova (it would have to be at least 1.4 times its own size).

In Choice A, there is no relationship suggested between the size of the Sun and its ability to have a white dwarf partner (per Type I). Choices B and D create unwarranted linkages between Type I and Type II supernovas. It is the white dwarf, not the Sun, which would undergo collapse and explosion as a supernova. In Choice E, even if the Sun does become a red giant before becoming a white dwarf, it does not mean that it will become a supernova. It would still need another star (i.e., binary star) which it could absorb en route to becoming a Type I supernova.

Question 193 - Choice A
Classification: Inference question
Snapshot: This question highlights the need to avoid choosing "reversed cause and effect relationships" and "fabricated cause and effect relationships" which are the hallmarks of some incorrect *inference* answer choices.

Choices B and D represent examples of reversed cause and effect relationships. In Choice B, it is the dense white dwarf that explodes as a supernova, not the companion star! Choice D is more subtle. We know in a Type II supernova that both energy from neutrinos and electromagnetic radiation is released. However the cause-and-effect relationship is also reversed. It is the collapsing of the star that *causes* the release of energy as neutrinos and electromagnetic radiation, subsequent to the exploding of the star as a supernova. Choice D suggests that it is the energy and electromagnetic radiation that *causes* the star to collapse and explode.

Choice A is readily inferable from the final sentence of the passage. The Sun cannot become a dwarf before becoming a red giant. We don't know whether all red giants become white dwarfs but we can infer that if a star becomes a white dwarf then it has previously been a red giant. In Choice C, the new classification scheme did not create the Type I and Type II distinctions; these were already defined by the old classification system. The new classification scheme serves to "refine" our understanding of Type I and Type II supernovas.

There is no indication from the information given in the passage that supernovas are rare events in the universe at large (Choice E). For all we know, they are common in some galaxies and rare in others. It is important not to draw upon outside knowledge when answering Reading Comprehension passages. You might say there is some humor to be found in the advice: "Don't try to use common sense to answer Reading Comprehension questions." Use logic—"yes"—but not common sense.

Question 194 - Choice B
Classification: Inference/Explicit-detail question
Snapshot: This question introduces the Roman Numeral question-type in Reading Comprehension.

The statement represented by Roman Numeral I cannot be proved or disproved from information gleamed from the passage. Although Type II stars appear bigger than Type I ("much more massive than the Sun" vs. "at least 1.4 times as big as the Sun"), it is not certain which Type releases the greatest amount of overall energy.

Roman Numeral II is true. To be a binary star, the Sun must have an orbiting partner. Because the Sun does not, it does not qualify as a binary star (see first sentence of second paragraph).

Roman Numeral III is false. The last line of the third paragraph clearly states: "Whereas Type I supernovas typically destroy their parent stars, Type II explosions usually leave behind the stellar core." Type II supernovas, therefore, do not result in "complete destruction of the exploding star."

CHAPTER 10

ANALYTICAL WRITING ASSESSMENT

"Put it before them briefly so they will read it, clearly so they will appreciate it, picturesquely so they will remember it and, above all, accurately so they will be guided by its light."
(Joseph Pulitzer)

For the purposes of reinforcing techniques used to answer *argument essays* and *issue essays*, write or sketch a response to the following questions and compare them to the proposed solutions presented. For the record, *Yuppie Café* and *Cars vs. Public Transportation* are classic examples of argument-type essays. Examples of issue-type essays include *Modernization, Is Success Transferable?*, *We Shape Our Buildings,* and *The Unexamined Life.*

ARGUMENT ESSAYS

195. Yuppie Café (〄 〄)

The following appeared as part of a campaign to sell advertising to local businesses through various Internet service providers.

"The Yuppie Café began advertising on the Internet this year and was delighted to see its business increase by 15 percent over last year's total. Their success shows that you too can use the Internet to make your business more profitable."

Discuss how well reasoned you find this argument. In your discussion, be sure to analyze the line of reasoning and the use of evidence in the argument. For example, you may need to consider what questionable assumptions underlie the thinking and what alternative explanations or counter examples might weaken the conclusion. You can also discuss what sort of evidence would strengthen or refute the argument, what changes in the argument would make it more logically sound, and what, if anything, would help you better evaluate its conclusion.

Identify the conclusion and evidence and choose three (or more) assumptions:

Conclusion:

Evidence:

Assumptions:

196. Cars vs. Public Transportation (🖋 🖋)

"People living in cities should switch from driving their cars to work on the weekdays to taking public transportation such as buses and subways. In large cities such as New York, London, and Shanghai, cars are an expensive and inefficient means of transportation and fossil fuel emissions are the major source of the city's pollution."

Discuss how well reasoned you find this argument. In your discussion, be sure to analyze the line of reasoning and the use of evidence in the argument. For example, you may need to consider what questionable assumptions underlie the thinking and what alternative explanations or counterexamples might weaken the conclusion. You can also discuss what sort of evidence would strengthen or refute the argument, what changes in the argument would make it more logically sound, and what, if anything, would help you better evaluate its conclusion.

Identify the conclusion and evidence and choose three (or more) assumptions:

Conclusion:

Evidence:

Assumptions:

ISSUE ESSAYS

197. Modernization (𝄞)

"Although most people would agree that historical buildings represent a valuable record of any society's past, municipal governments should resolve doubt in favor of removing old buildings when such buildings stand on ground that planners feel could be better utilized."

Discuss the extent to which you agree or disagree with the statement or opinion expressed above. Support your point of view with reasons and/or examples drawn from your own experience, observations, or reading.

Summarize the Pros and Cons

	Agree - Resolve doubt in favor of replacing old buildings	Disagree - Resolve doubt in favor of keeping old buildings
Quantitative factors	•	•
	•	•
	•	•
Qualitative factors	•	•
	•	•
	•	•

198. Is Success Transferable? (𝄞 𝄞)

"Personal success in one field or endeavor leads to success in other fields."

Discuss the extent to which you agree or disagree with the statement or opinion expressed above. Support your point of view with reasons and/or examples drawn from your own experience, observations, or reading.

Summarize the Pros and Cons

Yes - Personal or professional success in one field leads to success in other fields	No - Personal or professional success in one field does not lead to success in other fields
•	•
•	•
•	•

199. We Shape Our Buildings (⌡ ⌡ ⌡)

"First we shape our buildings then afterwards our buildings shape us."

Explain what you think this statement means and discuss the extent to which you do or do not agree with it. Support your views with reasons and/or specific examples from your experience, observations, or reading.

Summarize the Pros and Cons

Pros	Cons
•	•
•	•
•	•

200. The Unexamined Life (⌡ ⌡ ⌡)

"The life which is unexamined is not worth living."
(Plato)

Explain what you think this statement means and discuss the extent to which you do or do not agree with it. Support your views with reasons and/or specific examples from your experience, observations, or reading.

Summarize the Pros and Cons

Pros	Cons
•	•
•	•
•	•

PROPOSED SOLUTIONS

With respect to the two argument essays that follow, *Yuppie Café* and *Cars vs. Public Transportation*, the order in which assumptions and/or evidence appear may vary from outline to written solution. This is simply a matter of form, not substance.

195. Yuppie Café (⌡ ⌡)

Solution in Outline Form

The argument concludes that you can use the Internet to advertise and make your business more profitable. The author uses as evidence the fact that Yuppie Café advertised on the Internet and the company's business increased by 15 percent over last year's total. I do not find this argument to be well reasoned as it is resting on several debatable assumptions.

Attacking the assumptions:

- First, the argument assumes that a 15 percent increase in business is the same as a 15 percent increase in revenue or profit. We need clarification with respect to the term "business increase" in order to make a proper comparison.

- Second, the argument assumes that there is a cause and effect relationship between advertising on the Internet and the increase in business as stated.

- Third, the argument assumes that Yuppie Café is representative of all other businesses, i.e., your business.

- Fourth, the argument assumes that companies have access to the Internet in order to place company advertisements, as well as possess the company personnel capable of administering the system. The argument also assumes that a company has the money to spend on advertising on the Internet. These considerations create implementation assumptions. Moreover, the argument likely assumes that the costs of Internet advertising do not outweigh the revenues to be received.

Attacking the evidence:

- Achieving a business increase is easier for a younger business than it is for an older, more mature business within any given industry. The natural growth cycle of a typical business is characterized by an upward growth curve which flattens as the business matures. A high growth percentage is more easily achieved by a younger business which is more likely to have significant year-on-year growth. An increase in business will result in a higher percentage increase given that the increase is compared to a relatively smaller base.

Conclusion:

- In conclusion, in order to strengthen this argument, we need more information to substantiate the cause-and-effect assumption, representative sample assumption, comparison assumption, and implementation assumptions mentioned above.

- We could also strengthen the argument by softening the absolute-type wording as used in the original argument. The original sentence states, "Their success shows you how you too can use the Internet to make your business more profitable." The wording could instead read, "Their success shows how you too can probably use the Internet to make your business more profitable," or "Their success shows how a number of companies can use the Internet to make their businesses more profitable."

- Finally, we need clarification as to what exactly the word "success" means. How is it defined?

Solution in Essay Form (617 words)

The argument concludes that you can use the Internet to advertise and to make your business more profitable. The author uses as evidence the fact that Yuppie Café advertised on the Internet and that the company's business increased by 15 percent over last year's total. I do not find this argument to be well reasoned as it is resting on several debatable assumptions.

First, the argument assumes that there is a cause-and-effect relationship between advertising on the Internet and an increase in business. It could be that Yuppie Café saw an increase in business for reasons not related to advertising on the Internet. For example, a major competitor of Yuppie Café may have gone out of business, the company may have started serving a higher quality coffee product, business may have increased because word-of-mouth advertising lured customers, or perhaps there was a period of general economic prosperity.

Second, the argument assumes that Yuppie Café is representative of all other businesses, i.e., your business. This creates a representative sample assumption. It may even be true that the Internet does help highly customer-oriented companies with their businesses, e.g., coffee shops, health spas, and book distribution companies. But what about an oil and gas or mining company? Obviously, it is difficult to use a single example and then generalize it to all other companies.

Third, the argument assumes that other companies actually own computers, have access to the Internet in order to place company advertisements, and have company personnel capable of administering the system. Furthermore, the argument assumes that a company has the money or financial wherewithal to spend on advertising on the Internet. Moreover, the argument assumes that the money a company spends on Internet advertising does not outweigh the revenues to be derived from increased sales. These considerations create implementation assumptions.

Fourth, the argument assumes that a 15 percent increase in business is the same as a 15 percent increase in profit. The word "business increase" likely refers to revenues but, as we know, revenues and profit are not the same thing. Profit depends on the relationship between costs, revenues, and sales volume. Furthermore, the words "business increase" are vague. For example, a 15 percent increase in the number of customers served may not translate to a 15 percent increase in revenues or profits particularly if the retail price of a cup of coffee has been significantly reduced or the cost of a cup of coffee has risen substantially.

In conclusion, in order to strengthen this argument we need more information to substantiate the cause-and-effect relationship between advertising and an increase in business. We need more examples in order to show that Yuppie Café is not merely an exceptional business example. We need some assurance that companies have access to the Internet in the first place. We also need clarification as to whether an increase in business translates to an increase in revenues and/or whether an increase in revenues translates to an increase in profit. One word—"success"—is particularly vague and needs clarification. Is a 15 percent increase in business a worthy criterion for "success"? To a venture capitalist, success might be defined by a return of 50 percent or more. Furthermore, should success be measured merely along a quantitative dimension? What about the qualitative dimensions of employee or consumer satisfaction? Finally, softening the wording in the original argument could strengthen the argument. The original sentence states, "Their success shows you how you too can use the Internet to make your business more profitable." The wording could read, "Their success shows how you too can probably use the Internet to make your business more profitable," or "Their success shows how a number of companies can use the Internet to make their businesses more profitable."

196. Cars vs. Public Transportation (𝄃 𝄃)

Solution in Outline Form

The author concludes that people should switch from driving cars to work to taking public transportation such as buses and subways. The argument is based on the evidence that cars are an expensive and inefficient mode of transportation (in New York, London, and Shanghai) and fossil fuel emissions are the major source of the city's pollution. I do not find this argument to be well reasoned as it is resting on several debatable assumptions.

Attacking the assumptions:

- Cities? Do all people who live in cities necessarily live in *large* cities where pollution is a problem? This calls into question a scope issue—a city may not be a large city.

- Cars? The argument assumes that cars are the major source of the pollution in major cities. This may not be true. It could be that pollution comes from nearby factories or perhaps the toxicity of say bus emissions is much greater than the toxicity of car emissions.

- Weekdays? It also assumes (and much more subtly) that pollution is caused by cars driven on the weekdays as opposed to the weekends. Could it be that many people only drive short distances to work on the weekdays and then go for joy rides on the weekends, making weekends the time when pollution really adds up?

- Three cities? The argument assumes that New York, London, and Shanghai are representative of other major cities. But is the public transportation in these cities typical of all major cities?—Probably not. What about Rome, Bangkok, or São Paulo?

These cities likely do not have transportation systems as good as those of the cities mentioned in the argument.

- Own cars? The argument assumes first that people own cars. This may not be true.

- Available and convenient? It also assumes that public transportation is both available and convenient to use should a person decide to switch. What if there exists no convenient transportation in the far reaching suburbs of New York, London, or Shanghai? (we shall further assume that living in the suburbs still constitutes living in the city)

- Bottlenecks? The argument also assumes that if people do switch, the current system of public transportation will be able to accommodate all the "switchers."

Attacking the evidence:

- Expensive? The argument assumes that cars are an expensive means of transportation relative to public transportation. While this is quite compelling, it need not be necessarily true. First, there is car pooling in which more than one person rides in a car. Second, a person might have to take more than a single form of public transportation. Third, let's view things from the city's standpoint, not the consumer's standpoint. If the city has to build or maintain a large public transportation system (e.g., building a subway system), it could prove very costly indeed. From the city's standpoint, the cheapest means of transportation may be privatized transportation (e.g., let consumers pay for and drive their own cars).

- Inefficient? The argument also assumes that cars are an inefficient means of transportation. However, if a person uses a car to get to work in a shorter period of time, gains in productivity may offset otherwise higher transportation costs. This is particularly relevant for high wage earners, e.g., chief executives, managing directors, doctors, etc.

Conclusion:

Strengthening the argument would require:
- More data to strengthen each of the above assumptions.
- Clarification as to the definition of the word "pollution."
- Softening the absolute-type wording from "people should switch" to "people should probably switch."

Solution in Essay Form (845 words)

The argument concludes that people living in cities should switch from driving their cars to work on the weekdays to taking public transportation such as buses and subways. It uses as evidence examples drawn from New York, London, and Shanghai, where cars are found to be an expensive and inefficient means of transportation and fossil fuel emissions are the major source of each city's pollution. I do not find the argument to be well reasoned as it is resting on several debatable assumptions.

First, the argument suggests that cars are an expensive and inefficient means of transportation. While this assumption is quite compelling, it need not be necessarily true. In terms of efficiency, a person using a car could get to work more quickly. This extra time could spell gains in productivity, particularly for high wage earners such as chief executives, managing directors, and doctors, whose time might be more than offset by the increased costs of private transportation. Also, there might be ways to evaluate the costs of using private vehicles. For example, car-pooling would mean that people share a single vehicle. Also, in the event that a person needs to take more than a single form of public transportation (e.g., a bus and the subway) to get to work, costs would increase. Finally, let us view things from the city's standpoint, as opposed to the consumers' standpoint. If the city has to build or maintain a large public transportation system (e.g., building a subway system), it could prove very costly indeed. From the city's standpoint then, the cheapest means of transportation may be privatized transportation, i.e., let consumers pay for and drive their own cars.

Second, the argument assumes that exhaust fumes from cars are the major source of each city's pollution. This may not be true. It could be that large factories are the major cause of fossil fuel emissions, not cars. Furthermore, could it be that buses and minibuses contribute disproportionately more to air pollution than do cars? This could be the case if buses, for example, run on a different type of fuel such as diesel and emit more harmful toxic fumes than do cars. This argument also assumes, and much more subtly, that pollution is caused by cars driven on the weekdays as opposed to the weekends. Could it be that many people only drive short distances to work on the weekdays and then go for joy rides on the weekends, making weekends the time when pollution really adds up?

Third, the argument made assumes that people actually own cars and that public transportation is an option both available and convenient should a person wish to switch. A person may not own a car and, even if he or she does, a choice to switch to different modes of transportation may not be possible. This latter point may be the case where a person lives in an out-of-the-way place where public transportation is virtually non-existent and cars provide the only source of transportation. The argument also assumes that if people do switch, the current system of public transportation will be able to accommodate all the "switchers."

Fourth, there exists the assumption that people who live in cities, live in large cities. Even assuming this to be true, the situation in New York, London, and Shanghai regarding cars, public transportation, and pollution may not be representative of the situation in other cities. How comparable are these cities to other major cities? For example, it seems that these three cities have some of the most extensive public transportation systems in the world. Other major cities such as Rome, Bangkok, or São Paulo may not have an extensive, reliable, or convenient public transportation system. In the event that a person neither lives nor works in a major city, this argument quickly loses ground; cars may be the only efficient means of transportation.

In conclusion, strengthening this argument would require evidence to support the supposed cause and effect relationship between driving cars and exhaust fumes which are contributing the majority of the city's pollution. We also need some data showing just how expensive and efficient cars are particularly considering how expensive it might be from the city's standpoint to build a brand-new transportation infrastructure. Furthermore, we encounter a representative sample assumption. Is Shanghai's situation like other major cities? We need to be convinced that the public transportation in New York, London, and Shanghai is not just an aberration when compared to other major cities.

Lastly, the term pollution is inherently vague. Whereas cars might be the major source of the city's air pollution, they might not be the major source of the city's overall pollution if the term includes air, water, garbage, and noise. Lastly, this argument could be strengthened by softening the absolute way the original sentence is worded. Instead of saying, "People should switch...", we could say "People should probably switch..." or "A number of people should switch...." Also, instead of saying, "In major cities such as New York...", we could say, "In some major cities such as New York...."

ISSUE ESSAYS

197. Modernization (𝄐)

Solution in Outline Form

	Agree – Resolve doubt in favor of replacing historical buildings	Disagree – Resolve doubt in favor of keeping historical buildings
QUANTITATIVE	• Revenue streams: new buildings earn more money in rent or sales. • Revenue streams: new buildings earn more money in taxes. • Costs: old buildings have high maintenance costs which could be avoided if we built a new building.	• Revenue streams: old buildings earn money from tourists. • Revenue streams: wealthy individuals often donate money to preserve old historical buildings. • Costs: there is a huge capital outlay to begin construction on a new building which ties up valuable municipal funds.
QUALITATIVE	• Safety: new buildings are safer. • Architectural: new buildings are more visually harmonious with other modern buildings ("harmony in parity"). • Aesthetics: new buildings are a sign of power and progress.	• Educational: there is cultural, educational, and historical worth in old buildings. • Architectural: old buildings offer an interesting visual contrast to modern buildings ("harmony in contrast"). • Aesthetics: old buildings bear a sense of nostalgia.

Solution in Essay Form (463 words)

In general, I believe cities should err on the side of replacing older buildings with modern ones. According to an authoritative report released by researchers at the Council of Urban Planning & Cultural Preservation, revenue streams resulting from constructing new high-rise buildings earn more money in rent and taxes for the city while creating cost savings through the elimination of high maintenance costs associated with the upkeep of older buildings. More money means the city can sponsor more programs.

Who can dispute the monetary benefits? Although one could argue that there is a huge capital outlay required to begin construction on a new building, which ties up valuable municipal funds, the resulting revenue windfall in terms of rental and tax revenues is more than worth it from the city's standpoint. Tourism revenues and/or donation revenues received in support of historical buildings are small in comparison to potential rent and tax receipts derived from modern skyscrapers. In the recent *Time Magazine* article, "In with the New, Out with the Old," the journalist cites evidence for replacing old historical buildings including safety and aesthetics. New buildings are not only safer in terms of construction and fire prevention but also more harmonious with surrounding modern buildings. A new building is more likely to create a sense of architectural parity when standing alongside other modern buildings. To residents and visitors alike—"new"—is a sign of power and progress.

Old historical buildings do embody a sense of cultural, educational, and historical worth and their removal is regrettable. However, we cannot overlook the monetary and non-monetary benefits that come from their removal. In the city of Hong Kong, for example, downtown centers exist primarily to serve business needs; what people care about most is utility—safe and efficient usage of space. When the city is able to utilize valuable space in its downtown centers, additional revenues flow back to the community in the form of increased programs to the public.

In conclusion, I do feel some clarification is needed to determine the exact meaning of "better utilized." Not all things are measured in terms of money or volume. What about educational, historical, cultural, or aesthetic value? The more truly historical a building, the more this fact would come to bear on any decision to replace it. Is the building in question an architectural icon or perhaps the only building representing a specific era in the city's history? If the answer to either of these questions is "yes" then it is that much more unlikely we would try to replace it. If, however, the answer to both these questions is "no" then it is all the more likely that we would consider replacing the building. After all, who would argue that our cities do not exist for the utilitarian benefit of all their citizens?

198. Is Success Transferable? ($\int$ $\int$)

Solution in Outline Form

Yes – Personal or professional success in one field or endeavor leads to success in other fields	No – Personal and professional success in one field or endeavor does not lead to success in other fields
• Generally, true, people successful in one area of their lives tend to be successful in other areas as well.	• Michael Jordan (basketball star) tried playing professional baseball and failed.
• According to an article in the *Journal of Medicine*, individuals who are highly intelligent also tend to be more industrious and better adapted socially than people of average intelligence.	• Successful restaurateurs often try their hand at real estate or the stock market and flop.
• Leonardo da Vinci is considered the universal genius. He succeeded as a painter, architect, sculptor, and scientist.	• According to *Psychology Today* magazine, life comes down to priorities and few people can accommodate multiple priorities.
• Newton won acclaim in several areas including optics, mathematics, and mechanics.	• Bjorn Borg (5-time Wimbledon tennis champion) has failed miserably in virtually every aspect of his life outside of tennis.
• In my family, all members who are good at tennis tend to be good at golf.	• Looking at family friends, I observed successful businesspersons who are failures in their family lives.
• The same discipline and organizational skills required to be successful in one endeavor are applicable to a diverse number of endeavors.	• The same passion that some people have for one thing is absent in other areas.

Note: The distinction between quantitative and qualitative factors has been dropped because, in this particular issue, there does not exist a clear distinction between monetary and non-monetary considerations.

Solution in Essay Form (375 words)

I do not believe that, in general, personal or professional success in one field or endeavor leads to success in other fields. According to a recent article in *Psychology Today* magazine, life comes down to priorities and few people can accommodate multiple priorities. One need only look to the everyday world of sports. Michael Jordan, the basketball star, tried playing professional baseball and failed. Bjorn Borg, the former tennis star, has failed miserably in virtually every aspect of his life outside of tennis.

Although it is true that the more closely related a field or endeavor might be the greater the likelihood of success, it does not take much variation from a given field before any advantage is nullified. Someone good at math is probably good at physics, but we need only think back to grade school to realize that someone who is good at mathematics will not always be good at English. Even successful businesspersons can fall prey to the illusion that newfound success in one field will guarantee success in another field. Growing up, I saw Italian restaurateurs arrive in our city penniless and become wealthy from their restaurant operations. However, they later went on to lose a substantial amount of their wealth by playing the stock market and speculating in real estate.

Who can argue with the power of personal experience? Looking at my family and friends provides additional proof. One friend, Leilani, is a great artist but clueless when it comes to how to commercialize her talent. Another friend, Keith, is a marketing guru but lousy in his financial affairs. My brother did not have the passion or dedication to complete his undergraduate studies but seems to have endless energy to track commodity trends. I have observed friends of my father who are leaders in their professional lives but failures in their family lives. It is obvious that the same passion and dedication that so often foreshadows success in one field may be totally absent in another endeavor. In conclusion, I do not believe that success in one field or endeavor leads to success in other fields. Some allowance must be made with respect to differing definitions of "success" and the degree to which we are claiming success across differing fields.

199. We Shape Our Buildings (∫ ∫ ∫)

Solution in Outline Form

Pros - I agree with the statement	Cons - I disagree with the statement
• Statement (to me) indicates a type of reverse influence between types of buildings and society in general on an emotional and even physical level.	• Buildings cannot realistically shape the basic components of a person's personality.
• General examples: Europe, Papua New Guinea, New York.	• The people with which we surround ourselves, as well the political, economic, and social conditions around us, are much more important determinants of personality than are the buildings we find ourselves in.
• Interior of buildings, decorations, colors.	
• Key personal example, Lippo Center in Hong Kong.	
• Analogy for the way buildings shape us is that of weather and climate. Climate is likened to our basic personality traits; it is a long-term factor. Weather is likened to our emotions and moods; it affects us for the moment.	

Ambiguity: What does "shape" mean exactly? Does "buildings" include structures as well as monuments?

Solution in Essay Form (592 words)

In principle, I agree with the statement, "First we shape our buildings and afterwards our buildings shape us."

What this statement means to me is that there is a type of reverse influence that occurs between the types of buildings that a society builds and the emotional and even physical influence such buildings have on us as individuals. Certainly the words "shape us" are subject to interpretation. I assume that buildings cannot shape the basic building blocks of our personality but that they can shape our emotions, moods, and attitudes. The analogy might be one of weather and climate. Climate is likened to our personality; it describes a "broader" more comprehensive term. Weather is likened to our moods and emotions; it describes temporary conditions.

The way in which buildings may influence us can be seen in the differing architectural landscape as we travel from region to region in the world. Europe, for example, is full of old buildings and these older buildings help imbue people with a better appreciation of history. Knowing that we are in an old building makes us much more aware not only of time periods that have gone before but also of the contributions of individuals. I believe that historical buildings foster more historically minded people. Similarly, I feel "natural" buildings foster more ecologically minded people. In Papua New Guinea, native architecture embodies one-story thatched roof houses built of stone, mud, and clay.

In modern cities such as New York, tall glass buildings embody a sense of power and progress; they imbue tenants and visitors with a sense of professionalism and industriousness. Alternatively, they can also give the impression of being impersonal or superficial. Sometimes I get a feeling of helplessness when going up the elevator of an especially tall building. The collective effort required to build such a building means that no single individual could replicate such an engineering feat. Here is evidence of the futility of individual effort.

Feelings can change the minute we walk into a building. The Lippo Centre in Hong Kong happens to be one of my favorite buildings. The exterior of this building is constructed with a glass bubble look. These bubbles represent Koala bears crawling up the sides of a tree. I was told that the bubble design is economically more expensive because it is less efficient in terms of rental space. The Australian fellow who built this building went for aesthetics, not just economics. When walking inside this building, I feel my spirits pick up a little knowing that there was a considerable degree of personal care when planning and constructing the building.

The interior of buildings including, decorations may also have an affect on an individual. Imposing walls are a sign of alienation; open space is a sign of invitation. Modern art decorations indicate progressiveness whereas oil paintings are a sign of tradition. Coloring is also important. Green paint is a sign of calm energy; gray paint is a sign of submission; purples and reds elicit feelings of aggression.

In conclusion, whereas I do not believe that buildings influence our basic personality traits, there is little question in my mind that they affect our emotional outlook, moods, and attitudes over the short-run. Buildings may even shape us physically should we be forced to climb stairs or walk long hallways. Who can honestly say that the feeling that would accompany a visit to a chalet in the Swiss Alps would be no different from a visit to the top floor of the Empire State Building in New York?

200. The Unexamined Life (⌇ ⌇ ⌇)

Solution in Outline Form

Pros - Advantages of an examined life	Cons - Disadvantages of an examined life
• Let me relate this question to my experiences with golf: "the more I looked into golf the more the game looked into me".	• Being able to draw finer distinctions among the things in our lives means that we may become more dissatisfied with our experiences, especially the mediocre ones.
• Ability to make finer distinctions in the game of golf, and by analogy life, means we can experience more and have richer lives.	• Too much "examination" in our lives leads to imbalances, e.g., seriousness vs. spontaneity.
• Examination is a tool to extract the best things in life while hopefully minimizing the negative effects.	
• Conclusion – the examined life leads to a higher life which is ultimately more rewarding.	

Ambiguity: What does "examination" mean exactly?

Solution in Essay Form (754 words)

In general, I believe in the quote that the life which is unexamined is not worth living. However, the word "examination" is open to interpretation. Does this mean quiet reflection on the subway or does it mean active journalizing and perhaps fervent discussion with friends or peer groups to understand better the nature of our lives and interactions? In any event, to me the statement, "The unexamined life is not worth living," means that people should stop and reflect on various aspects of their lives. I also believe there are costs involved in living life in a manner which requires frequent introspection and self-analysis.

To analyze the costs and benefits of living the examined life, I would like to draw on an example taken from the world of golf and relate it, by analogy, to life in general. During high school, I had no interest in playing golf. I preferred to play tennis which I excelled in, and thought of golf as not only boring but reserved for older persons. Since my parents played golf, not tennis, I forced myself to take up the game of golf in order to spend more time with them. At first, my desire was weak. Needless to say, my golf outings felt awkward and unnatural. But a funny thing happened about one month into my practice. I found I was starting to like golf. Moreover, I was finding the game interesting. Off the course, I caught myself thinking about all the different clubs, the strokes, the stances, the different lies of the ball, the differences among local golf courses, and I even began watching golf on TV—the very thing I once thought was ridiculously boring and inconsequential. My experience could be described as, "The more I looked into golf, the more the game looked into me."

I wondered for a moment what I would give to have the shot-making ability of a great golfer and what it would be like to consistently shoot par golf. Shortly afterward, I read a golf article about why a number of former golf greats stopped playing golf when they retired because they could not bear shooting simply par golf since they had been used to shooting sub-par golf during the peak of their careers. It was as if having played professional golf and knowing how to shoot sub-par golf had somehow ruined their ability to be satisfied that they were still "great" golfers in the eyes of the average golfer. Knowing what it is to play truly superb golf had made playing "poor" golf unbearable. By analogy, for a person who lives the examined life, he or she comes to know the finer distinctions of "good and better," and "better and best" in the things that he or she does. Being able to draw such distinctions brings both satisfaction and dissatisfaction.

There are tradeoffs in life. The businessperson does not achieve recognition without hard work; the artist does not achieve glory without pain. We do not know highs unless we know lows. Knowing, for instance, how to play classical music lends a person a sense of higher enjoyment as compared with the person who does not know how to play or listen to such music. However, it also allows the same person to feel dissatisfaction when hearing a mediocre piece because he or she is cognizant of the difference.

Ultimately, "The more we look into life the more life looks into us." If we are clever, we can use examination as a tool to extract the best things out of life while minimizing the negative effects. For example, running a business with too much emphasis on numbers and not enough on people creates imbalances. If we plan our personal lives too much, we may lose our spontaneity and compassion. If we place too much emphasis on money, we may find ourselves looking withered and sickly—the all too ominous signs of material wealth without balance. Lastly, even a person who examines life too intensively may develop a serious demeanor at the detriment of an easy-going manner and carefree attitude. Such a person will see more in life compared with others but at a cost.

The question of whether one "should" lead an examined life is largely a conundrum. Consciously or unconsciously, once we start to examine our lives, we cannot go back. The examined life cannot be as free as the unexamined life—which lives a life of bliss—but an examined life can lead to a higher life, which is ultimately more rewarding.

A complete review of strategies and approaches is contained in *Chapter 2*.

Problem Solving

1. Identify the type of problem and the appropriate math principle behind the problem at hand.

2. Decide which approach to use to solve the problem—algebra, picking numbers, backsolving, or approximation and eyeballing.

3. After performing calculations, always check again for what is being asked for.

4. Employ guessing or elimination strategies, if necessary, and when possible.

Data Sufficiency

1. Evaluate each stem independently (one at a time); if each stem is insufficient then evaluate both stems together as if they were a single stem.

2. In a *Yes/No Data Sufficiency* question, each stem is sufficient if the answer is "always yes or always no" while a stem is insufficient if the answer is "sometimes yes and sometimes no." In a *Value Data Sufficiency* question, each stem is sufficient if the answer results in a single value while a stem is insufficient if the answer results in a range of values.

3. When picking numbers, think first in terms of the "big seven" numbers.

4. Employ guessing or elimination strategies, when possible.

Sentence Correction

1. Glance at answer choices looking for vertical patterns.

2. Try to determine what the pivotal grammar issue is and if the pivotal issue falls under one of the "big six" grammar categories.

3. Read each answer choice looking for horizontal patterns.

4. Choose the best answer—the answer which is grammatically correct, idiomatically correct, and effective in terms of style.

Critical Reasoning

1. Read the question.

2. Read the passage.

3. Analyze the argument and try to anticipate what the likely answer is.

4. Eliminate common wrong answer choices including out-of-scopes, irrelevancies, distortions, and opposites.

Reading Comprehension

1. Read for content, noting topic, scope, and purpose.

2. Read the first sentence *first*, then scroll down and read last sentence *next*.

3. Read for structure, noting important transition words as well as the number of viewpoints and relationship among viewpoints.

4. Eliminate common wrong answer choices including out-of-scopes, distortions, and opposites.

Analytical Writing

Analysis of an Argument Essay:

1. Visualize the *solutions template* for an Analysis of an Argument essay.

2. Identify the conclusion and evidence in the argument.

3. Choose three (or more) assumptions contained in the argument.

4. Begin by restating the argument and by answering the original question.

5. Use transition words to structure your argument essay.

6. Question the use of one vague term used in the argument and ask for clarification.

7. Suggest strengthening the argument by softening its absolute-type wording.

8. Write (or type) a response and proofread your argument essay.

Analysis of an Issue Essay:

1. Visualize the *solutions template* for an Analysis of an Issue essay.

2. Summarize the pros and cons for your issue.

3. Choose three (or more) pieces of evidence.

4. Begin by restating the issue and by answering the original question.

5. Use transition words to structure your issue essay.

6. Question the use of one vague term used in the issue and ask for clarification and/or draw attention to ambiguity inherent in the issue itself.

7. Use one rhetorical question.

8. Write (or type) a response and proofread your issue essay.

QUIZ - SOLUTIONS

Page numbers provide a point of reference.

1. False. The ratio of gold coins to total coins is $\frac{1}{6}$ or $16\frac{2}{3}$%.

Page 139
(Problem 51)

2. False. The probability of getting a six on either the first <u>or</u> second toss is $\frac{11}{36}$, calculated as $\frac{1}{6} + \frac{1}{6} - \left(\frac{1}{6} \times \frac{1}{6} \right) = \frac{11}{36}$.

Page 161
(Problem 88)

3. False. The store item is now selling for a 44% discount or 56% of its original price. Example: $100 less 20% equals $80 and $80 less 30% equals $66. A $44 discount is 44%.

Page 135
(Problem 43)

4. False. The ratios of the length of the sides of a scalene right triangle with corresponding angle measures of 30°-60°-90° is 1-$\sqrt{3}$ -2.

Page 30

5. False. Multiplying a number by 1.2 is the same as dividing that number by the reciprocal of 1.2, which is 0.83, not 0.8.

Page 132
(Problem 38)

6. False. The following are grammatically correct sentences: "Jonathan <u>likes</u> not only tennis but also golf" or "Jonathan not only <u>likes</u> tennis but also <u>likes</u> golf."

Page 205
(Problem 134)

7. False. In formal logic, the phrase "Every A is a B" must be translated as "Only B's are A's." Case in point: The statement "Every cat is a mammal" must be translated as "Only mammals are cats." It is not true to say that if every cat is a mammal then only cats are mammals.

Page 58 & 248
(Problem 180)

8. False. Unlike the Analysis of an Issue essay which is made better by the use of personal examples and anecdotes, the Analysis of an Argument essay does not require personal examples or anecdotes.

Page 81

9. False. Whereas the conclusion and evidence of an argument are always explicit, the assumption is always implicit. The assumption is never explicit. It is invisible, existing in the mind of the speaker or the hand of the writer (author).

Page 49

10. False. Arguably the best way to read a GMAT Reading Comprehension passage is to "read the first sentence first but the last sentence next." Then proceed to read the whole passage. The author might either conclude on the bottom line or hint at the passage's overall meaning, so reading the last sentence sooner rather than later is deemed advantageous.

Page 16